The Heritage of American Catholicism

A TWENTY-EIGHT-VOLUME SERIES DOCUMENTING THE HISTORY
OF AMERICA'S LARGEST RELIGIOUS DENOMINATION

EDITED BY

Timothy Walch

ASSOCIATE EDITOR
U.S. Catholic Historian

A Garland Series

The Building of an American Catholic Church

THE EPISCOPACY OF JOHN CARROLL

JOSEPH AGONITO

Garland Publishing, Inc.
New York & London
1988

LIBRARY OF CONGRESS CATALOGING-IN-PUBLICATION DATA

Agonito, Joseph.
  The Building of an American Catholic church.
  (The Heritage of American Catholicism)
  Origianally presented as the author's thesis (Ph. D.--Syracuse University, 1972).
  Bibliography: p.
  1. Catholic Church--United States--History--18th century. 2. Catholic Church--United States--History--19th century. 3. United States--Church history--18th century. 4. United States--Church history--19th century. 5. Carroll, John, 1735-1815. I. Title. II. Series.
BX1406.2.A36 1988   282'.73   88-9788
ISBN 0-8240-4084-8 (alk. paper)

DESIGN BY MARY BETH BRENNAN

PRINTED ON ACID-FREE, 250-YEAR-LIFE PAPER.
MANUFACTURED IN THE UNITED STATES OF AMERICA

to my mother
Gertrude Telesco Agonito
for her love and encouragement

PREFACE

Several years ago, while taking a seminar in
American History at Syracuse University with Dr. Robert J.
Rayback, I reviewed for the course Monsignor John Tracy
Ellis' splendid little volume <u>American Catholicism</u>, in the
Chicago History of American Civilization series. Dr.
Rayback posed a set of questions for me to consider: what
is the nature of American Catholicism? What effect has
the American environment had--an environment overwhelmingly
Protestant in population, democratic in spirit, and frontier
in social complexion--in forming the American Catholic
Church? Since then I have added for consideration several
related questions. What modifications did the Catholic
Church have to make in order to become a part of its new
world environment? What is American about the Church?
What of the Roman element has remained? It is around these
questions, then, that the present work revolves. They
serve as the major thread, tying together into a unified
whole, the multi-facet character of this study.

It appeared that the episcopacy of John Carroll, the first Bishop of Baltimore (1789-1815), was the best place to begin such a study. By all accounts this was the formative period in the history of the Catholic Church in America--a time when, under the influences of the new world, the very foundations of the American Catholic Church were being laid. John Carroll played a significant role in this great drama. He is, accordingly, the central figure in this study. Still, he was not alone. There were many other Catholics--clerics and lay--who, like Carroll, were as eager to shape their Church to its new surroundings. They also find a place in these pages.

I do not presume that this work, which attempts to analyze the very nature of American Catholicism, is definitive; rather, it is an exploratory work which, by investigating the impact of the American environment on the development of the Catholic Church in America during the episcopacy of John Carroll, hopes to point out some new directions that scholarship might take for a better understanding of the history of the American Catholic Church.

* * * * * * * * * *

No historical work can ever be a solitary endeavor.
My own experience indicates otherwise. Throughout this
investigation I have been generously assisted by archivists,
librarians, and fellow historians. My appreciation to the
following individuals: to Dr. William D. Hoyt, Jr., former
editor of the John Carroll Papers, who shared with me the
hospitality of his home and his collection of John Carroll's
letters; to Monsignor John Tracy Ellis, past President of
the American Catholic Historical Association, and Reverend
Robert Trisco, secretary of the association, who willingly
gave me permission to reproduce their entire collection of
the John Carroll Papers; to Dr. Joseph Herman Schauinger,
Professor of History at the College of St. Thomas, who made
available from his own collection the translated letters
of Benedict Joseph Flaget, the first Bishop of Bardstown,
Kentucky, and his fellow-missionaries, Stephen Theodore
Badin and John Baptist David; to Dr. Hugh Davis, and
especially Reverend Donald Clark, from the Classics
Department at LeMoyne College, Syracuse, for their help in

translating various materials; to Reverend Robert F.
McNamara, Professor of Church History at St. Bernard's
Seminary, Rochester, New York, for his interest and
encouragement; and, special thanks to Reverend Thomas
O'Brien Hanley, editor of the John Carroll Papers, who
always gave graciously of his time, his ideas and his
knowledge of the period.

The assistance rendered by archivists was equally
indispensable to this work. I want to express my thanks to
Moreau B.C. Chambers at Catholic University, whose personal
warmth and professional skill always made my visits to the
archives there so pleasant and rewarding; to Reverend
John Tierney of the Archdiocese of Baltimore, who despite a
busy schedule, opened up the archives for my use; to
Reverend Vincent Bellwoar at Georgetown University, who
shared with me the valuable holdings in the Georgetown
archives; to Reverend Thomas E. Blantz at the University of
Notre Dame, for sending photo-copies of materials necessary
for this work; and, to the Jesuit Fathers at the Provincial's
House, Maryland Province of the Society of Jesus, who made

my short stay there so rich in research and companionship.

I am also indebted to the many libraries and librarians that made this work possible. The libraries of Georgetown University, Catholic University of America, and St. Bernard's Seminary were especially generous in honoring the many requests that I made for inter-library loans. I want to thank Dr. Taisto J. Niemi and his competent staff at LeMoyne College in Syracuse--especially the ever helpful Michael McLane--for allowing me free use of their rich holdings in Catholic Church history. A special note of appreciation must be made to Mrs. Grace MacDonald and her wonderful staff at Onondaga Community College--especially Jeannette Woodward, Sally Potter, and Frances Baker--who spent many long hours tracking down the numerous requests I made for information and books. I cannot thank them enough for their interest in my work, their determination to find materials, and their friendliness despite all the burdensome tasks that I placed upon them.

I want to express my gratitude to Nelson M. Blake, my major advisor, for the warm interest he has shown over the years towards my work; to my colleagues at Onondaga Community College and to the administration for granting me a sabbatical leave to complete this study; and, above all, to my wife and companion, Rosemary Giambattista Agonito, who despite her many professional responsibilities found the time to listen to the trials and joys of a would-be historian.

CONTENTS

INTRODUCTION

The American Revolution had a profound impact on the position of the Roman Catholic Church in the United States. As a result of the forces set loose by the revolution the various states emancipated Catholics from the penal legislation of the colonial period. Everywhere Catholics could now worship freely and, in several of the states, they gained as well full political equality. Even the age-old Protestant animosity against Catholics and their Church diminished during this period.

This new-found freedom and these changing attitudes presented the Catholic Church with its first real opportunity to prosper in the English speaking "new world." But the Catholic Church could not take advantage of this opportunity unless it shook off some of its "old world" characteristics and became acculturated to the American environment.

As a native American, John Carroll, the first Roman Catholic Bishop in the United States, understood the

need for his Church to become "Americanized." He realized
that so many of his fellow Americans viewed his Church,
however wrongly, as a "foreign" institution, alien to
America. He resented most the accusation that the loyalty
and allegiance that Catholics owed to Rome detracted from
their attachment to the United States. In the post-
revolutionary period--a time of rising nationalism--these
charges were especially damaging to the cause of Catholicism
in America.

Unlike most other American churches, however, the
Catholic Church in the United States was only one part of
an ancient, world-wide, tradition-bound, highly-structured
organization governed from Rome, the ecclesiastical center
and font of authority for Catholicism throughout the world.
For American Catholics any change must take place within
the context of Roman Catholic doctrines and practices.
This was always the controlling and, in some cases, the
limiting factor, for one could not conceivably make changes
in the fundamentals of the faith--such as in doctrine or
ecclesiastical structure--and still remain Roman Catholic.

Carroll's task--and that of the many Catholics, cleric and lay, who shared his concern for the future of their Church in America--was to shape the Catholic Church into an American institution without, however, abandoning its peculiar "Roman" or "Catholic" character. This would prove a delicate and difficult task.

In 1784, when Rome appointed John Carroll Superior of the Catholic missions in the United States, the Catholic Church was numerically small, lacking priests and religious facilities. In the years ahead the religious life of Catholic congregations would have to be awakened, priests found, churches and schools built. These tasks alone were sufficient to tax the strength of the Catholic community. Still, in addition to these practical demands, the Catholic Church was confronted with grave and delicate problems that could affect its very success in America. The manner in which Carroll and his fellow Catholics handled these special problems constitutes the basis for this work.

* * * * * * * * * *

American independence from Great Britain presented Catholics with their first formidable difficulty. No longer could they remain under the spiritual authority of the Vicar-Apostolic of London, who had assumed jurisdiction over the affairs of the Catholic Church in America throughout the eighteenth century. With full understanding of American conditions, Catholics recognized the need to establish a form of church government which would make them independent of any "foreign" jurisdiction, save the spiritual authority of the Holy See to which Catholics everywhere owed obedience. Accordingly, they would have to resist any plan that placed them under "outside" jurisdiction, such as that of the Roman Congregation for the Propagation of the Faith which had been founded by the Holy See in 1622 to govern the life of the Church in those parts of the world where no established hierarchy or significant body of Catholics existed. Such an arrangement meant that Propaganda (as the Congregation was called) could designate, appoint, and delineate the powers of the superior for the

Church in America--clearly a dependency which would only intensify the suspicions many Americans already entertained about the loyalty of Catholics. Instead, the American clergy would have to work for the establishment of a regular hierarchy controlled by themselves. The selection by the American clergy of their first diocesan bishop, whose power and right to govern came not by delegation from Rome, but from his office as a descendant of the apostles, was the necessary first step in the building of an American Catholic Church. Furthermore, ever sensitive to the charges, made by critics of the Catholic Church, that the Pope's claims to temporal power and infallibility were detrimental to the safety of any state in which Catholics lived, Catholics would have to instruct their fellow citizens that their fears were unfounded, for American Catholics did not recognize any pretensions Rome might have made to temporal power, nor consider papal infallibility an article of their faith. At the same time, however, Catholics could not deny (as some would ask) the spiritual authority of Rome, without forfeiting the name Roman

Catholic. They would have to assure their critics that spiritual dependence on the Holy See did not in any way detract from the loyalty and allegiance that Catholics owed to their native land.

After establishing the formal structure of their Church and determining her proper relationship with Rome, the American clergy could turn to questions affecting the internal life of the Church. An immediate problem concerned the role of the laity. Living in a Protestant, republican, and generally more open society than anywhere in Europe, the laity came to envision for themselves a more significant role in the affairs of the parish church. The "trustee" problem, as it was called, would disturb the peace of Carroll's entire episcopacy. While Carroll and the clergy would have to recognize that the climate of opinion in America demanded that the laity exercise some voice in the affairs of the parish church, they had to guard against any lay invasion of the traditional spiritual authority of the priest and bishop.

The spiritual needs of Catholics, and non-Catholics also, deserved special attention. In order to awaken the religious life of Catholics, and to attract converts, the Church's message and services would have to be made more intelligible. Accordingly, Carroll and some members from the clergy and laity gave careful consideration to changing the liturgy from the Latin to the vernacular, and to cultivating good preaching by the clergy. Liturgy in the vernacular and eloquent preaching (which the Protestants so admired) could serve as a bridge to the non-Catholic world.

Internal problems, though, could not dominate the whole attention of Catholics. They had to consider their relationship with the outside world as equally crucial to the success of the Catholic Church in America. As a minority group living in a society overwhelmingly composed of non-Catholics, Catholics could not avoid mixing with those of different faiths in their everyday life. Carroll and the clergy could hope that out of these meetings non-Catholics would come to realize that their fears and suspicions about Catholics were groundless. Still, there were dangers as well, for contact between the two religious groups could possibly lessen the faith of Catholics or, worse still, lead to the idea of theological tolerance. The faithful, then, would have to be carefully instructed in the traditional teachings of their Church, which taught that Catholicism was the only true religion.

There were certain areas where Catholics could, without any serious difficulty, fully demonstrate their "Americanism," and in so doing silence the accusations which non-Catholics leveled against their Church. Catholic love for their native land--a land in which the Church was more free to carry out its mission than in Catholic countries in Europe--came easy, and brought no conflict with traditional Catholic teachings. Actually, the Roman Catholic Church, which has existed in almost every conceivable type of civil society, has generally encouraged in her members the principle of patriotism to their homeland. America would place no dilemma before Catholics who saw no incompatibility between the spiritual allegiance they owed Rome and their Church, and the political allegiance they owed to America.

Even the developing religious policy of America-- religious toleration and separation of church and state-- posed no special problems for Catholics. While the Roman Catholic Church considered neither concept as ideal, there were admittedly circumstances under which they could be positively supported as necessary and even desirable. As a minority group Catholics in America naturally understood the benefits that would accrue to their faith from the implementation by the state, and national, governments of religious freedom. During Carroll's episcopacy, Catholics would also come to accept, on other than pragmatic grounds, the principle of religious toleration and separation of church and state.

Catholics understood the need to create in America-- a country overwhelmingly non-Catholic, democratic, and frontier--a Church that was suited to its environment yet, at the same time, still faithful to its traditional heritage. How well they succeeded in this difficult task forms the basis for this work.

PART I

THE ESTABLISHMENT OF AN AMERICAN CATHOLIC CHURCH

CHAPTER I

THE ELECTION OF A BISHOP

The signing of a definitive peace treaty between
Great Britain and the United States on September 3, 1783,
was of crucial importance to the small number of Catholics
living in America. The recognition of American independence
rendered untenable any further dependency by American
Catholics on the **Vicar-Apostolic** of London who claimed
jurisdiction over Catholics living in English America. [1]

---

[1] The Reformation in England brought to an end the
Catholic hierarchy in that country. In 1685, after experi-
menting with several different forms of ecclesiastical
government for the remaining Catholics living in England,
the Holy See established the office of Vicar-Apostolic,
subject to the Sacred Congregation for the Propagation of
the Faith which exercised control over all mission territory.
The Vicar-Apostolic received his appointment and spiritual
faculties from the Pope and Propaganda. The Vicar-Apostolic
was a titular bishop--a bishop without a diocese. Nonetheless, his powers were similar to that of a diocesan bishop,
and all missionary activity in the vicariate was subject to
his authority. In 1688, England was divided into four
vicariates, one centered in London. From this year, down
to the appointment of John Carroll in 1784 as Prefect-Apostolic
of the Catholic Missions in America, the London Vicar-Apostolic
presumably had jurisdiction over Catholics in English America.
The spiritual powers of Catholic missionaries who came to
the colonies in the eighteenth century were derived from the
London Vicar-Apostolic. A simple priest could not validly
exercise his office without authorization from his bishop.
Peter Keenan Guilday, A History of the Councils of Baltimore
1791-1884 (New York: Macmillan Co., 1932), Chap. IV, "The
London Jurisdiction 1634-1783," pp. 37-49. (Hereinafter
referred to as Councils); Francis Joseph Winslow, "Vicar-
Apostolic," New Catholic Encyclopedia, XIV (1967), 638-39.

Actually, the two Vicars-Apostolic of London--
Richard Challoner (1758-1781) and James Talbot (1781-1784)--
who exercised supervision over the American Catholics
during the revolutionary period had little desire to
perpetuate this relationship. Challoner had long complained
that America was too far away, too remote for him to
exercise proper spiritual administration, and he had
recommended to Rome that a separate Bishop Vicar-Apostolic
be appointed to reside in the English colonies. His
efforts did not materialize, in part because the Catholics
in America protested, for they feared the recriminations
that would follow if a Catholic bishop were to come to
Protestant America.[2] During the colonial struggle for
independence Challoner and Talbot, as patriotic and prudent
Englishmen, practically ceased relations with the Catholic
clergy and laity in rebellious America. In 1783, Talbot
claimed that he would no longer exercise ecclesiastical
jurisdiction in the newly-independent United States, and

---

[2]John Gilmary Shea, History of the Catholic Church
in the United States, Vol. II: The Life and Times of the
Most Reverend John Carroll (New York: John G. Shea, 1888),
pp. 51-52, 54, 56-57. (Hereinafter referred to as John
Carroll); Peter Keenan Guilday, The Life and Times of John
Carroll: Archbishop of Baltimore 1735-1815 (New York:
The Encyclopedia Press, 1922), Chap. XI, "Opposition to
the American Bishopric," pp. 151-62. (Hereafter referred
to as John Carroll)

refused faculties to two ex-Jesuits who were returning to America.[3]

The American clergy also realized that an official break from the ecclesiastical jurisdiction of the London Vicar-Apostolic was necessary and desirable. Such a separation, however, presented certain difficulties. The spiritual authority of Father John Lewis, the present vicar-general in America of the Vicar-Apostolic of London, would automatically come to an end with the break. There would, then, be no priest in America with the requisite power of jurisdiction to govern the Catholic clergy and laity. Accordingly, Lewis convened a meeting of the First General Chapter of the Clergy in November, 1783, to devise a new form of ecclesiastical government for the Catholic Church in America. The Chapter appointed a Committee of Five to petition Rome and request that Lewis be retained with certain "episcopal" privileges--that of administering the sacrament of confirmation, blessing chalices, holy oils, and altar stones, and granting faculties to new priests coming into the missions. The petitioners informed Rome

[3]Charles F. McCarthy, "The Historical Development of Episcopal Nominations in the Catholic Church of the United States 1784-1884," Records of the American Catholic Historical Society of Philadelphia, XXXVIII (December 1927), 310. (Hereinafter referred to as Records.)

that since independence had been achieved it was no longer advisable for the American clergy to remain under the spiritual jurisdiction of the London Vicar-Apostolic; in fact, officials of the new government had intimated as much to them. It was imperative that Rome designate Lewis as superior of the missions in America with the necessary religious powers to provide for the spiritual life of the Catholic flock. Such a step would avoid offending the civil government and would provide for proper ecclesiastical government in America.[4]

Since several members of the clergy were not satisfied with the tone of the first petition, another committee was appointed to draft a second. This petition differed from the former in that the clergy now requested the privilege of electing their own superior and pointed out that a bishop would not be well received in the United States.[5] The committee instructed one of its members, Father John Carroll, to send this statement to the Pope

---

[4]Clergy's Petition to the Pope, 1784. Propaganda Archives. Scritture Riferite nei Congressi, America Centrale. Vol. II, Fol. 238. John Carroll Papers, Transcript. Catholic University of America Archives.

[5]Guilday, John Carroll, pp. 171-72.

through an intermediary in Rome.[6] Carroll enclosed a personal note explaining to his correspondent the sentiments of the American clergy toward the establishment of the hierarchy in the United States. "You are not ignorant," he wrote, "that in these United States our Religious system has undergone a revolution, if possible, more extraordinary than our political one." In all states, Catholics were granted religious liberty; and, in four states, civil liberty as well. In order to preserve these newly-won liberties, Carroll argued that Catholics must avoid giving offense to American sensibilities by being dependent on any foreign jurisdiction, save that ". . . which is

---

[6]John Carroll was born into an old and distinguished Maryland Catholic family on January 8, 1735. In 1748 he left his native land for a long stay in Europe where he completed his education in the English refugee colleges on the continent and became a member of the Society of Jesus. In 1774, a year after Pope Clement XIV suppressed the Jesuits, Carroll returned home. He was forty years old, having been away for twenty-seven years. Despite this long absence, Carroll remained a loyal American. He played a small role in the events of the American Revolution by accompanying in 1776 a delegation from Congress whose mission was to win over Canada to the American side. The attempt was unsuccessful and Carroll returned to Maryland to administer to the Catholics in his area and to concentrate on the larger affairs of the Catholic Church in America. In this capacity he served as a delegate to the First General Chapter of the Clergy which met in November, 1783, to develop a plan of ecclesiastical organization for the Catholic Church in America. Richard J. Purcell, "Carroll, John," Dictionary of American Biography, III (1929), 526-28.

essential to our Religion, an acknowledgment of the Pope's Spiritual Supremacy over the whole Christian world." The spiritual jurisdiction of the London Vicar-Apostolic was, he pointed out, no longer acceptable; therefore, the American clergy were requesting that Rome allow them the right to choose one of their own as ecclesiastical superior, with designated "episcopal" powers.[7]

Rome was equally aware that independence created a new situation for Catholics in the United States. Months before the first meeting of the General Chapter of the Clergy (November, 1783), Rome had already begun to devise a plan of ecclesiastical government for Catholics living in America.[8] On January 15, 1783, the Prefect of the Congregation of Propaganda, Cardinal Leonardo Antonelli

---

[7]John Carroll to Roman agent, November 10, 1783. Archives of the Archdiocese of Baltimore, Special Case C-A4. (Hereinafter referred to as AAB.)

[8]The original Italian, French, and Latin documents relative to the appointment by Rome of an ecclesiastical superior for the Catholic Church in the United States were translated by Edward I. Devitt under the title "Propaganda Documents: Appointment of the First Bishop of Baltimore," Records, XXI (December, 1910), 185-235. (Hereinafter referred to as Propaganda Documents.)

wrote to Archbishop Doria Pamphili, the Apostolic Nuncio

at Paris.[9] Antonelli informed Pamphili that the dissolu-

tion of the political ties between Great Britain and the

United States would carry over into the religious sphere

as well, and the dependence of American Catholics on the

Vicar-Apostolic of London would come to an end. Propaganda

proposed to establish in one of the principal cities in

America ". . . a Vicar-Apostolic, with episcopal character,

chosen from among the subjects of the new republic, who

should receive from the Holy See powers for the spiritual

government of the Catholics of all those regions. . . ."

Such a course was desirable since a Vicar-Apostolic had the

power to administer the sacraments of Confirmation and Holy

Orders, and ". . . national jealousy would thus be obviated,

by not constraining these new republicans to receive those

---

[9]The Sacred Congregation for the Propagation of the Faith was established by Pope Gregory XV in 1622. It was entrusted with the administration, expansion, and protection of the missionary system of the Catholic Church. The United States was considered in 1784 as missionary territory subject to Propaganda, since it did not have an ecclesiastica hierarchy that would allow it to be brought within the regular administrative order of the Catholic Church. Even with the establishment of the American hierarchy, however, Rome allowed the Catholic Church in the United States to remain under Propaganda's jurisdiction until 1908. Elizabeth M. Lynskey, The Government of the Catholic Church (New York: P.J. Kenedy and Sons, 1952), pp. 46-51; Heinrich Scharp, How the Catholic Church is Governed (New York: Herder and Herder, 1960), pp. 77-79.

sacraments from foreign bishops." Of course, if the
leaders of the American Congress should be reluctant to
admit a bishop into the country, Rome was willing to
appoint a Prefect Apostolic (who would have broad powers,
but not episcopal title). Antonelli concluded that in all
cases ". . . if natives should be found available, they
should always be preferred, . . . but, if available natives
should not be found, there should be permission to appoint
foreigners, always, however, from among the most impartial
and acceptable to the government."[10]

During the year and a half which followed,
Antonelli's plan for the government of the Church in
America was challenged by several other schemes, all of
which failed to materialize.[11] The ecclesiastical

---

[10]Antonelli to Pamphili, January 15, 1783, Devitt,
"Propaganda Documents," pp. 186-90.

[11]Devitt's article contains many of the primary
documents that are necessary for an understanding of the
"ecclesiastical negotiations" that took place during this
period. The most careful and acceptable secondary study
was that by Jules A. Baisnée, France and the Establishment
of the American Catholic Hierarchy: The Myth of French
Interference 1783-1784 (Baltimore: John Hopkins Press,
1934). Baisnée's major task was to examine the charges made
by Shea, John Carroll, pp. 212-25, and Guilday, John Carroll,
pp. 178-201, that French officials--civil and ecclesiastical--
interferred in the ecclesiastical affairs of the young
Catholic Church in America. After reviewing critically all
the relevant documents, Baisnée properly concluded that the
charges were unfounded.

negotiations however, came to an end on June 9, 1784, when

Rome appointed John Carroll as Prefect-Apostolic of the

Catholic missions in America.[12]

Rome's reasons for appointing John Carroll as

Prefect, instead of John Lewis, were twofold. First, Rome

wanted to please Benjamin Franklin, the United States'

minister to France, who had warmly recommended John Carroll

for the position.[13] Franklin had been a good friend of

Carroll since the two had served on an ill-fated delegation

which tried in 1776 to win Canada over to the America

cause. Secondly, Rome considered Lewis, who was then

sixty-three years of age, as too old for the difficult task

---

[12] In the eighteenth century Rome normally established a Prefecture-Apostolic for those regions where the
ecclesiastical organization of the Catholic Church was still
in its infancy. The Prefect-Apostolic received his appointment and spiritual faculties from the Holy See and Propaganda. While not a bishop the Prefect still exercised wide
powers--he could consecrate chalices, patens, and portable
altars, administer Confirmation, confer tonsure and minor
orders--and all missionary activity in the prefecture was
subject to his authority. Francis Joseph Winslow, "Prefect-
Apostolic," New Catholic Encyclopedia, XI (1967), 727.

[13] Pamphili to Antonelli, May 17, 1784, Devitt,
"Propaganda Documents," p. 210; Antonelli to Pamphili,
June 9, 1784, Ibid., p. 213; Franklin noted in his "Diary":
"The Pope's Nuncio called, and acquainted me that the Pope
had, on my recommendation, appointed John Carroll, superior
of the Catholic clergy in America." Albert Henry Smyth,
(ed.), The Writings of Benjamin Franklin (10 vols.; New York
Macmillan Co., 1905-1907), X, 349.

of organizing the Catholic Church in America.[14] Evidently,

Rome had decided to appoint Carroll as Prefect (and not

bishop Vicar-Apostolic) in light of the known anti-prelacy

sentiment that existed in America, among Protestants and

Catholics alike. Since the Prefect-Apostolic did not carry

episcopal title, it should not offend the sensibilities of

Americans.[15]

The official notice from Rome of his appointment

did not reach Carroll until November 26, 1784. Antonelli

congratulated Carroll on his designation as Prefect of the

missions in America, and pointed out that in the exercise

of his office, he was independent of ". . . any ecclesiastical

power, except the same Sacred Congregation of Propaganda. . . ."

Antonelli assured Carroll that this arrangement was only

temporary, for Rome would soon establish in the United

States a Vicar-Apostolic.[16]

Carroll was reluctant to accept the appointment,

and it was a full three months before he notified Rome of

his willingness to do so. It placed him in an embarrassing

position, for several months earlier he had told his fellow

---

[14]Antonelli to Pamphili, June 9, 1784, Ibid., p. 214.

[15]Guilday, Councils, p. 56.

[16]Antonelli to Carroll, June 9, 1784. As quoted by Shea, John Carroll, pp. 243-45.

Jesuit and lifelong English friend, Charles Plowden, that
". . . this you may be assured of, that no authority
derived from the Propaganda will ever be admitted here."[17]
Carroll was disturbed by the temporary nature of his
appointment, his absolute dependency on Propaganda, and the
extremely limited powers given him, especially that which
forbade him from granting faculties to priests coming to
America save by express permission of Propaganda. He
feared that this arrangement would only confirm the worst
suspicions entertained by so many Americans that his Church
was unduly dependent on foreign authority.

Carroll used the time prior to his acceptance of
the Prefectship to consult with his fellow clergy, to
clarify his own objections, and to formulate his thoughts
on the best form of church government in an America,
overwhelmingly Protestant, anti-Catholic, and jealous of
its independence from all forms of "foreign" control.

In a Circular Letter to the American clergy,
probably drafted in early December, 1784, Carroll developed
his position at length. He noted that the limited faculties

[17]Carroll to Plowden, April 10, 1784. Maryland
Province Archives of the Society of Jesus, Box 202-B6.
(Hereinafter referred to as Maryland Province Archives.)

granted him as Prefect were inadequate to the needs of the
country, and further questionable because they came from
the Congregation of Propaganda which claimed jurisdiction
over the Catholic "missions" in America. Carroll proceeded
to list his objections to such an arrangement. He considered the exercise of any power by Propaganda in this
country ". . . not only as improper, but as dangerous
here." America, having recently won its independence, was
rightly jealous of any foreign interference, and the
appointment of a Superior by Propaganda could prejudice the
cause of Catholicism in America by exposing ". . . it to
the reproach of encouraging a dependence on a foreign
power. . . ." The only authority which Catholics should
accept was that ". . . which being purely spiritual, is
essential to our Religion, to wit, an acknowledgment of the
Pope's spiritual supremacy and of the See of St. Peter
being the center of Ecclesiastical unity." None other
should be accepted. Propaganda was wrong to designate
America as "mission" territory. Perhaps this was true in
earlier times, but not now when Catholicism has been

accorded by ". . . the Constitution . . . equal rights and privileges with that of other Christians: . . ." "We form," Carroll added, ". . . a permanent body of national clergy, with sufficient powers to form our own system of internal government, and I think, to choose our own Superior. . . ." As for the future, he would recommend to Rome that a diocesan bishop chosen by the clergy in America--not a Vicar-Apostolic dependent on Propaganda--would be the best way to avoid recriminations.[18] The distinction between a diocesan bishop and a Vicar-Apostolic was a significant one for Carroll. Whereas a diocesan bishop received his power of jurisdiction to govern from his office, a vicar-apostolic's powers were delegated from Rome. Furthermore, the vicar-apostolic was nominated by the Holy See and Propaganda, whereas this was not always the case of a diocesan bishop.[19]

---

[18] Carroll to Clergy, no date. Draft of a Circular Letter. AAB, Case 9-06.

[19] As successors of the apostles the bishops, by divine institution, are placed over particular churches, which they rule with ordinary power under the authority of the Holy See. While the Pope, as supreme pastor of the Catholic Church, may limit the exercise or territorial extent of the bishop's right of jurisdiction--the power to govern--he cannot suppress or change its essential character. A diocesan bishop then exercises ordinary and immediate jurisdiction. His jurisdiction is called "ordinary" because it is vested in him by reason of his office and not by delegation; it is "immediate" because he may exercise it without need of an intermediary. Thomas A. Faulkner, "Bishop (Canon Law)," New Catholic Encyclopedia, II (1967), 586-88; Lynskey, The Government of the Catholic Church, pp. 17-19, 50-51; Francis Joseph Winslow, Vicars and Prefect Apostolic (Maryknoll, N.Y.: Catholic Foreign Mission Society of America, 1924), pp. 8-10.

Father Robert Molyneux, pastor of St. Joseph's Church in Philadelphia and a close friend of Carroll, shared the latter's objections to the limited nature of the Prefect's power, especially the "cramping clause" which forbade Carroll from granting faculties to new priests coming to America save by express permission of Propaganda. Molyneux pointed out to his friend that when Pope Gregory sent St. Augustine to England the latter was given power to act on his own, ". . . and was he a meer servile tool to a Propaganda"?[20]

Despite the objections, Carroll accepted the appointment. He had been urged to do so by several of his fellow clergy, who felt that the Prefecture, despite its limitations, was a necessary first step in the development of a ecclesiastical government in America.[21] Evidently, Carroll was moved by similar sentiments as he explained to the clergy ". . . that nothing but the present extreme necessity of some spiritual powers here could induce me to act under a commission, which may produce, if long continued, and it should become public, the most dangerous

[20]Molyneux to Carroll, December 7, 1784. AAB, Case 5-K8.

[21]Shea, John Carroll, p. 251; Guilday, John Carroll, p. 214.

jealousy."[22]   Besides, Rome had promised that this arrange-

ment was only temporary in nature, and Carroll could hope

that his arguments would convince Rome to develop the

ecclesiastical structure as recommended by himself and the

clergy.

He finally accepted the appointment in a letter to

Cardinal Antonelli dated February 27, 1785. Carroll hoped

that what he had to say would not be misunderstood in Rome,

but he realized that the organization of the Church in

America could not be safely or wisely begun unless Rome

fully understood the situation in an America suspicious of

Catholics and foreign powers. Carroll pointed out to

Antonelli that in all the states religious liberty was

granted to Catholics; yet, many of the states still denied

them full civil rights ". . . unless they renounce all

foreign jurisdiction, civil or ecclesiastical. . . ." In

those few states where religious and political liberty had

been granted, many Catholics feared that all could be lost

if they showed an undue dependence on Rome. Carroll

assured Rome that the clergy and laity ". . . will never be

[22]Carroll to Clergy, no date. Draft of a Circular
Letter. AAB, Case 9-06.

swayed from obedience due to the Sovereign Pontiff." Still,

to avoid the dangers they fear, the Catholics

> . . . therefore, desire that the adversaries
> of our religion be given no handle for
> incriminating us on the grounds that we
> depend more than is proper on a foreign
> power. Let some reason be found, by which,
> later on, some ecclesiastical superior
> could be appointed to this area so that the
> spiritual jurisdiction of the Holy See may
> be altogether maintained. At the same time
> all occasion would be removed for objecting
> that we were admitting something harmful to
> the Independence of our country.

Carroll realized that this could best be accomplished by

the establishment of a diocesan bishop with ordinary powers,

elected by the American clergy, and subject to the Pope

only in spiritual matters, and he proceeded, in an indirect

and subtle fashion, to lead Antonelli to the same conclu-

sion. If, as Antonelli had remarked in an earlier letter,

Rome planned in the future to appoint a bishop for America,

Carroll asked whether it would be a Vicar-Apostolic or a

diocesan bishop? The decision, Carroll thought, should

depend on the answer to the following question: ". . . What

person will serve more for the betterment of the Catholic

position, for the removal of hatred toward Catholics, for

removing the alarm over foreign jurisdiction"? For Carroll there was no doubt that the appointment of an ordinary bishop with the right of jurisdiction inherent in his office and not delegated from Rome would be more acceptable in the United States. As to the method of nominating a bishop Carroll preferred the choice be left to the American clergy; but, if this was not allowed, he hoped that they could at ". . . least decide upon some way of nominating a bishop by which offense to our people both Catholic as well as sectarian may be averted."[23]

Carroll had made two basic points: first, that his limited powers, especially that which prevented him from granting faculties to new priests coming into the country save without express permission from Propaganda, seriously hampered him in the exercise of his duties as Prefect; and secondly, that only the appointment of a diocesan bishop would be most conducive to the cause of Catholicism in America. Rome soon rectified the first problem. Antonelli later notified Carroll that the clause in question had been removed, that he had the power to grant faculties to any

[23]Carroll to Antonelli, February 27, 1785. Propaganda Archives. Scritture Riferite nei Congressi, America Centrale. Vol. II, Fol. 306. John Carroll Papers, Transcript. Catholic University of America Archives.

priest coming to America that he chose to.[24] As for the

second point--the appointment of a diocesan bishop, subject

to the Pope only in spiritual matters, and elected by the

American clergy--this would not come to pass until

November 14, 1789, when Rome confirmed John Carroll as the

first Bishop of Baltimore.

* * * * * * * * * *

On the question of establishing a "bishopric"

Carroll had to proceed with caution, for he knew that some

members of the clergy were against it.[25] At the last

session of the General Chapter of the Clergy's meeting

(October 11, 1784) the delegates considered Father Thorpe's

letter from Rome announcing Carroll's appointment as

Prefect. Since the majority of those present felt that a

Prefect with certain "episcopal" powers was adequate to the

present needs of the Catholic missions in the United States,

---

[24]Antonelli to Carroll, July 23, 1785. Propaganda
Archives. Lettere della S. C., Vol. 246, Fol. 437.
Guilday Transcripts. Catholic University of America
Archives. Father John Thorpe, the American clergy's agent
in Rome, wrote Carroll that he had a meeting with Cardinal
Borgia, the Secretary of the Congregation of Propaganda,
who apologized for the restrictive clause which was left in
merely by ". . . an oversight in the Secretary's Office. . . ."
Thorpe to Carroll, August 31, 1785. AAB, Case 8-H5.

[25]Carroll to Thorpe, February 17, 1785. AAB,
Case 9A-F1.

the Chapter declared that a Bishop was at present unnecessary, and that if any were sent by Rome he would not be
supported from the estates of the clergy. A committee was
appointed, composed of Fathers Bernard Diderick, Ignatius
Matthews, and Joseph Mosley, to notify Rome of the
Chapter's sentiments.[26] The committee's Memorial to Rome
(in which Father Diderick, the leader of the anti-episcopal
faction, emerged as the main spokesman) informed the Pope
of the Chapter's opinion ". . . that there is not the least
necessity for a bishop in this country, because there is
no institution as yet for the education of youth, and
their subsequent preparation for holy orders." Diderick
also pointed out that such an appointment could be harmful
to Catholicism in the United States because "The majority
of the Protestant population here are adverse to a Roman
Catholic prelate, and for this reason the episcopal office

[26]Thomas Aloysius Hughes, History of the Society of
Jesus in North America, Colonial and Federal. Documents
(London: Longmans, Green, and Co., 1910), I, Part ii, 633.
(Hereinafter referred to as Documents.)

if introduced would most likely awaken their jealousy against us."[27]

Carroll was displeased with Diderick and with certain parts of the Memorial.[28] It was perhaps to offset Diderick's remarks that Carroll now told Antonelli how the Protestant fear of prelacy was subsiding, and that the decision of the Episcopal Church to appoint a bishop was not censured by the Congress. Carroll assured Antonelli that:

> . . . there would not now be any disturbance
> if a bishop should be appointed, because the
> Protestants are thinking about appointing one

---

[27]Clergy's Memorial to Rome, December, 1784. As quoted in Bernard U. Campbell, "Memoirs of the Life and Times of the Most Rev. John Carroll," United States Catholic Magazine, III (1844), 797-98. Campbell argued that an equally important reason (though not one mentioned to Rome) for opposing the establishment of a bishopric was the fear that a bishop would come to exercise control over the Jesuit estates in the United States. Such a fear was not imaginary. Guilday, in John Carroll, pp. 51-52, 167 fn. 2, pointed out that Challoner, Vicar-Apostolic of the London District, was instructed by Propaganda to take temporary possession of all the property belonging to the suppressed Society, but this order Challoner did not care to enforce in the United States. But the fear of such "confiscation" was always there in the minds of some Jesuits, and explains the reason for Article 19 of the General Chapter's Form of Government: "The person invested with spiritual jurisdiction in this country shall not in that quality have any power over or in the temporal property of the clergy." Hughes, Documents, I, Part ii, 622.

[28]Carroll to Thorpe, February 17, 1785. AAB, Case 9A-F1.

themselves. Secondly, just as they hope to
derive some esteem among the people of their
sect from this Episcopal dignity, we also
are confident that not only the same will
hold true for us, but other great benefits
will follow when the Church is administered
the way Christ our Lord established it.[29]

He again stated his preference for a bishop with ordinary

powers, chosen by the American clergy.

Antonelli's reply to Carroll was significant, for

it demonstrated the willingness on the part of Rome to

satisfy, as much as possible, the peculiar needs of

Catholics living in Protestant America. Cardinal Antonelli

told Carroll that Rome had decided to establish, in the

near future, a Vicar-Apostolic with the title and character

of bishop, and to confer this dignity upon himself.

Evidently, Propaganda was not yet prepared to declare for

the appointment of a diocesan bishop (as Carroll had

requested) who would be more independent of the Congrega-

tion. But, Rome was willing to make a generous offer as

to the method of selection, and Carroll was informed that

". . . if, however, you judge it more expedient and more

consistent with the constitution of that Republic that

[29]Carroll to Antonelli, February 27, 1785.
Propaganda Archives. Scritture Riferite nei Congressi,
America Centrale. Vol. II, Fol. 306. John Carroll Papers,
Transcript. Catholic University of America Archives.

the missionaries themselves, at least for the first time,

recommend some individual to the Sacred Congregation to be

promoted to the office of Vicar-Apostolic the Sacred

Congregation will not hesitate to perform whatever you

consider to be most expedient.[30]

Carroll shared Antonelli's letter with his fellow

priests at the Second General Chapter of the Clergy

meeting at Whitemarsh in November, 1786. After due

deliberation the Chapter's majority set forth the funda-

mental principles necessary for the good government of the

Catholic Church in the United States:

> 1. That the form of spiritual government to
> which alone they do submit shall be properly
> Episcopal, depending only on the Holy See in
> matters essentially belonging and universally
> acknowledged to belong to the Holy See as its
> undoubted prerogative.
> 2. That a Diocesan Bishop alone is adequate
> to the above purpose.
> 3. That the representatives of the Clergy of
> the United States . . . are the only proper
> persons to chuse the same.

The assembled clergy then created a committee of three,

composed of Fathers Robert Molyneux, John Ashton, and

---

[30]Antonelli to Carroll, July 23, 1785. Propaganda
Archives. Lettere della S. C., Vol. 246, Fol. 437.
Guilday Transcripts. Catholic University of America
Archives.

John Carroll, to incorporate its sentiments in a memorial
to Rome.[31]

Shortly after the meeting adjourned Father Charles
Sewall, Secretary of the Chapter, issued a Circular Letter
to the Clergy, explaining the reasons behind the Chapter's
resolution on the bishopric. Sewall reminded the clergy
that the political leaders of the country, as well as the
Protestants, ". . . will be confirmed in their prejudices,
if we admit for our chief ecclesiastical Superior a person
appointed by a foreign Congregation, responsible to them
for the exercise of his authority, and removable at their
pleasure." He pointed out that since ". . . the clergy
and the faithful here constitute a National Church . . .
they have therefore a right to the same ecclesiastical
government, as has been used from the days of the Apostles
in every National Church. . . ."--a superior, chosen by
themselves, independent of any jurisdiction save the
spiritual authority of the Holy See. Another factor to
consider was that in time the new clergy coming into the
country may constitute a ". . . sufficient number to carry

[31]Minutes of the Second General Chapter of the
Clergy, November 13-22, 1786. Maryland Province Archives,
Box 2-N7.

measures contrary to our wishes and destructive of the good, which our longer experience of the temper and government of America, enable us to perform."[32]

One additional reason for the appointing of a bishop was the growing realization by many of the clergy that stronger ecclesiastical authority was necessary in America to curb the turbulent spirits of dissident clergy and laity involved in the trustee movement that first emerged in New York City.[33] In the Clergy's Petition for a Bishop, which Fathers Molyneux, Ashton, and Carroll sent to

---

[32]Charles Sewall's Circular Letter to the Clergy, November 24, 1786. As printed in Hughes, Documents, I, Part ii, 670-71. In order to answer the doubts of those Jesuits who feared that the coming of a bishop would prove detrimental to their hopes of reviving the Society, Sewall said that this point had been considered by the Chapter and, ". . . so far from conceiving it harmful to the Society's recovering her rights in this country, we are clearly of opinion, that a Bishop chosen by ourselves, while we constitute a majority, would greatly facilitate so desirable an end."

[33]Carroll told Father William O'Brien that it was the Nugent "affair" in New York City which provided a note of urgency for a request to Rome to establish an episcopacy in America. (Carroll to O'Brien, May 10, 1788, AAB Case 9-S1.) And, in a letter to the Spanish envoy to the United States, Don Diego de Gardoqui, Carroll reminded him of their earlier conversation in which they had concluded that a bishop's authority would be necessary in America where republican institutions were more conducive to claims of independence from authority. (Carroll to Gardoqui, April 19, 1788. AAB, Case 9A-G1.)

the Pope on March 12, 1788, the petitioners expressed their

grave concern over the growing defiance of the Prefect's

authority in America.   Rebellious clergymen, they explained

to the Pope,

> . . . offer as the reason for their unruliness
> and disobedience that they are bound to obey a
> bishop who wields personal authority, but not a
> simple priest who has only delegated authority,
> such as is forbidden by our laws. This was
> recently done in New York by those who wished
> to throw off the yoke of authority. In seeking
> an excuse for their obstinacy they stressed a
> reason most likely to win favor with the
> heterodox, namely, that the authority of the
> ecclesiastical superior put over us by the
> Sacred Congregation was illegal, because it
> was set up by a foreign tribunal and was
> dependent on this tribunal both as regards its
> exercise and its duration.

The petitioners wanted to establish in America a form of

ecclesiastical government which would encompass spiritual

unity with Rome and conformity to the temper of America.

Two points would help to reach this end: first, that the

Pope erect a new episcopal see in the United States, under

his authority; and, secondly, that the election of the

bishop, at least for the first time, be permitted to the

American clergy.[34]   Carroll followed this Petition with a

---

[34]Fathers Carroll, Molyneux, Ashton to the Holy
See, Clergy's Petition for a Bishop, March 12, 1788.
Propaganda Archives. Scritture Riferite nei Congressi,
America Centrale, Vol. II, Fol. 358. John Carroll Papers,
Transcript. Catholic University of America Archives.

personal plea of his own, in which he stressed that the
". . . authority of a bishop will be more weighty in church
government . . ." and ". . . more effective in coercing
those of intractable disposition."[35]

Rome was moved by these arguments, and Antonelli
informed the petitioners that their request for the
election of a diocesan bishop by the American clergy was
approved. Antonelli noted, however, that this privilege
of "election" was granted for the _first_ time only.[36] When
Antonelli's letter of approval arrived, the committee sent
a Circular Letter to the Clergy to notify them of Rome's
decision. Accordingly, the clergy were assembled at
Whitemarsh on May 18, 1788, where John Carroll was almost
unanimously elected as bishop. Carroll's name was forwarded
to Rome where the Pope confirmed the choice of the American
clergy, and on September 14, 1789, the Sacred Congregation
concurred in Carroll's election. The Brief _Ex hac
apostolicae_, establishing the See of Baltimore with John
Carroll as its head, was issued on November 6, 1789. The
following summer Carroll left for England to be consecrated

[35]Carroll to Antonelli, March 18, 1788. AAB,
9A-G1.
[36]Antonelli to Carroll, Molyneux, Aston, July 12,
1788. As quoted in Shea, _John Carroll_, pp. 333-34.

on August 15, 1790, in the Chapel of Thomas Weld at

Lulworth Castle--thereby becoming the first Bishop of

Baltimore.[37]   The first step in the building of an American

Catholic Church had been achieved.

[37]Guilday, John Carroll, pp. 352-54, 356-57, 373.

CHAPTER II

WHO SHALL GOVERN THE

AMERICAN CHURCH

The papal brief _Ex hac apostolicae_ establishing the
See of Baltimore did not reach Carroll until April, 1790.
Upon reading it Carroll became disturbed by certain passages in which the Pope declared that he had granted
permission for the American clergy to elect the Bishop of
Baltimore for the first time only, and that all future
vacancies in this office were to be filled by him.[1]
Evidently, Rome had chosen to ignore the American clergy's
earlier request that the mode of election for future
appointments should not be made without prior consultation

---

[1]The Papal Brief _Ex hac apostolicae_ was later
printed in _A Short Account of the Establishment of the New
See of Baltimore_ (Philadelphia: Carey, Stewart, and Co.,
1791), pp. 14-16. By the common law of the Roman Catholic
Church the Holy See had the right to designate all bishops
for new and vacant sees. (Evidently the Pope intended to
assert his prerogative in the United States.) Actually,
in many parts of the Catholic world, the Holy See had not
chosen to exercise this right. Throughout the centuries
the Papacy has provided for several different ways in
which others--princes, bishops, cathedral chapters--have,
in fact, designated episcopal candidates. Even in these
cases, though, the final appointment of all bishops was
subject to the approval of the Holy See.

with the priests in the United States who best understood
the temper of America.[2] Father John Ashton, Procurator-
General of the Select Body of the Clergy, expressed to
Carroll his dismay over the Pope's presumptions as stated
in the brief, and Carroll assured him that he too opposed
the Holy See's claim because ". . . the exercise of such a
power by the Pope would draw on our Religion a heavy
imputation from the government under which we live."
Carroll was confident that despite the Pope's pretensions
". . . the clergy will have as good right to say, that the
election shall be held by members of their own body, and
that they never can, with safety, or will admit any Bishop
who is not so constituted."[3]

Carroll found the passages in question so objec-
tionable, he feared that the publication of the brief in
America, without certain modifications, would be unwise.
When Plowden informed Carroll that the English printer
Coghlan wanted to publish a pamphlet account of the

---

[2]Carroll, Molyneux, Ashton to the Holy See, Clergy's
Petition for a Bishop, March 12, 1788. Propaganda
Archives. Scritture Riferite nei Congressi, America
Centrale. Vol. II, Fol. 358. John Carroll Papers, Trans-
cript. Catholic University of America Archives.

[3]Carroll to Ashton, April 18, 1790. AAB,Case
9A-H2.

consecration ceremonies (including a translated version of the brief) Carroll immediately replied that Coghlan should print only part of the papal brief for ". . . certain passages . . . should not be printed."[4] Evidently, the passages were not omitted, for Carroll later told Plowden that "I have left [in] the clauses of the bull, for which you contend. . . ." Carroll, however, took his friend gently to task, for in his zeal to defend the just pre-rogatives of the Holy See Plowden ended up justifying expressions ". . . which certainly were introduced for the sake of usurpations on the rights of the . . . Diocesan clergy."[5] Carroll returned to America with a few copies of Coghlan's pamphlet, but after the observations made by some of the leading non-Catholics (to whom he showed the brief) against those passages which secured for Rome control over future appointments to the See of Baltimore, he thought it best to disseminate no more copies.[6]

The Pope's claim to fill all future vacancies in the See of Baltimore presented a serious barrier to the

---

[4]Carroll to Plowden, September 7, 1790. Maryland Province Archives, Box 202-B28.

[5]Carroll to Plowden, October 4, 1790. Maryland Province Archives, Box 202-B33.

[6]Carroll to Plowden, February 22, 1791. Maryland Province Archives, Box 202-B34.

realization of the American clergy's desire to control the selection of their superiors. The Third General Chapter of the Clergy (May 11-18, 1789) had proposed such a plan. In order to establish a permanent mode of appointing bishops best suited to the character of the United States, the Chapter called for the division of the diocese into three districts, each of which was to be represented by two "electors." Whenever a vacancy occurred the electors were to convene and elect a new bishop. If the bishop decided in favor of a Coadjutor, he could summon the electors, and recommend to them the person he favored for the position. The mode of election in this case was to follow that proscribed for that of the bishop, except that now the bishop would also have a vote. The Chapter's plan was subject to the approval of the electors, and, if this was obtained, the plan was to be ". . . powerfully recommended at Rome to be confirmed by the authority of the Holy See.[7]

Carroll was familiar with the plan for he had attended the last day's session of the Chapter's meeting.

[7]Hughes, Documents, I, Part ii, 686-87.

Although he left no written observations concerning this particular proposal, Carroll probably approved of it, for he favored the participation of the clergy in the selection of their ecclesiastical superiors--a step he deemed all the more necessary in republican America. He did not, however, want the whole body of the clergy to participate in future elections; that would be too impractical and, perhaps, too democratic as well.[8] He summarized his philosophy in this way to Plowden:

> For, tho I am much opposed, as you and Mr. Milner to Ecclesiastical democracy, yet I wish sincerely, that Bishops may be elected, at this distance from Rome, by a select body of clergy, constituting, as it were a Cathedral chapter. Otherwise, we shall never be viewed kindly by our government here, and discontent, even amongst our own clergy, will break out.[9]

For whatever the reason the Chapter's plan was not pressed at Rome; instead, Carroll was negotiating with Antonelli on a different plan. Carroll told Antonelli that at the Synod of 1791 the clergy, with whom he had consulted, had declared in favor of a second episcopal see, though if Rome thought otherwise, a coadjutor to the Bishop of

[8]Carroll to Ashton, April 18, 1790. AAB, Case 9A-H2; Carroll to Plowden, November 12, 1788. Maryland Province Archives, Box 202-B19.

[9]Carroll to Plowden, 1791. Maryland Province Archives Box 202-B40.

Baltimore would be acceptable. He shared with Antonelli his fears that if the Pope reserved the right to choose the successors to the Bishop of Baltimore or the Coadjutor ". . . this will seriously displease the civil authorities, and that it will arouse much opposition to us." Carroll's suggestion, and that of the clergy, was that the future election of a bishop or coadjutor should be left to fifteen priests--ten of whom to be the oldest missionaries in America, and the rest to be chosen by Carroll. If Rome granted this request, Carroll was prepared to concede ". . . that the Holy See retain the right to reject candidates until someone is chosen who meets the full approval of the Pope."[10] He was conceding a great deal, but he did so, as he told Plowden, out of his ". . . sollicitude [sic] to provide for a close and intimate union with the Holy See."[11]

On September 29, 1792, Antonelli responded to Carroll's request. As to the question of creating another episcopal see or appointing a bishop-coadjutor, the Pope and Propaganda preferred the latter as more conducive to

[10]Carroll to Antonelli, April 23, 1792. AAB Case 9A-I.

[11]Carroll to Plowden, April 30, 1792. Maryland Province Archives, Box 202-B42.

maintaining ecclesiastical unity and uniformity of disci-

pline. Antonelli's reason for this decision was that:

> . . . the appointment of a coadjutor will avoid
> another appreciable difficulty which could
> arise from the election of a new bishop. While
> on the one hand His Holiness could never
> [italics mine] agree that a new bishop be freely
> chosen from among the members of your clergy, on
> the other, as you yourself fear, an unwelcome
> choice by the Roman Pontiff would arouse great
> opposition among them. Therefore, with the
> designation of a simple coadjutor, this diffi-
> culty will be removed and will even disappear,
> since no one can complain if a bishop requests
> the Holy See to grant him a coadjutor.

Evidently, Rome had no intention of retracting her state-

ment in the papal brief Ex hac apostolicae "for this first

time only," and accordingly rejected a free election of a

coadjutor by the American clergy. Rome was not, however,

insensitive to, or unaware of, the reasons why the American

clergy desired a voice in the selection of their superiors.

Therefore, Antonelli instructed Carroll to ". . . consult

with the older and more experienced members of your clergy

and then to propose a suitable and experienced American

missionary whom the Holy Father will designate as your

coadjutor."[12] By allowing Carroll and the American clergy

---

[12] Antonelli to Carroll, September 29, 1792.
Propaganda Archives. Lettere della S. C., Vol. 262, Fol.
558. Guilday Transcripts, Catholic University of America
Archives.

the right to propose a person ". . . whom the Holy See would designate [italics mine] as . . . coadjutor," Rome granted in fact, what she denied in principle, the right of the American clergy to select their second ecclesiastical superior. After consulting with some of the clergy Carroll proposed, and Rome accepted, the name of Father Lawrence Graessel as Coadjutor to the See of Baltimore with the right of succession.[13]

Looking ahead to the day when the bishop-coadjutor would be consecrated, Carroll felt it necessary to ask Rome for still another privilege, this time to modify the traditional oath to be taken by bishops upon assuming their

---

[13]Carroll to Antonelli, June 17, 1793. AAB Case 9A-I. After Graessel's premature death, Carroll repeated this procedure and then proposed to Rome the name of Father Leonard Neale as coadjutor. Guilday, John Carroll, pp. 570-72, stated that Graessel was elected as coadjutor by the clergy, and Francis J. Weber, "Episcopal Appointments in the U.S.A.," American Ecclesiastical Review, CLV (September, 1966), 179, does the same. I am inclined to agree with Shea, John Carroll, p. 409, that Carroll "consulted" with some of the clergy, and that no formal election took place. This interpretation seems more consistent with the language of Carroll's letter to Antonelli just quoted.

office.[14]   Carroll explained to Antonelli that non-

Catholics would attend the consecration of the coadjutor,

and they would take exception to certain parts of the oath,

especially that passage where the bishop-elect said: "I

will to the utmost of my power seek out and oppose

schismatics, heretics, and the enemies of our Sovereign

Lord and his successors." Carroll wanted this declaration

deleted; failure to do so would arouse ill-will towards

the Catholic Church which the Protestants ". . . decry as

so opposed to the religious liberty to which we Catholics

in the United States are so indebted."[15] Carroll wanted

the bishop's oath to be changed to that as taken by the

Bishops of Ireland.[16]

---

[14]Some of the documents pertaining to the Bishop's
oath were translated by Thomas Middleton, and published
under the title "Documents Relating to the Appointment of
Rev. Lawrence Graessel as Coadjutor to the Right Rev.
John Carroll, First Bishop of Baltimore," American Catholic
Historical Society of Philadelphia Researches, XXI (April,
1904), 59-64. (Hereinafter referred to as Researches.)
Evidently, Carroll had himself objected to taking this
oath. Thorpe wrote Carroll from Rome twice in August,
1790, to share his feelings, but since it was so close to
the time of Carroll's consecration Thorpe did not press
the matter with Antonelli. Thorpe to Carroll, August 11,
1790. AAB, Case 8-K6; Thorpe to Carroll, August 21, 1790.
AAB, Case 8-K8.

[15]Carroll to Antonelli, September 20, 1793. AAB,
Case 9A-I.

[16]Carroll to Antonelli, October 15, 1794. AAB,
Case 9A-I.

The Congregation of Propaganda discussed Carroll's
petition at a General Meeting on June 16, 1794. In the
hope of avoiding any further prejudice towards the
Catholic Church in America (as predicted in the Bishop of
Baltimore's letter), permission was granted for Carroll to
replace the traditional oath with that allowed the Bishops
of Ireland and the Bishop of Mohilow, Russia, which deleted
the objectional passage.[17] Propaganda notified Carroll of
its decision allowing him to use the oath taken by the
Bishops of Ireland and Mohilow, so that ". . . every
pretext for finding fault and bringing charges may be
unavailable to . . . [those] malevolent persons. . ." who
provoke hostility against Catholics and the Holy See.[18]

On December 7, 1800, Father Leonard Neale (whom
Carroll and the clergy had chosen after Graessel's death)
was consecrated as Bishop of Gortyna, and Coadjutor to the
Bishop of Baltimore. Carroll and the clergy had succeeded
in designating their coadjutor, and in having changed the
traditional consecration oath of the bishop-elect, all of
which they deemed necessary to lessen the prejudice of

[17]Propaganda Archives. Acta (1794), Fol. 442,
Num. 8. Guilday Transcripts. Catholic University of
America Archives.
[18]Propaganda to Carroll, August 10, 1794. Propa-
ganda Archives. Lettere Della S. C., Vol. 226, Fol. 490.
Guilday Transcripts, Catholic University of America Archives

their fellow Americans against the Catholic Church in this country. Still, the designation of Neale, was a privilege, not a right, granted at Rome's pleasure. Rome had not accepted Carroll's request to establish a permanent procedure by which the designation of episcopal candidates would come from America. Events connected with the division of the diocese of Baltimore and the creation of four new episcopal sees confirmed this fact.

* * * * * * * * * *

By the papal bull Ex debito pastoralis officii, issued on April 8, 1808, the Holy See divided the Diocese of Baltimore and erected four new episcopal sees in the United States. In 1806, at Rome's request, Carroll had submitted to Propaganda a proposal calling for this very same division of his diocese. Carroll also forwarded at that time a list of nominees for the proposed bishoprics, save that of New York, which he preferred to remain vacant until an acceptable candidate could be decided upon. Rome approved of Carroll's plan and accepted his recommended candidates, except for New York where, upon its own authority, Father Luke Concanen, an Irish Dominican living

in Rome, was appointed as bishop.[19] In appointing

Concanen, Rome had chosen a man whom Carroll knew and

respected.[20] Still, considering Carroll's often stated

position on the need for the American clergy to have a

voice in the selection of their ecclesiastical superiors,

it was surprising that he did not voice any objection to

Rome over the appointment of Concanen.

What must have disturbed Carroll even more, however,

was that passage in the papal bull Ex debito pastoralis

officii in which the Holy See declared:

> We by the apostolical authority . . . erect and
> constitute four new episcopal sees in the said
> States, for four respective bishops, now and
> hereafter whenever a vacancy occurs in any of
> the said sees, to be elected and constituted by
> us and the apostolic see. . . .[21]

In November, 1810, Carroll met for several weeks with his

fellow bishops--Neale, Cheverus of Boston, Egan of

---

[19]McCarthy, "Historical Development of Episcopal
Nominations," pp. 321-23; Guilday, John Carroll, Chap.
XXIX, "The Division of the Diocese of Baltimore (1808),"
pp. 567-601.

[20]Victor F. O'Daniel, "Concanen's Election to the
See of New York (1808-1810)," Catholic Historical Review,
II (April, 1916), 19-20, 22-23.

[21]A copy of the Papal Bull Ex debito pastoralis
officii can be found in the Records, XVIII (September,
1907), 296-98.

Philadelphia, and Flaget of Bardstown, Kentucky. They

discussed the problem of hierarchical appointments, and

obviously dissatisfied over the present state of affairs in

which the American ecclesiastical leaders had no official

right to control the nomination of future bishops, they

resolved that:

> In case the Holy See will graciously permit
> the nomination to vacant Bishoprics to be made
> in the United States, it is humbly and respect-
> fully suggested to the Supreme Pontiff of the
> Church to allow the nomination for the vacant
> Dioceses to proceed solely from the Archbishop
> and Bishops of this Ecclesiastical Province.[22]

The bishops made no mention of the clergy's right to

participate in the selection of the hierarchy. The General

Chapter of the Clergy (May, 1789) had proposed, with

Carroll's approval, such an approach; and Carroll had

introduced a similar plan to Rome in 1792. Perhaps now

that an ecclesiastical hierarchy existed in the United

States such an approach was no longer necessary or appro-

priate. In any case, Carroll did not rule out some voice

for the clergy in the selection of their bishops, for he

did consult with certain priests in the diocese of

---

[22]Regulations, Bishop's Meeting, November, 1810.
AAB, Case 11-I2.

Philadelphia when he attempted to find a replacement for the late Michael Egan. But Carroll did not take up again the earlier, more democratic plans, in which the clergy officially participated in the selection of their bishops. The Bishops submitted a joint letter to Rome, in which they requested the sole right to nominate in all future cases where an episcopal vacancy occurred, but the disturbed state of Europe and the imprisionment of Pius VII by Napoleon made communications so difficult that as late as 1814 their petition went unanswered. It is not known whether Rome ever received it. In any case, the Holy See appointed, in 1814, without consulting the American hierarchy, Father John Connolly, an Irish Dominican, to succeed the late Luke Concanen, as the second Bishop of New York.[23] Carroll did not learn of Connolly's appointment until the summer of 1815.[24] He complained in a

---

[23]McCarthy, "Historical Development of Episcopal Nominations," p. 324; Weber, "Episcopal Appointments in the U.S.A.," p. 180.

[24]When Carroll heard of Connolly's appointment he may have remembered with some bitterness the assurances which Luke Concanen gave him after having conferred with the Pope: "On this subject permit me to add, and to assure your grace, that no appointment, no arrangement of any importance regarding the Church of the United States will be adopted by the Holy See without your previous advice, and consent. This I have taken special care to be determined on." Concanen to Carroll, August 9, 1809. AAB Case 2-W7.

private note to Plowden: "I wish this may not become a very dangerous precedent, fruitful of mischief by drawing censure upon our religion, and a false opinion of the servility of our principles.[25] Yet when he wrote to Cardinal Litta, Prefect of the Sacred Congregation of Propaganda, he did not take the opportunity to protest Rome's appointment of Connolly without consulting the American hierarchy.[26]

Failure to press more strenuously at Rome for the right to control nominations, opened the way for more difficulties in the American Church, as actually happened in 1814-1815 when the See of Philadelphia fell vacant with the death of Bishop Michael Egan. The church at Philadelphia was in such a disturbed condition because of the trustee controversy that Carroll suggested to his fellow bishops that they send a list of recommended names to Rome for the immediate appointment of a new bishop. Carroll knew that this could not be done in an authoritative manner, since

---

[25] Carroll to Plowden, June 25, 1815. Stonyhurst Archives. Guilday Collection, Catholic University of America Archives.

[26] Carroll to Litta, October 10, 1815. Propaganda Archives. Scritture Riferite nei Congressi, America Centrale. Vol. III, Fol. 350. John Carroll Papers, Transcript. Catholic University of America Archives.

Rome had not granted the request which they had made in
December, 1810, but the situation called for prompt action.[27]
There was still another, and equally important reason for
action--the attempt of foreign prelates to influence the
appointment of the rebellious Father William Vincent Harold
as Bishop of Philadelphia.[28] Carroll replied with anger to
Plowden: "How any of these Prelates, and particularly the
Ven. Abp. of Bourdeaux could determine themselves to
interfere in an affair so foreign to their concern, and to
which they are so incompetent, is a matter of surprise."[29]
Jean Louis Ann Magdalen Lefebvre de Cheverus, the first
Bishop of Boston, expressed his own annoyance to Carroll:
"It is certainly astonishing that Prelates in France or
Ireland should recommend subjects for the Mission here and
be listened to rather than you and those here you are
pleased to consult."[30]

---

[27]Carroll to American Bishops, August 23, 1814.
AAB, Case 9-K5.

[28]Carroll to Flaget, Bishop of Bardstown, Kentucky,
August 12, 1815. AAB, Case 9-M4.

[29]Carroll to Plowden, June 25, 1815. Stonyhurst
Archives. Guilday Collection, Catholic University of
America Archives. In this same letter, Carroll accused the
Archbishop of Dublin, John Troy, as one of those prelates
who had recommended Harold. Troy later denied the charge.
A good account of the controversy, sympathetic to Troy,
is that of Daniel Joseph Connors, "Archbishop Troy and the
American Church (1800-1823)," United States Catholic
Historical Society, Historical Records and Studies, XXII
(1932), 168-83.

[30]Cheverus to Carroll, May 11, 1815. AAB, Case 2-P(

Harold was never named to the See of Philadelphia.
Perhaps Carroll's arguments had persuaded Rome against
Harold's proposed appointment. Still, the aged Bishop
of Baltimore (Carroll was eighty years old in 1815, the
year of his death) must have been apprehensive about the
future. Granted, there had been successes in the past--
the election of a diocesan bishop by the clergy, the
designation of the coadjutor, the changing of the oath.
All of these steps were necessary if the Church was to
become an acceptable institution in an America republican
in spirit, proudly independent, and suspicious of all
things Catholic. Carroll had served as bishop for a
quarter of a century, and throughout his episcopacy he
tried to obtain, without success, Rome's approval to
establish a permanent procedure by which the independence
of the Catholic Church in America could be secured from
outside control. The clergy's plan to allow for the
election of ecclesiastical superiors never survived
Carroll's own election; and even the bishop's resolution of
1810 which called for the American hierarchy to control the

nomination of bishops was not granted. The Pope claimed the sole right (which he exercised on several occasions) to fill, on his own authority, all episcopal vacancies in America; and foreign prelates tried to influence the selection of candidates for American bishoprics. Such actions only served to keep alive the suspicions of many Americans that the Catholic Church could never become a truly American institution. The selection of the hierarchy by the American bishops themselves was crucial, then, in overcoming non-Catholic prejudices. But this had not been achieved. Perhaps Guilday's words are too harsh, but on this question at least, there was a degree of sad truth in his statement that Carroll ". . . died with the consciousness of failure and defeat."[31]

[31]Guilday, John Carroll, p. 685.

CHAPTER III

AMERICAN CATHOLIC RELATIONSHIP

WITH ROME

Throughout the 1780's John Carroll had consistently
maintained that it was essential for American Catholics to
accept no foreign jurisdiction over their affairs, save
the spiritual authority of the Pope, and even in this
realm he sought certain privileges which would reduce
Rome's influence in the American Church to a minimum. As
Carroll told Archbishop Doria Pamphili, Papal Nuncio at
Paris, any undue dependence on Rome would only confirm many
Americans in their mistaken opinion that ". . . our faith
demands a subjection to His Holiness incompatible with the
independence of a sovereign state. . . ."[1] Non-Catholics
believed that the demand for allegiance which Rome claimed
from all its members was such that Catholics could not be
fully loyal to their country. Carroll realized that this
prejudice of so many Americans would only serve to make

[1]Carroll to Pamphili, November 26, 1784. AAB,
Case 9A-F1.

more difficult the acceptance of the Catholic Church in the United States. He also knew that it was this same jealousy against all kinds of "foreign authority" (which was what most Americans took Rome to be) that had served to exclude Catholics from civil rights in many of the states. It was therefore crucial that such prejudices, entertained for so long against Catholics, be eradicated. This could be accomplished in two ways. First, by making Rome's influence in the ecclesiastical affairs of the church in this country as light and inconspicuous as possible, and this Carroll strove to do throughout his episcopate; secondly, by assuring their fellow Americans, that Catholics denied, in principle and practice, any claims that Rome possessed temporal authority. Catholics must make it clear that they gave only allegiance to the spiritual authority of Rome, and that they did not credit Rome with any temporal power to intervene in any way in civil affairs.

Carroll had strongly opposed placing the ecclesiastical affairs of the Catholic Church in America under the jurisdiction of Propaganda, for this in itself could

be defined as undue foreign influence. When he learned,
however, from his friend Charles Plowden, that Propaganda
had designs going beyond the ecclesiastical, that the
Congregation intended to possess the Jesuit estates in
America, he replied with anger against any intrusion by
Rome in the temporal concerns of the clergy:

> For they may be assured, that they will never
> get possession of a sixpence of our property
> here, and if any of our friends could be weak
> enough to deliver any real estate into their
> hands or attempt to subject it to their
> authority, our civil government would be
> called upon to wrest it again out of their
> dominion. A foreign temporal jurisdiction
> will never be tolerated here. . . . They may
> therefore send their agents when they please;
> they will certainly return empty-handed. My
> only dread . . . would be the scandal that
> would result from the assertion of unjust
> pretensions. . . .[2]

Carroll's fears proved unfounded, for Antonelli later
assured him that Propaganda had no intention to interfere
in temporal matters.[3]

---

[2]Carroll to Plowden, September 26, 1783. Maryland
Province Archives, Box 202-B5. During the seventeenth
century Jesuit priests and lay brothers who came to Maryland
received land under the headright system. In addition,
pious Catholics bequeathed land to the Jesuits for purposes
of keeping the faith alive in the American missions. The
Jesuits supported themselves and their missionary labors
from the proceeds of these estates.

[3]Antonelli to Carroll, June 9, 1794. As quoted by
Guilday, John Carroll, pp. 203-04.

Carroll stressed to his constituency that the Pope's powers were purely spiritual, and in no way did the Pontiff's powers carry over into the temporal realm. When the trustees of Holy Trinity Church, Philadelphia, refused to accept Carroll's spiritual authority because it derived from a "foreign jurisdiction" he pointed out, with some annoyance, that this reproach would be warranted if Catholics acknowledged in the Pope ". . . any power or prerogative, which clashed in the least degree with the duty, we owe to our country, or its laws." Catholics owe to their country loyalty and support; to the Pope ". . . obedience in things purely spiritual." "Happily," Carroll noted, "there is no competition in their respective claims on us, nor any difficulty in rendering to both the submission, which they have a right to claim."[4]

Carroll's statement that American Catholic allegiance to Rome served to bar them from civil office in some of the states was most true in New York. Here, according to the State Constitution of 1777, all those assuming civil or military office in the state were required to take an

[4]Bishop's Carroll's Pastoral Letter to the Congregation of Holy Trinity Church, February 22, 1797. Printed Copy. AAB, Case 10-W2.

oath to ". . . renounce and abjure all allegiance and
subjection to all and every foreign king, prince, potentate
and State, in all matters ecclesiastical as well as
civil. . . ."[5]

In 1806 Francis Cooper, a prominent New York City
Catholic, won election to the State Assembly--the first
Catholic to be sent to that body. Cooper, as a loyal
Catholic, could not take the oath, which, in effect,
included a denial of the spiritual supremacy of the Pope.[6]
The Catholics of New York City petitioned the New York
State Legislature on January 6, 1806, to protest against
an oath which barred Catholics from their common rights of
citizenship. In their defense, the petitioners, clearly
and boldly stated their position on the kind of allegiance
Catholics owed to Rome:

> They are willing . . . to swear, that they
> renounce and abjure all allegiance and subjec-
> tion to every foreign power however titled, in

---

[5]Francis Newton Thorpe, The Federal and State
Constitutions (7 vols.; Washington: Government Printing
Office, 1909), V, 2637-38.

[6]The story of Cooper and the "oath" is well told
by William H. Bennett, "Francis Cooper: New York's First
Catholic Legislator," Historical Records and Studies, XII
(1918), 31-32; and Leo Raymond Ryan, Old St. Peter's:
The Mother Church of Catholic New York 1785-1935 (New York:
United States Catholic Historical Society, 1935),
pp. 83-86. (Hereinafter referred to as Old St. Peter's.)

all matters not only civil, but also
ecclesiastical, as far as they may interfere
with, or in the smallest degree affect the
freedom, independence, or safety of the
state; but as the Bishop of Rome is the
acknowledged head of the profession of which
they are members, they cannot renounce and
abjure all subjection to the decrees of the
Roman Catholic Church, as promulgated by him,
in matters purely and solely spiritual, and
which cannot interfere either with the civil
or religious rights of their brethren of
other denominations, without a total derelic-
tion of the religious principles they
profess. . . .[7]

The petitioners were successful. The New York State

Legislature in February, 1806, eliminated that section

which read "in all matters ecclesiastical," thereby allow-

ing Cooper to take the oath and assume his seat.[8]

Other American Catholic writers, addressing them-

selves to this question of temporal power, drew similar

conclusions. Father Demetrius Augustine Gallitzin, a

convert to Catholicism and missionary priest to the settlers

of western Pennsylvania, repudiated charges made by

Protestant critics that Catholics believed in the temporal

authority of Rome. Gallitzin replied that the Pope's

---

[7]Petition of the Catholics of New York City to the
New York State Legislature, January 6, 1806, as printed in
the American Citizen, February 12, 1806. Copy found in
AAB, Case 10-Y7.

[8]Laws of the State of New York (Albany: John
Barber, 1806), Chap. III, p. 10.

jurisdiction was purely spiritual, and not of this world.
This alone Catholics accepted. As for their temporal
allegiance, Catholics gave that only to their government.
Consequently, if the Pope, as a temporal prince, was to
invade the United States, ". . . our principles, as Roman
Catholics would oblige us, in compliance with our oath of
allegiance, to take up arms and defend our country against
the forces of his holiness as bravely as we would against
the armies of Great Britain."[9] Gallitzin's conclusions
were obvious. The Pope had no power to depose civil
rulers, to absolve subjects from their oaths of allegiance
to their governments. Granted, some Popes, moved by pride
and ambition, had acted in this manner, but this was an
abuse. "The Catholic Church," he asserted, ". . . commands
us to give to God what is God's, and to Caesar what is
Caesar's."[10]

Father Francis Anthony Fleming, of St. Mary's
Church, Philadelphia, writing under the pen-name "Verax,"
denied the charges of "Verus" that Catholics adored the

[9]Demetrius Augustine Gallitzin, "A Defence of
Catholic Principles," Gallitzin's Letters: A Collection of
the Polemical Works, ed. by Grace Murphy (Loretto, Pa.:
Angelmodde Press, 1940), pp. 89-90. (Hereinafter referred
to as "A Defence of Catholic Principles.")

[10]Ibid., p. 89.

Pope.[11] "We reject," Fleming remarked, ". . . all [Papal]

pretensions to temporal powers. We revere in the Pope,

[only] a spiritual preeminence and authority. . . ."[12]

Fleming admitted that were the Pope ". . . to renew the

antiquated pretensions of some of his predecessors, by

intermeddling in the temporal concerns of America, the

American Catholics would imitate the conduct of their

English brethren under Queen Elizabeth."[13]

Out on the frontier Father Stephen Theodore Badin,

a refugee from France and the first Catholic priest

ordained in this country, had printed a politico-religious

tract to enlighten Kentucky Catholics on the true principles

---

[11]According to Joseph L.J. Kirlin, Catholicity in
Philadelphia (Philadelphia: John Jos. McVey, 1909),
pp. 135-36, it was Fleming who collected the literature
of the controversy from the different newspapers in which
they appeared, and published them. At some point in the
controversy with "Verus," Fleming was joined by Matthew
Carey, a noted Catholic publisher in Philadelphia. Carey
soon withdrew from the contest, much to the disappointment
of Bishop Carroll who liked Carey's polemical style.
Carroll to Carey, March 7, 1792, as printed in "Selections
from the Correspondence of the Deceased Matthew Carey,
Writer, Printer, Publisher," Records, IX (September, 1898),
371-72.

[12]Francis Fleming and Matthew Carey, The Calumnies
of Verus (Philadelphia: Johnston and Justice, 1792),
pp. 46-47.

[13]Ibid.

of Catholics in reference to God and country.[14] Badin

pointed out that where Catholics recognize the Pope as the

visible head of the whole Catholic Church, they do not

". . . believe that the Pope has any direct or indirect

authority over the temporal power and jurisdiction of

foreign Princes or States." Hence, the Pope had no right

to depose civil rulers, or to absolve subjects, living

under heretical or schismatical rulers, of their allegiance;

Catholics would be ". . . bound in conscience to defend

their Prince and Country, at the hazard of their lives and

fortunes . . . even against the Pope himself, should it be

possible for him to attempt an invasion."[15]

---

[14]Robert Gorman, Catholic Apologetical Literature
in the United States 1784-1858 (Washington: Catholic
University of America Press, 1939), pp. 17-18, fn. 46,
pointed out that the first section of Badin's book, which
deals in part with the question of Rome's spiritual and
temporal authority, was not written by Badin. He had taken
these sections from a work originally composed by an
English Benedictine, a Father James Maurus Corker, who
had published it in London in 1680, under the title Roman
Catholic Principles, in Reference to God and the King.
The extensive notes, however, which follow these short
three sections, are Badin's.

[15]Stephen Theodore Badin, The Real Principles of
Roman Catholics, in Reference to God and the Country
(Bardstown: F. Peniston, 1805), pp. 8-9. (Hereinafter
referred to as Real Principles of Roman Catholics.)

* * * * * * * * * *

Protestants often charged American Catholics with
holding, as an article of their belief, to the doctrine of
papal infallibility.[16] Protestants chose to interpret the
doctrine of papal infallibility in its broadest terms,
applying to all the Pope's utterances (even in areas beyond
faith and morals) an authority which had to be obeyed by
all Catholics. This enhanced power of the Pope who,
according to the Protestants, also claimed temporal
authority, posed a further danger to the independence and
safety of every state in which Catholics lived. It
constituted one more reason to doubt the allegiance of

---

[16]The doctrine of Papal Infallibility was <u>not</u> an
official part of Catholic teaching at this time. It was
not proclaimed as an article of belief, binding on all
Catholics, until the Vatican Council of 1870. As
finally decided on by the Council, the doctrine of Papal
Infallibility declared that: "The Roman Pontiff when
he speaks <u>ex cathedra</u>, that is, when exercising the office
of pastor and teacher of all Christians, he defines with
his supreme apostolic authority, a doctrine concerning
faith or morals to be held by the universal Church,
through the divine assistance promised to him in St. Peter,
is possessed of that infallibility with which the divine
Redeemer willed his Church to be endowed in defining
doctrine concerning faith and morals: and therefore such
definitions of the Roman Pontiff are irreformable of
themselves and not from the consent of the Church." As
quoted in Dom Cuthbert Butler, <u>The Vatican Council</u>,
(2 Vols.; London: Longmans, Green and Co., 1930), II
133.

Catholics, who were compelled by their faith to obey an "infallible" Pope.[17]

No American Catholic accepted the broad definition that Protestants gave to infallibility.[18] A few Catholics were personally willing to recognize that the Pope could not err in matters of faith and morals (which was to accept by indirection the doctrine of papal infallibility), though they would not say that such a belief was a part of the official teachings of the Catholic Church. Many denied that papal infallibility (even in its limited sense of applying only to faith and morals) constituted a part of Catholic doctrine, and the insistence with which they did so was probably motivated by a desire to counter the harmful consequences to their church that could result from Protestant charges.

Father Charles Nerinckx, a Belgian missionary who came to America in 1804, made the strongest statement in support of papal infallibility. In an address to his

---

[17]Sister Mary Augustina Ray, American Opinion of Roman Catholicism in the Eighteenth Century (New York: Columbia University Press, 1936), pp. 133, 137, 270. (Hereinafter referred to as American Opinion of Roman Catholicism.)

[18]Carroll to Plowden, September 2, 1790. Stonyhurst Archives. Guilday Collection, Catholic University of America Archives.

fellow Belgians, Nerinckx implored them to always

". . . show solemn respect to His [Christ's] Vicar and let

us always take for a rule the latter's voice and behavior

in questions of doctrine."[19] On another occasion, prior

to his departure from Belgium (where he had gone in 1815

for a visit), he left his countrymen the following pointed

suggestion:

> And let me here also add the further advice,
> which I myself have always tried to practice,
> to cling steadfastly to the Head of the
> Church--the Pope of Rome; to accept his
> decisions as the words of Him whose place he
> fills. . . . There never sprang up an error
> or heresy of which the Pope was head, and
> never will there be true faith where the Pope
> is not at the head.[20]

Carroll was inclined to agree with Nerinckx that

the Holy See had been the guardian of the faith throughout

the centuries. His few utterances on this subject

demonstrate that he was close to the traditions of the

Society of Jesus which accepted the infallibility of the

---

[19]Charles Nerinckx, _Einen Oogslag op dem Tegenwoordigen Staet der Roomsch-Catholyke Religie in Noord-America_ (Louvain, 1816), p. 14. Unpublished translation by Magdeleine Wellner for my personal use.

[20]As quoted in William J. Howlett, _Life of Rev. Charles Nerinckx_ (Techny, Ill.: Mission Press, 1915), pp. 313-14. (Hereinafter referred to as _Nerinckx_.)

Pope in matter of faith and morals.[21] Carroll assured

Antonelli that as bishop he would lay the ". . . most

solid and enduring foundation not merely of union with

the Holy See but also of conformity, obedience and love."

Experience had taught him ". . . that faith and morals are

kept intact if there is a close union with Christ's Vicar

on earth, and that nearly every lapse in either originates

in a diminution of respect for the See of Peter."[22]

Father John Thayer, a New England minister who

converted to Catholicism in 1783, pointed out that some

divines carried their respect for the Holy See so far that

they supposed that Christ would never allow the Pope to

propose anything to the Church in matters of faith that

was contrary to divine revelation--in other words, that the

Pope was infallible. But Thayer knew the doctrines of

Catholicism well enough to reply to his critics that

". . . this is only an opinion, which every one is free to

---

[21]Carroll to Plowden, September 2, 1790. Stonyhurst Archives. Guilday Collection, Catholic University
of America Archives; W.J. Sparrow-Simpson, Roman Catholic
Opposition to Papal Infallibility (Milwaukee: Young
Churchman Co., 1910), pp. 72-79.

[22]Carroll to Antonelli, July, 1790. Propaganda
Archives. Scritture Riferite nei Congressi, America
Centrale. Vol. II, Fol. 390. John Carroll Papers,
Transcripts. Catholic University of America Archives.

believe or reject. . . ."[23] Gallitzin, who was a good

theologian, flatly denied Protestant charges that

infallibility of the Pope was an article of the Catholic

faith. Cardinal Bellarmine and other divines to the

contrary, he concluded that the Catholic Church never

taught such a doctrine.[24] Fleming dismissed Protestant

accusations that Catholics adored the Pope by simply

saying: "We do not worship the Pope. It is not an article

of our faith, that he is infallible. . . ."[25] Father

Anthony Kohlmann, a learned Jesuit stationed in New York

City, noted: "It is no article of Catholic faith that

the Pope is himself infallible, separated from the Church,

---

[23]John Thayer, Controversy Between the Rev. John
Thayer, Catholic Missionary of Boston, and the Rev. George
Lesslie, Pastor of a Church in Washington, New Hampshire
(Newburyport: John Mycall, 1793), p. 14. (Hereinafter
referred to as Controversy.)

[24]Gallitzin, "A Defence of Catholic Principles,"
p. 89.

[25]Fleming and Carey, Calumnies of Verus, pp. 46-47.

even in expounding the faith."[26]   Badin, evidently drawing

from the same source as Kohlmann, quoted the same passage

against Papal infallibility.[27]

* * * * * * * * * *

The refusal on the part of American Catholics to

attribute to the Pope any temporal power or infallibility,

in no way resulted in a denial of the Pope's spiritual

supremacy over the whole Church.   American Catholics

maintained the warmest feelings of respect and veneration

for the Holy See, and they called for a close spiritual

union with Rome as essential to Catholicism.

Fleming, Gallitzin, and Badin--all of whom seriously

limited Papal power in temporal concerns and infallibility--

---

[26]Anthony Kohlmann, The Catholic Question in
America (New York: Edward Gillespy, 1813), Appendix,
p. cxiii. Since Kohlmann is listed in most accounts as
the author of this work, I have continued, for convenience
sake, to do so here. While Kohlmann may have been the
moving force behind the work, it was William Sampson, his
defense counsel, who actually prepared the report of the
famous "confessional" trial, printed in the first part of
The Catholic Question. The "Treatise on Penance" (placed
in the Appendix of this book), usually attributed to
Kohlmann, was written by a fellow Jesuit, Father Benjamin
Joseph Fenwick, though with assistance from Kohlmann.
Gorman, Catholic Apologetical Literature, pp. 28-29;
Francis X. Curran, "The Jesuit Colony in New York 1808-1817,"
Historical Records and Studies, XLII (1954), 64-65.

[27]Badin, Real Principles of Roman Catholics, p. 9.

willingly recognized the Pope's spiritual preeminence and authority over the whole Catholic Church.[28]

A stronger assertion still of Papal Supremacy was to be found in one of the questions in Bishop's Hay's Catechism, published with Carroll's approval:

> Q. What duty do the people owe to the chief pastor of the Church?
>
> A. Considering his high station, we owe him the greatest respect and veneration, and considering his supreme authority, we owe an entire obedience to his decrees and orders in all things relating to religion.[29]

Carroll subscribed fully to that simple catechetical question. While he denied Papal claims to temporal power, and sought to limit the influence of Rome in the internal ecclesiastical affairs of the American Church, Carroll was an ardent defender of the spiritual authority of the Holy See, and he would not allow any detraction from the Pope's spiritual prerogatives. He told Father Andrew Nugent, temporary pastor of St. Peter's Church, New York City, that the New York State oath, which demanded one to renounce all foreign authority ". . . in all matters ecclesiastical

---

[28]Fleming and Carey, Calumnies of Verus, pp. 46-47; Gallitzin, "A Defence of Catholic Principles," pp. 89-90; Badin, Real Principles of Roman Catholics, p. 9.

[29]Bishop John Hay, An Abridgement of the Christian Doctrine (Baltimore: Bernard Dornin, 1809), p. 31.

as well as civil. . . ." was unacceptable since it resulted

in a denial of the Pope as the visible head of the Church.[30]

On another occasion Carroll refused to send young boys to

study at a seminary in Mainz, for he did not want to

expose them to dangerous teachings, since missionary priests

coming from Germany held lax views concerning the spiritual

authority of the Holy See.[31]

Carroll sought to maintain a close union with Rome,

the center of ecclesiastical unity. He assured Pius VI,

shortly after his consecration as bishop, that he would

". . . never fail in that fidelty and obedience to the

Holy See, without which, as I have learned from ecclesiastical

history and the Holy fathers, faith totters." Carroll added

that he would make every effort, so that those committed to

his care--clergy and laity alike--would be animated by the

same spirit.[32]

---

[30]Carroll to Nugent, July 18, 1786. AAB, Case 9A-Gl.

[31]Carroll to Pastor in Mainz, July 17, 1783, as quoted in Lloyd Paul McDonald, The Seminary Movement in the United States: Projects, Foundations, and Early Developments 1784-1833 (Washington: Catholic University of America Press, 1927), p. 7; Carroll to Antonelli, July, 1790. Propaganda Archives. Scritture Riferite nei Congressi, America Centrale, Vol. II, Fol. 559V. Carroll Papers, Transcript. Catholic University of America Archives.

[32]Carroll to Pius VI, September 27, 1790. Propaganda Archives. Scritture Riferite nei Congressi, America Centrale. Vol. II, Fol. 404. John Carroll Papers, Transcripts. Catholic University of America Archives.

Soon after Carroll returned home from his consecration in England he summoned the American clergy to meet with him in the first Synod of the Clergy, November, 1791. Realizing that the distance which separated America from Rome--geographically and culturally--was so great, Carroll feared ". . . the danger of a propension to a schismatical separation from the center of unity." He called the synodial meeting so that ". . . an uniform discipline may be established in all parts of this great continent; and every measure so firmly concerted, that as little danger, as possible, may remain of a disunion with the Holy See."[33]

Under pressure, then, from their fellow Americans, who considered Rome's claims to temporal authority and papal infallibility as further proof that Catholics could never become fully American, many Catholics spoke against these concepts. But Catholics could never renounce their spiritual union with the Pope, the supreme pastor of the Catholic Church. They could not turn away from

[33]Carroll to Plowden, October 12, 1791. Maryland Province Archives, Box 202-B39.

the spiritual authority of the Holy See without a painful surrender of the name "Roman Catholic." And this they were not prepared to do.

PART II

CLERIC-LAY RELATIONS: TRUSTEEISM

CHAPTER IV

THE TRUSTEE CONTROVERSY--WHO SHALL

GOVERN THE PARISH CHURCH?

In the early centuries of Christianity the Church
was the sole proprietor of its possessions, with the
administration of its goods residing in the hands of the
diocesan bishop. A new practice developed in the sixth
century. Each parish church claimed its patrimony as
distinct from that of the cathedral (bishop's) church; the
pastor and his assistants managed the goods of each church.
During the Middle Ages a system of lay administration of
church revenue emerged in parts of Western Europe--France,
Spain, Germany and England. These committees of laymen,
known by various names--fabriques or marquilliers in
France, kirchenältester in Germany--were elected by the
more prominent members of the parish. They administered
the temporal concerns of the church, but had no authority
to interfere in ecclesiastical affairs. Even in their own

sphere they were essentially subject to the clergy, for the pastor assumed the chief place on the board. The legitimacy of the fabricae (board of lay managers) was recognized by the Council of Trent.[1]

The practice, then, of some lay influence in the area of church temporalities had not been entirely foreign to the Roman Catholic Church. In America, however, laymen came to play a more significant role in parish affairs. Actually, such a development was inevitable, for the very nature of American law decreed the rise of trusteeism--lay control over church revenue and property.

Under American law the Catholic Church was not recognized as a corporation; its dioceses were not judicially noticed as corporate entities, and the bishop qua bishop was not accorded any authority outside of the spiritual. The ecclesiastical system of the Catholic Church had neither ". . . legal capacity nor legal existence and [was] incapable sui juris of having legal rights or temporal property."[2]

---

[1] Patrick J. Dignan, A History of the Legal Incorporation of Catholic Church Property in the United States 1784-1932 (Washington: Catholic University of America Press, 1933), pp. 67-71. (Hereinafter referred to as Legal Incorporation of Catholic Church Property.) Robert F. McNamara, "Trusteeism," New Catholic Encyclopedia, XIV 323-25.

[2] Carl F.G. Zollmann, American Church Law (St. Paul: West Publishing Co., 1933), p. 112; Chester Joseph Bartlett, The Tenure of Parochial Property in the United States (Washington: Catholic University of America Press, 1926), pp. 1, 6-11, 21-22, 25.

American law created a distinction between the
Church--the spiritual entity--and the religious society--
the temporal body of members. Only the latter could be
recognized by the law; only the latter could be incorporated so as to acquire legal tenure of Church properties.[3]

Catholic congregations, or elected members thereof,
were incorporated either by special act of the State
legislature or under general incorporation laws. The law
authorized religious corporations to govern the temporal
concerns of the churches; they were not empowered, though,
to interfere in its spiritual affairs. As Zollmann, a
leading authority on American church law, stated: "The
religious corporation has no spiritual capacity, or
denominational character, is not ecclesiastical in its
functions, and has nothing to do with the church except as
it provides for its wants. It cannot alter the church's
faith and covenant. . . ."[4]

The principle of incorporation in America was more
congenial to the Protestant churches with their long
tradition and practice of lay control, than to the Catholic

[3]Zollmann, _American Church Law_, pp. 143-45.
[4]_Ibid._, pp. 133-34, 144-46.

Church with its limited experience in this area.[5] Nevertheless, during the late eighteenth century more and more
Catholic congregations found incorporation a more
advantageous way of securing ecclesiastical church properties and, perhaps, a better way to exercise control over
the management of the church. Carroll allowed (some say
tolerated) this practice. Incorporation entrusted
considerable power to trustees--power which, to Carroll's
consternation, they soon misused. The limited experience
of Catholics with lay involvement in church affairs put
the trustees at a disadvantage. They did not know how to
handle the power which American law gave them <u>within</u> the
context of Roman Catholic doctrine and practice.

* * * * * * * * * *

The first major outbreak of "trusteeism" occurred
at St. Peter's Church, in New York City. The pastor of
St. Peter's was Father Charles Whelan, an Irish Capuchin.
Many members of the congregation were not impressed with
Whelan, of whom a fellow priest said that he was not
". . . eloquent when speaking in public, nor has he the

---

[5]Dignan, <u>Legal Incorporation of Catholic Church
Property</u>, pp. 51-52.

gift of ingratiating himself."[6] In the fall of 1785,
Father Andrew Nugent, a fellow Capuchin, arrived in New York
City where he became assistant pastor at St. Peter's.
Nugent, a good preacher, soon won a following among the
trustees and members of the congregation. The Nugent
"faction" insisted that Whelan resign. The trustees
refused to pay Whelan any further salary as of Christmas,
1785, and they even threatened to take legal measures to
remove him if necessary. On December 18, 1785, two
adherents of Nugent seized the Sunday collection--and so
began the first schism in an American Catholic parish
church.[7]

The situation in New York disturbed Carroll. He
sent a strong protest to the trustees. He expressed his
dismay that some members of the church held to the opinion
that the congregation could choose and discharge the parish
priest without the consent of the bishop or ecclesiastical
superior. "If ever the principles, there laid down,"
Carroll exclaimed, "should become predominant, the unity
and catholicity of our Church would be at an end; and it

[6]Farmer to Carroll, May 10, 1785, AAB, Case 3-P9.

[7]Ryan, Old St. Peter, pp. 47-49; Guilday, John
Carroll, pp. 262-64.

would be formed into distinct independent societies, nearly in the same manner as the congregational Presbyterians of your neighboring New England states." So as not to appear ungenerous, Carroll indicated his willingness, when future circumstances permitted, to satisfy their wishes by appointing Nugent as "joint-chaplain." Meanwhile, Whelan was still their pastor. Any attempt to remove him by legal means would be strongly resisted, and Carroll declared that ". . . no clergyman, be he who he may, shall receive any spiritual powers from me, who shall advise or countenance so unnecessary and prejudicial a proceeding. . . ."[8]

Carroll's letter did not quiet the affair. The trustees continued to press Whelan, finally forcing him to leave St. Peter's in February, 1786. Carroll reluctantly accepted Nugent as temporary pastor. Still, peace did not come to troubled St. Peter's. Nugent, in turn, fell out with the trustees over the question of salary. In October, 1786, Carroll went to New York City to deal with Nugent who, he now found out, the Archbishop of Dublin had suspended from his priestly functions before he came to

[8]Carroll to Trustees of St. Peter's Church, January 24, 1786, AAB, Case 9A-F2.

America. Carroll removed Nugent, and appointed in his place Father William O'Brien.[9]

Nugent refused to accept Carroll's authority. On Sunday morning, as Carroll prepared to say mass at St. Peter's, Nugent intervened and said that he had the right to celebrate the mass. When Carroll started to speak against Nugent in his sermon a scene developed. Later Carroll told Antonelli what happened: "And when I attempted to do this he shouted in a still louder voice. When he charged his accusers with perjury some of the parishioners accused him of the gravest misconduct. A tumult ensued, abusive language, most unbecoming the sacredness of the place, was exchanged between him and others."[10] Carroll suspended Nugent because of his contumacy, and then left the church followed by most of the congregation.

Carroll published an address to the Catholics of New York City so as to answer the erroneous view of his authority expounded by Nugent. He reminded them that their

[9] Ryan, Old St. Peter's, pp. 51-53; Guilday, John Carroll, pp. 267, 277-78.

[10] Carroll to Antonelli, March 18, 1788, Propaganda Archives. Scritture Riferite nei Congressi, America Centrale. Vol. II, Fol. 363. John Carroll Papers, Transcripts, Catholic University of America Archives.

forefathers had maintained, despite all obstacles, the

purity of the faith as passed down from the first apostles:

> And how did they obtain this great effect?
> Was it by intruding themselves into the
> sanctuary? Did they, did you before you
> crossed over into this country, assume to
> yourselves the rights of your first pastors?
> Did you name those clergymen who were charged
> with the immediate care of your souls? Did
> you invest them with their authority?
> . . . No, dear Christians; neither your fore-
> fathers nor you assumed to yourselves those
> prerogatives: you never plunged that fatal
> dagger into the vitals of true religion.

Carroll reiterated the teachings of the Church on this

subject--that the power to preach the gospel, to administer

the sacraments, to appoint pastors for the care of souls

was bestowed by Jesus Himself on the Apostles, and they in

turn passed down this divine commission to their successors.

His authority, then, as ecclesiastical superior, came from

Christ through the apostles; therefore, he <u>alone</u> had the

power to constitute and appoint pastors, and not the

congregation.[11]

The trustees of St. Peter's accepted Carroll's

authority to suspend Nugent and to appoint O'Brien in his

place. In order to regain possession of the church building,

[11]Carroll's Address to the Catholics of New York
City. Maryland Province Archives.

they were forced to take Nugent into court. The judge ruled in favor of the trustees, since the New York State law of incorporation specifically provided that it was not intended to affect any change in the religious government of any church so far as it related to doctrine or discipline.[12] Nugent had broken with church doctrine and discipline. The judge declared that Nugent, having been dismissed by his lawful superior according to the established discipline of the Catholic Church, was no longer ". . . fitted for the pastoral office."[13] St. Peter's found its desired peace.

The most serious trustee disturbance took place in Philadelphia. Many of the German Catholics at St. Mary's were dissatisfied with their position there. They were jealous of the Irish whom they felt discriminated against them.[14] More important, however, was their disappointment that Carroll had not appointed the priest of their choice, Father John Charles Helbron, as pastor of St. Mary's.[15] Unhappy at their defeat, and displeased with their position

[12] Shea, John Carroll, pp. 323-26.

[13] Carroll to Antonelli, April 14, 1789. AAB, Case 9A-G3.

[14] Molyneux to Carroll, February 8, 1788. AAB, Case 8A-T1.

[15] Carroll to Beeston, March 22, 1788. AAB, Case 9-E

in St. Mary's, some of the Germans, led by James Oellers and Adam Premir, decided to form a new church. They purchased a site, collected funds for construction, and elected trustees who, in October, 1788, were allowed to incorporate as the "Trustees of the German Religious Society of Roman Catholics of the Holy Trinity Church." On March 22, 1789, the parishioners of the new church, exercising what they thought to be their rights under the principle of jus patronatus--that those who build and maintain a church have the right to present the name of a pastor for confirmation by the ecclesiastical superior-- elected John Chalres Helbron as pastor, and submitted his name to Carroll for his approval. Carroll refused even to consider Helbron's name, for he rejected the claim made by the congregation at Holy Trinity to the jus patronatus.[16]

Despite Carroll's objections, the trustees moved ahead with their plans. They fixed the solemn opening of the church for Sunday, November 22, 1789. They invited John Charles Helbron to serve as pastor, and he accepted. In early December, 1789, Carroll revoked Helbron's

[16]Carroll to Trustees of Holy Trinity Church, October 11, 1789. AAB, Case 9A-H1.

faculties and forbade him to exercise any pastoral functions. Carroll journeyed to Philadelphia during that same
month to try and resolve the problem. His threat to
suspend the dissident priest was effective, for Helbron
signed a statement that neither he nor any other clergyman
could lawfully exercise the priestly ministry in America
without the approval of the ecclesiastical superior.
Helbron advised the trustees to give up their claim to the
jus patronatus, but this they refused to do. Still,
Carroll had made his point. On January 6, 1790 he read
Helbron's statement to the congregation of Holy Trinity,
and then, in a generous offer, he appointed Helbron as
their pastor.[17]

Helbron did not remain for long in Philadelphia.
In November, 1791, he left for Europe (from where he never
returned) to collect money to pay the debts of Holy
Trinity. His brother, Father Peter Helbron, came to
Philadelphia where, with the permission of Carroll and the

---

[17]Vincent J. Fecher, A Study of the Movement for
German National Parishes in Philadelphia and Baltimore
(Rome: Apud Aedis Universitatis Gregorianae, 1955),
pp. 21-24, 30-32. (Hereinafter referred to as German
National Parishes.) Francis Hertkorn, A Retrospect of Holy
Trinity Parish 1789-1814 (Philadelphia: F. McManus, Jr.
and Co., 1914), pp. 38-39. (Hereinafter referred to as
Holy Trinity Parish.)

approval of the congregation, he served as pastor of Holy

Trinity Church. All went well until July, 1796, when the

proud and ambitious Father John Nepomucene Goetz arrived

in Philadelphia. With the approval of the congregation

Carroll appointed Goetz as assistant pastor. But Goetz

protested; he wanted to be a co-pastor with equal rights

as Peter Helbron. A dispute broke out between the two

priests. The trustees intervened, and in late September,

1796, they drew up a set of Resolutions which, in effect,

established their authority to regulate the activities of

the priests in the parish. Goetz signed willingly; Peter

Helbron refused on the grounds that the trustees had

exceeded their authority by usurping spiritual jurisdiction.

The trustees replied by electing Goetz pastor pro-tempore,

and dismissing Peter Helbron.[18]

Peter Helbron refused to accept the trustees'

decision for he still considered himself as the lawful

pastor of Holy Trinity. He was supported by Leonard Neale,

Carroll's Vicar-General, who initiated a lawsuit to have

Goetz removed. Neale's lawyer, a Mr. Lewis, was of the

[18]Fecher, German National Parishes, pp. 34-38;
43-45; Hertkorn, Holy Trinity Parish, pp. 41-43, 48-51;
Martin I.J. Griffin, "The Rev. Peter Helbron, Second Pastor
of Holy Trinity Church, Philadelphia," Records, XXIII
(March, 1912), 2-13.

opinion that the trustees, by departing from the discipline of the Catholic Church, had violated provisions of the law under which they were incorporated.[19] The trustees replied to this line of argument by asserting their independence of ecclesiastical authority. Neale summarized for Carroll's benefit the affidavit which James Oellers, on behalf of the trustees, submitted to the court: "It stated that the German Roman Catholics separated from St. Mary's and built themselves a Church with no other intention than to choose and appoint what priest they pleased for their pastor independently of St. Mary's and the Bishop and of all foreign jurisdiction and to govern themselves by the laws of God and those of the land where they lived."[20]

While the case dragged on in the courts, Neale issued a public address to the congregation of Holy Trinity. "Why did you," he asked, "arrogate to yourselves the power of discarding him [Helbron]. Who gave you this power? Or has the Catholic Church in any case whatever, acknowledged in the laity a power of discharging their lawful Pastor at will? No. She neither has, nor ever will." Neale denied

[19] Neale to Carroll, November 7, 1796. AAB, Case 11-B4.

[20] Neale to Carroll, January 4, 1797. AAB, Case 11-B2.

that they ever possessed the right of _jus_ _patronatus_:
"You can have none, because your church has no FIXED,
PERMANENT, and UNALIENABLE fund for the support of a
pastor." Besides, even _if_ they possessed the right of
patronage, it only meant the right to present, and not to
appoint or discharge a pastor:

> For according to the doctrine and practice of
> the Catholic Church, from the apostolic days
> down to the present time, all pastors are
> appointed by their respective Bishops, without
> whose concurrence and approbation they can
> have neither mission nor jurisdiction. And
> therefore to assert and obstinately maintain
> the contrary would be Schismatical and
> Heretical.[21]

Carroll followed with a firm, but conciliatory letter, in
which he pleaded for a return of the congregation to the
true principles of the Catholic Church--that the bishop
alone exercises spiritual authority over the clergy.[22]

The trustees and priests (Goetz had meanwhile been
joined by a Father William Elling) at Holy Trinity did not
receive favorably Neale and Carroll's appeals. Therefore,
in February, 1797, Carroll excommunicated the two dissident
priests. Neale read the sentence of excommunication before

[21]Neale's Address to the German Roman Catholics
Frequenting Trinity Church in Philadelphia, December 8,
1796. AAB, Case 10-U2.
[22]Carroll's Address to the Congregation of Trinity
Church, Philadelphia, February 27, 1797. AAB, Case 10-W2.

the congregation at St. Mary's Church, and he performed the traditional ceremony--the ringing of a bell, the closing of a book, and the blowing out of a candle--which such a sentence demanded.[23]

Carroll went to Philadelphia in 1798 with the hope that he could personally heal the schism. Instead, the trustees served him with a writ, and brought him into court where a lawyer for the schismatics denied his episcopal authority and jurisdiction over Holy Trinity Church.[24] Evidently, Holy Trinity was not yet ready to return to the fold.

The affair dragged on for a few more years. In 1801, the trustees, perhaps tired of the fight and of their anomalous position, sought a reconciliation with Carroll. Carroll was more than willing to be reconciled, provided, of course, that they recognized his episcopal authority. On January 28, 1802, Elling (Goetz had left Holy Trinity in 1797) made his act of submission; the

---

[23]Martin I.J. Griffin, "The Reverend John Nepomucene Goetz, Third Pastor and William Elling, Assistant of Holy Trinity Church, Philadelphia," Records, XXXIII (June, 1912), 116-19.

[24]Shea, John Carroll, pp. 419-21; Annabelle M. Melville, John Carroll of Baltimore: Founder of the American Catholic Hierarchy (New York: Charles Scribner's Sons, 1955), p. 207.

trustees did so the next day. Carroll removed the ban of

excommunication against Elling, and appointed him pastor of

Holy Trinity Church. The schism was over.[25]

Carroll was not the only bishop to have his

episcopal authority challenged by lay trustees. Michael

Egan, the first Bishop of Philadelphia had his own share

of troubles, first with his trustees, and then with his

clerical assistants. Father William Vincent Harold and

his uncle, Father James Harold, assisted Egan at St.

Mary's Church. The three priests pressed the trustees for

an increase in their salary, but the trustees refused.[26]

The younger Harold then assumed a hostile and overbearing

attitude toward the trustees, and at one time said:

". . . that the Church belonged to the clergy, and with it

the whole of the income." The trustees considered Harold's

claim as "absolutely untenable," for, in their opinion, the

property of the Church belonged to the congregation.[27]

Egan came to realize that the Harolds were formenting

---

[25]Hertkorn, Holy Trinity Parish, pp. 57-58.

[26]Martin I.J. Griffin, History of the Right Reverend
Michael Egan, First Bishop of Philadelphia (Philadelphia: By
the Author, 1893), pp. 27, 51, 54, 61-64. (Hereinafter
referred to as Egan.)

[27]Sunday Documents Submitted to the Consideration of
Pewholders of St. Mary's Church by the Trustees of that
Church (Philadelphia: Lydia R. Bailey, 1812), p. 14.
Printed copy found in AAB, Case 11B-K2.

trouble, and to prevent a serious rupture between the clergy and the trustees from taking place, he sought a reconciliation with the lay leaders of the church. His conciliatory tone made the trustees withdraw a petition they were sending to the Pennsylvania legislature which would have called for the removal of the clergy from the Board of Trustees.[28]

By the end of 1812 Egan reached an accord with the trustees, but now his differences with the Harolds became more pronounced. Egan was displeased with the elder Harold who refused an order to leave for Pittsburgh; and, he resented the pressure of the younger Harold to become his coadjutor. The trustees supported their bishop in this quarrel. On February 21, 1813, the Harolds informed the congregation they were resigning. They did not believe Egan would accept their resignation, or that the congregation would allow him to do so. To their surprise Egan accepted their resignation, and he would not reinstate them despite a petition signed by 534 members of the congregation

[28]John Ashley and Edward Carroll to Carroll, December 22, 1812. AAB, Case 11B-L4.

A great part of the congregation had turned against Egan and the trustees.[29]

The Haroldite supporters organized, and in the election of April, 1813, they overthrew the old (bishop's) board of trustees. Egan feared that the Haroldites, who sought to control the affairs of the church were infected with "the spirit of presbyterianism."[30] The new board, alleging the need for economy, reduced the annual salary of Egan and his assistants. Egan thought differently. He saw the trustees move as a way of forcing out his new assistant, so that the Harolds could return. He assured Carroll that he would resist the trustees' decision, for it was "subservive of all ecclesiastical authority."[31]

Egan held firm, but the fight was cut short by his premature death in 1814. Father Patrick Kenny, his assistant, said of him: "He is, incontestably, a martyr of the following truly Catholic principle, that the laity never had, nor ever will acquire by any means, the right of nominating and appointing the Priests or Pastors, in

---

[29] Griffin, Egan, pp. 68-70, 76-80, 81-84.
[30] Egan to Carroll, March 4, 1813. AAB, Case 11-010.
[31] Egan to Carroll, July 7, 1813. AAB, Case 3-J3.

defiance of the will and approbation of a Catholic

bishop."[32]   Kenny's eulogy was overdone and unfair to the

trustees. While the latter did try to pressure Egan to

reinstate the Harolds, they never considered installing the

priests in defiance of Egan's authority.[33]

Even Baltimore, Carroll's episcopal city, did not

escape from such ecclesiastical disturbances. In 1797,

Frederick Cesarius Reuter, a young, ambitious, intensely-

nationalistic German priest was approved by Carroll to

serve the German Catholics of Baltimore. Reuter remained

only a year, after which he returned to Europe. He visited

Rome where he charged (quite falsely) that the Bishop of

Baltimore was hostile to the nationalistic aspirations of

German Catholics in the United States. In early 1799,

when Reuter reappeared in Baltimore, Carroll was not

pleased. It was only under pressure from the German

Catholics of the city that he reluctantly granted Reuter

religious faculties, severely limited in time and scope.

When these faculties expired in July, 1799, Carroll refused

to renew them. The German Catholics, over the bishop's

[32]Kenny to Carroll, July 10, 1814. AAB, Case 4-L2.

[33]Cf. Letter of Harold's supporters to Carroll,
April 28, 1813. AAB, Case 11B-N3.

objections, decided to build their own church with Reuter as pastor. Carroll sought a compromise. He would sanction the building of the church if the trustees would agree (among other things) not to accept any priest whom he did not approve; the trustees rejected these conditions as an infringement upon their legal right of patronage. Carroll later sought an agreement with Reuter; the latter was willing to accept the bishop's authority, provided he could serve as pastor to the Germans in Baltimore. This qualification Carroll found unacceptable. In 1802, the trustees informed Carroll that the new German church of St. John the Evangelist was completed; moreover, they had elected Reuter as their pastor, and they hoped for the bishop's approval. Despite Carroll's refusal, Reuter served the Germans at St. John's for the next three years.[34]

In 1805, Carroll decided to challenge Reuter and the trustees in the courts. He appointed Father Francis X. Brosius as pastor of St. John the Evangelist, and then obtained a court order to compel the trustees to accept him. The Germans replied that they ". . . have the sole

[34]Fecher, German National Parishes, Chapter III, "Father Reuter and the Baltimore Germans 1797-1802," pp. 58-87.

and exclusive right of nominating and appointing their pastor, and that no other person, whether bishop or pope have a right to appoint a pastor without the assent and approbation of the congregation. . . ." Having placed the Church under the jurisdiction of the Minorites Conventuals of the Order of St. Francis, they argued that Reuter ". . . owed obedience to the civil magistrates and to his order," and to no other ecclesiastical person or body whatever."[35] The General Court ruled against the trustees and, in compliance with this judicial decision, St. John's accepted the bishop's choice for pastor. Reuter disappeared, and was heard of no more.

Further south, in Charleston, S.C., there was another incident of "trusteeism." The pastor of St. Mary's Church was the eloquent, but lax, Simon Felix Gallagher. Some members of the congregation complained to Carroll that Gallagher's proneness to drink brought scandal to the church. Carroll pressed Gallagher to resign the pastorate, but this he refused to do. In the spring of 1803 Gallagher went to Rome to plead his case.[36]

---

[35] Brosius v. Reuter, Report of Cases--General Court and Court of Appeals of the State of Maryland, 1800-1805, Harris and Johnson, I, 551-558.

[36] Peter Kenan Guilday, The Life and Times of John England: First Bishop of Charleston 1786-1842 (2 vols.; New York: America Press, 1927), I, 142-49.

Carroll sent Father LeMercier to Charleston, but the trustees would only accept him as a temporary pastor until Gallagher returned. LeMercier was not one to accept a rebuff. On Sunday, January 29, 1804, LeMercier shared with the congregation Carroll's letter which stated that he, and not Gallagher, was the lawful pastor. As he returned home from mass he was confronted by several members of the board of trustees who asked him several questions. In faltering English LeMercier shared with Carroll the conversation that took place:

> The first [question] was this. Mr. LeMercier who sent you here? The Right Rev. Bishop of Baltimore said I. Who desired him to send you here? Don't know said I. Well, Sir, as we did not ask for you nor for any body else we shall never acknowledge you our pastor and are determined to acknowledge of none but Mr. Gallagher. I attempted to make a short reply to them [and] their answer was that they would not care more about the bishop than about me and another added nor would [he] care of the pope himself if he was to send another but Mr. Gallagher.[37]

With Gallagher's return from Rome, ecclesiastical affairs at St. Mary's deteriorated. In July, 1805, the trustees informed Carroll that LeMercier's conduct was so

[37]LeMercier to Carroll, January 30, 1804. AAB, Case 4-V8.

objectionable that they forbade him to officiate any longer
at the church. Carroll wrote sharply on the back of their
letter: "His ecl. superior alone could acquit or condemn
him as unfit for the pastoral charge--the laity are neither
the source of sprl. jurisdiction, nor can stop its course--
opposite pretensions would reduce us to a level with other
sects."[38]

Carroll responded by suspending Gallagher, who was
forbidden to perform religious services in the church.
The congregation split over the issue; most members,
however, including the trustees, sided with Gallagher.[39]
Fortunately for St. Mary's, LeMercier returned to France in
1806. Gallagher and the trustees sought a reconciliation
with Carroll, and, in December, 1806, Gallagher was
reappointed as pastor of St. Mary's. For the moment peace
was restored in Charleston.[40]

The trustee movement was not restricted to the east
coast. It spread, with the expanding frontier, to the west
as well. In Kentucky, the lay Catholics of Scott County,

---

[38]Secretary of the Charleston Church to Carroll,
July 27, 1805. AAB, Case 11A-F3.

[39]Edward Lynch to Carroll, April 23, 1804. AAB,
Case 5-B11; Mrs. J. McDonald to Carroll, January 18, 1804.
AAB, Case 5-C13.

[40]Guilday, John England, I, 149-50.

under the leadership of the independent-minded James Gough,

attempted to establish a form of ecclesiastical government

under which they would control the temporal affairs of

St. Francis Church. They hoped to accomplish this by

having title to the church's property vested in their name,

and by having laymen constitute the Board of Trustees.

Badin strongly opposed this effort to create a "presby-

terian" constitution for the church. He argued (quite

incorrectly from the American experience at least) that

church property was to be held and administered by the

clergy. Badin's will prevailed, and title to the property

of St. Francis was made out to Bishop Carroll, with Badin,

Father Robert Angiers, and a layman, Cornelius Fenwick, as

trustees. The pastor escaped, in the words of Judge

Twyman, being made the laity's "humble submissive tenant

at will."[41]

The newly acquired territory of Louisiana was also

touched by the spirit of trusteeism. In March, 1805,

---

[41] Sister Mary Ramona Mattingly, The Catholic Church
on the Kentucky Frontier 1785-1812 (Washington: Catholic
University of America Press, 1936), pp. 93-94, 139-40;
Joseph Herman Schauinger, Stephen Theodore Badin, Priest
in the Wilderness (Milwaukee: Bruce Publishing Co., 1956),
pp. 65, 125-26, 130; Twyman to Carroll, April 4, 1808.
AAB, Case 10-D10.

Father Patrick Walsh, who claimed to be the Vicar-General
of the Diocese of Louisiana, suspended Pere Antoine de
Sedella as pastor of St. Louis Cathedral, New Orleans.
The congregation, refusing to accept Walsh's decision,
voted overwhelmingly to restore Sedella to his position,
and Sedella accepted this appointment by the people.
Walsh took the matter to the Supreme Court of the territory,
charging that Sedella, as a suspended priest, no longer had
any right to remain at the cathedral. The court, in a
rare decision, ruled that Sedella was the lawful pastor,
and that the marguilliers were the administrators for the
real owners of the church--the Catholics of New Orleans.[42]
Walsh died in 1806. Carroll then appointed Father Jean
Olivier to serve as his Vicar-General. Olivier suspended
Sedella for not recognizing his authority, but the marguilliers would not allow Olivier to suspend the pastor
whom they had appointed and whom the law recognized.[43]
The marguilliers of St. Louis Cathedral, like their counterparts in so many parish churches throughout the country,
had assumed the right to control the temporalities of the

[42]Roger Baudier, The Catholic Church in Louisiana
(New Orleans, 1939), pp. 255-58.
[43]Ibid., pp. 260-61.

church and the designation of its pastor.[44]   The signifi-

cant difference was, that in their case, the court upheld

their right to do so.

---

[44]Sibourd to Carroll, December 10, 1815.   AAB,
Case 7-R9.

CHAPTER V

THE TRUSTEE CONTROVERSY:

AN ANALYSIS

While lay influence in the administration of church
temporalities was not unknown to the Roman Catholic Church,
the trustee movement in the United States allowed for the
more significant practice of lay ownership and control over
church property. The very nature of American law, which
did not recognize the Catholic Church, or its hierarchy,
as having legal existence, made possible the trustee system.
Church property could be held in the name of individuals,
but since this approach presented certain disadvantages
(e.g., what if the legal owner died without a will, or
bequeathed the estate to someone for whom it was not
intended?), it was not encouraged. In order to provide a
greater security for ecclesiastical property, the law
allowed for the congregation, or an elected part thereof,
to incorporate and thereby secure the protection of civil

authority. During the episcopacy of John Carroll most Catholic parishes adopted this practice.

Lay trustees fully understood the powers they possessed under the law of incorporation--for instance, legal title to parish property. When Father William Vincent Harold said ". . . that the Church belonged to the clergy, and with it the whole of the income . . . ," the trustees of St. Mary's Church replied: "But that the claim thus set up is absolutely untenable, and that the property of the church is in the congregation, is beyond all question."[1] Despite the protestations of Bishop Egan, the trustees of St. Mary's lowered the salary of the priests at the church. When Egan condemned their act as a violation of ecclesiastical authority, they boldly declared their legal right to do so under the charter of incorporation.[2] At Holy Trinity, Elling disagreed with the trustees over the question of his pension. Elling requested that Carroll be allowed to arbitrate the issue. Adam Premir, one of the trustees, replied that this was unnecessary since Elling's demand was temporal in nature, and, as such, the trustees

---

[1] Sundry Documents Submitted to the Consideration of the Pewholders of St. Mary's Church by the Trustees of that Church (Philadelphia: Lydia R. Barley, 1812), p. 14. Printed copy found in AAB, Case 11B-K2.

[2] Griffin, Egan, pp. 87, 92-94, 99-101.

alone should decide the question.[3]   Later, when a Mrs.

Shindler told James Oeller to settle with Elling according

to the bishop's advice, Oellers was reported to have said:

". . . all the clergymen are rascals, they have not to

interfere in our temporal concerns."[4]   Many laymen, who

served as trustees, would have agreed with their colleagues

at St. Mary's--that the property of the parish church

belonged to the congregation, with the trustees serving as

legal guardians.

Once incorporated under state law the trustees

could turn to the courts in their struggles with priests

and bishops. At Holy Trinity the trustees threatened the

dismissed Peter Helbron with a lawsuit if he did not return

certain items taken from the church.[5]   And, when Carroll

went to Philadelphia in 1798 to resolve the dispute, he

was served a writ and brought into court where a lawyer for

the trustees denied his episcopal authority over Holy

Trinity.[6]   Nugent was warned by the trustees of St. Peter's

---

[3]Elling to Carroll, August 9, 1806. AAB, Case 3-02.

[4]Elling to Carroll, September 17, 1806. AAB,
Case 3-07.

[5]Trustees of Holy Trinity Church to Peter Helbron,
October 15, 1796. AAB, Case 11B-U5.

[6]Shea, John Carroll, pp. 419-20.

that they would take legal measures to remove him if he did not go willingly.[7]

In all these cases the trustees depended for legal protection on the specific provisions of their charters of incorporation; there were times, however, when they appealed to state constitutional law, or American "law" in general, for protection against what they considered ecclesiastical tyranny. The Nugent faction argued that they need not obey Carroll's authority, since as Prefect-- Apostolic he received his jurisdiction from Rome--a juris- diction contrary to the laws of the state of New York which, in effect, forbade all foreign jurisdiction whether civil or ecclesiastical.[8] In their affidavit to the court, the trustees of Holy Trinity stated that they built their Church with no other intention than to name their own pastor independently of the ". . . Bishop and of all foreign jurisdiction, and to govern themselves by the laws of God and those of the land where they lived."[9] And when

[7]Ryan, Old St. Peter's, p. 49.

[8]Carroll to Antonelli, March 18, 1788. Propaganda Archives. Scritture Riferite nei Congressi, America Centrale, Vol. 11, Fol. 363. John Carroll Papers, Trans- cript; Carroll to Plowden, November 12, 1788. Maryland Province Archives, Box 202-B19.

[9]Neale to Carroll, January 4, 1796. AAB, Case 11-B2.

the Papal brief was shown them, in which all the Catholics in the United States were subject to Carroll's authority, ". . . they impudently dared to assail the brief as imposing a yoke on them contrary to the American laws."[10]

Trustees brooked little interference in their affairs from the clergy. It was for this reason that many preferred not to have any priest sitting on the board. The leading figures of St. Francis' Church wanted the board of trustees to be composed solely of laymen; while Robert Abell and Bennet Spalding protested a legislative bill incorporating the church at the Pottinger Creek settlement which made the pastor serve as President of the Board of Trustees.[11] Angered by their dispute with the clergy of St. Mary's, the trustees threatened to submit a petition to the Pennsylvania legislature calling for the removal of clerics from the board.[12] In Charleston, at St. Mary's Church, the pastor was actually excluded from the board of trustees.[13]

---

[10] Carroll to Propaganda, no date. As quoted in Shea, John Carroll, pp. 420-21, fn. 3.

[11] Mattingly, Catholic Church on the Kentucky Frontier, pp. 93-94, 139-40.

[12] John Ashley and Edward Carrell to Carroll, December 22, 1812. AAB, Case 11B-L4.

[13] Guilday, John England, I, 150-51; Thomas F. Hopkins, "St. Mary's Church, Charleston, S.C.," Yearbook, 1897, City of Charleston, S.C. (Charleston: Walker, Evans, and Cogswell Co., 1897), pp. 448, 451-52.

Actually, the laws of incorporation were not one-sided in favor of the trustees, and Carroll need not have complained to the Prefect of Propaganda that ". . . we live among hostile sects of non-Catholics, so that there is no hope of gaining assistance from the civil magistracy or the secular arm to reduce stubborn men to order."[14] State laws of incorporation did not countenance lay insubordination to ecclesiastical discipline, nor leave the religious superior without recourse. Lay trustees, while possessing certain temporal powers under the law, were not authorized to interfere in purely spiritual or ecclesiastical affairs. Most states adopted language similar to that found in the New York State Incorporation Act of 1784:

> And be it further Enacted by the Authority aforesaid, That nothing herein contained, shall . . . alter or change the Religious Constitutions or Governments of either of the said churches, congregations, or societies, so far as respects or in any wise concerns the Doctrine, Discipline, or Worship thereof.[15]

---

[14]Carroll to Brancadoro, August 20, 1799. Propaganda Archives. Scritture Riferite nei Congressi, America Centrale. Vol. III, Fol. 66. John Carroll Papers, Transcript. Catholic University of America Archives.

[15]New York State Incorporation Act of 1784, Laws of the State of New York 1777-1784 (Albany: Weed, Parsons and Co., 1886), Chap. XVIII, pp. 613-18.

It was this side of the incorporation laws that
afforded Carroll the protection he needed to maintain
ecclesiastical order. And Carroll made as ample use of
the law, as did the dissident trustees he opposed, and
with more success, too. It was under provisions of this
kind, then, that Carroll challenged Nugent in New York,
Reuter in Baltimore, and Fromm at Sportsman's Hall,
Pennsylvania. The courts upheld Carroll in all three
cases. Nugent was forced to leave St. Peter's because, in
the opinion of the court, having been suspended by his
ecclesiastical superior for breach of the Catholic Church's
faith and discipline, he was no longer "fit" for office;
St. John's was compelled to receive Brosius as pastor since,
according to the court, he (and not Reuter) had the
bishop's approval; and Fromm was removed from Sportsman's
Hall for the same reason.[16]

The Fromm case was typical. Father Francis Rogatus
Fromm arrived at Sportsman Hall, near Greensburg, Pennsylvania, on May 2, 1791. The congregation acknowledged him
as their new pastor to succeed the late Father Theodore

[16]For the Nugent and Reuter "cases" see above,
pp. 77-82, 92-94.

Brouwers who had founded the church. Fromm also assumed possession of Sportsman's Hall, which Brouwers had left in his will to the priest who succeeded him. Carroll would not recognize Fromm's right to the pastorate of the church, nor to the possession of Brouwer's estate. Fromm refused to relinquish control, and, in 1795, Carroll suspended him. Later, the congregation sought to remove him from the church, and they took the case to court.[17] The court's decision, which upheld the bishop's authority, was significant:

> The bishop of Baltimore has . . . had the sole episcopal authority over the Catholic Church of the United States. Every Catholic congregation within the United States is subject to his inspection; and without authority from him no Catholic priest can exercise any pastoral function over any congregation. . . . Without his appointment or permission to exercise pastoral function over this congregation no priest can be entitled, under the will of Browers [sic] to claim the enjoyment of this estate, Fromm had no such appointment or permission, and is therefore incompetent to discharge the duties, or enjoy the benefits, which are the objects of the will of Browers.[18]

---

[17] Shea, John Carroll, pp. 449-50; Felix Fellner, "Trials and Triumphs of Catholic Pioneers in Western Pennsylvania," pp. 206-21.

[18] Lessee of Executors of Theodore Browers v. Franciscus Fromm, Pennsylvania Supreme Court Report, Addison, V, 361-71.

* * * * * * * * * *

Inasmuch as American law granted certain powers to lay trustees which they used in their struggles with church authorities, it was a contributing factor in the rise of trusteeism. But, in itself, American law would not have caused the movement to develop. There was nothing in the law which allowed trustees to interfere in purely spiritual or ecclesiastical affairs (e.g., the appointing or dis- missing of pastors), and when challenged in the courts the trustees generally lost because they had committed acts that exceeded the temporal powers which incorporation charters granted to them. Actually, there were other forces at work, more potent still, and without which trusteeism--the movement by laymen to control the parish property and priest--may not have arisen. The influence of the Protestant experience of lay control was of crucial importance to the movement.

Carroll understood all too well the influence which the Protestant tradition of lay control exerted upon Catholic lay trustees. He shared with Antonelli his anxiety over the Nugent schism in New York City, and he

warned of the consequences if this first attempt at

resistance to episcopal authority was not quickly

suppressed:

> Here Catholics live among every variety of the
> heterodox, so that I greatly fear that unless
> this be done priests of unruly character,
> guided by this example, will throw off the
> yoke of obedience, and the laity will be
> flattered into believing that they too should
> claim the power of determining their pastors
> just as they see [italics mine] the sectarians
> do.[19]

That the laity were often flattered into believing

that they could choose their pastors as did the Protestants

was all too evident to Carroll and his fellow clergy.

Carroll viewed the principles set down by the trustees at

St. Peter's as similar to the Congregationalists of New

England; and he considered the ideas on church government

advanced by the trustees at Holy Trinity as closer to the

---

[19]Carroll to Antonelli, March 18, 1788. Propaganda
Archives. Scritture Riferite nei Congressi, America
Centrale. Vol. 11, Fol. 363. John Carroll Papers,
Transcript; Maréchal, writing thirty years later, said the
same thing: "Likewise all the Protestant sects . . . elect
and dismiss their pastors at will. Catholics in turn,
living in their midst, are evidently exposed to the danger
of admitting the same principles of ecclesiastical govern-
ment." Ambrose Maréchal, "Ambrose Maréchal's Report to
Propaganda, October 16, 1818," in John Tracy Ellis, ed.,
Documents of American Catholic History (2d ed., rev.;
Milwaukee: Bruce Publishing Co., 1962), p. 214.

principles of Luther and Calvin than to the Catholic Church.[20] Egan thought that the Haroldites at St. Mary's had adopted a "spirit of presbyterianism."[21] In Lancaster, several of the trustees opposed their pastor, Father Francis Fitzsimmons. Fitzsimmons said that these men looked upon themselves as "Calvinistical Elders."[22] and Gallitzin, who fled to western Pennsylvania, in part to establish a Catholic settlement far removed from Protestant influence, remarked to his assistant and early biographer, Father Peter Henry Lemcke:

> I came here in order to get away from trustees
> and pew-renting and all the other evils con-
> sequent upon such a system. There was no other
> way but to begin something new on a code of
> principles different from those hitherto in
> force. Wherever something had already been
> undertaken, it had been spoiled from the
> beginning because of the universal tendency
> to imitate the Protestants.[23]

---

[20]Carroll to trustees of St. Peter's Church, January 24, 1786. AAB, Case 9A-F2; Carroll's Address to the Congregation of Trinity Church, February 22, 1797. Printed copy. AAB, Case 10-W2.

[21]Egan to Carroll, March 4, 1813. AAB, Case 11-O10.

[22]Fitzsimmons to Carroll, February 20, 1804. AAB, Case 3-T5.

[23]As quoted in Peter Henry Lemcke, _Life and Work of Prince Demetrius Augustine Galltizin_ (New York: Longman's Green and Co., 1940), p. 102.

There were few places one could go to get away from
Protestants, and few Catholics cared to do so. Contact
between members of the two sects was inevitable in a
society where Catholics were so few, Protestants so many.
In countless ways, in public and private, for business or
pleasure, Catholics met with Protestants. And perhaps from
these contacts they learnt about, perhaps even came to
admire, the Protestant practice of lay control in the
church.

Some of the laymen who served as trustees had
established relationships with Protestants that may have
been an influential factor in shaping their positions.
James Oeller, a leading trustee at Holy Trinity, had
Protestant in-laws, since his son had married a Baptist
woman.[24] The German Catholics of Holy Trinity were
friendly with the German Protestants of Philadelphia, as
demonstrated by the time, labor, and materials which the
latter group donated to the building of Holy Trinity
Church.[25] Picot de Clorivière, assistant pastor of
St. Mary's, Charleston, S.C., blamed the problems of that

[24]Griffin, Egan, p. 29.
[25]Hertkorn, Holy Trinity Parish, pp. 29-30.

church, in part, on the trustees who had married outside the faith: ". . . this is the fault of the trustees-- whose Catholicity or fervour is much cooled by being married with protestants--and they think our rules must be more _liberal_ than they were formerly."[26]

* * * * * * * * * *

Political conditions in the United States were also responsible for the independence which the trustees showed toward their ecclesiastical superiors. The democratic philosophy of America and its republican form of government impressed many native and immigrant Catholics, who then attempted to carry this spirit over into the Church.[27]

Maréchal informed Rome that the Americans carried over their love of civil liberty--especially the principle that all officials were subject to the people--into the religious sphere as well, as evidenced by the Protestant sects which allowed for the congregations to elect and remove the pastors. Maréchal thought that Catholics living in America would be exposed to this prevailing spirit, and

[26]Clorivère to Carroll, November 2, 1813. AAB, Case 2-Q6.

[27]Clestine Joseph Nuesse, _The Social Thought of American Catholics 1634-1829_ (Westminister, Md.: Newman Book Shop, 1945), p. 176.

might admit similar principles in their ecclesiastical government.[28] Carroll also implied that there was a connection between the idea of civil liberty in America and the disobedience of some members of the clergy and laity to religious authority. Speaking of Fromm and his followers Carroll remarked: "They seemed to think that by coming to America, besides attaining civil liberty, they could now, with impunity, oppose the pastor of souls."[29]

Catholic laymen and priests often supported their struggle against ecclesiastical authority by reference to this spirit of American liberty. A Mr. Little, a member of the troubled St. Peter's Church, told the pastor, Father William O'Brien that he (and others) opposed the removal of Father John Thayer. Little went on to say: ". . . that the congregation who was in favor of Mr. Thayer would not be priest ridden, that this was a country of liberty [italics mine], and they had a right to choose a priest for themselves. . . ."[30] Elling assured Carroll that if he

---

[28] Maréchal, "Ambrose Maréchal's Report to Propaganda October 16, 1818," in Ellis, Documents of American Catholic History, p. 214.

[29] Carroll to Antonelli, April 23, 1792. AAB, Case 9A-I.

[30] O'Brien to Carroll, August 15, 1796. AAB, Case 5-U5.

recognized the right of the congregation at Holy Trinity to choose their own pastor, ". . . which they claim as free and independent citizens . . ." then all would be well.[31] The trustees of Holy Trinity complained to Rome that the papal brief establishing the diocese of Baltimore granted such full powers to Carroll that he could act as sole and independent judge over the Catholics in the United States; this, they pointed out, was not an acceptable practice in the United States.[32] A Mrs. McDonald, who, though a Protestant, was one of the early supporters of the Catholic Church in Charleston, S.C., informed Carroll that she would continue to support Gallagher over LeMercier. She defended her stand by referring to the social compact theory of government, so familiar to Americans: "Altho the Catholic religion enjoins submission, it could never be supposed to give up our just Rights--this Church was first formed by a few in mutual compact for their individual good and the good of their fellowman."[33]

---

[31]Elling to Carroll, December 1, 1801. AAB, Case 11B-W9.

[32]Trustees of Holy Trinity Church to Rome, October, 1797. As quoted by Fecher, German National Parishes, pp. 154-55.

[33]McDonald to Carroll, February 27, 1804. AAB, Case 5-C14.

* * * * * * * * * *

In addition to American influences on the rise of
trusteeism, there were certain "old-world" forces at work--
the concept of nationality and the canonical principle of
jus patronatus.

The principle of nationality was the most important
factor in the trustee controversy at Holy Trinity and
St. John the Evangelist. The German Catholics of these
two churches ultimately challenged Carroll's authority
because they considered him (quite falsely) ". . . an
enemy of their nation and of their language, and thought
he neglected their spiritual welfare by failing to supply
them with a German clergy." The Germans did not want to
be assimilated; they wanted to preserve their language,
their culture, their very nation from the attacks by
native and other Catholic nationality groups, and from

Carroll as well.[34]   Therefore, the Germans formed their

separate, "national" churches.[35]

The jus patronatus was long recognized in the

Church. As finally defined it allowed for the patron of a

church--one who gave the land, erected the building, and

provided for the continual support of the church and its

pastor--the right to present the name of a person for

pastor to the ecclesiastical superior for his approbation.[36]

The Germans of Holy Trinity and St. John the

Evangelist made use of the jus patronatus in their struggle

---

[34]Fecher, German National Parishes, pp. 93-99;
Kirlin, Catholicity in Philadelphia, pp. 123-25.

[35]Actually, the "national" or "ethnic" parish
church was, in an indirect way, the product of the
American environment. The Catholic immigrants who came
to America hoped to preserve their old way of life, above
all symbolized in their churches. The new world, however,
presented certain difficulties in this area. Here they
were thrown into already existing churches controlled
by native Americans or other nationality groups. Dissatisfied, they banded together with their fellow
countrymen who spoke the same language (regardless of
the district in the old country from which they came),
to form their own, separate ethnic-churches. For a more
complete explanation of this development consult Will
Herberg, Protestant-Catholic-Jew: An Essay in American
Religious Sociology, Anchor Books (New York: Doubleday and
Co., 1960), pp. 11-16.

[36]Dignan, Legal Incorporation of Catholic Church
Property, pp. 77-78; R. Chaput, "Patronage, Canon Law of,"
New Catholic Encyclopedia, X (1967), 1113.

with Carroll.[37]   In March, 1789, the trustees of Holy

Trinity notified Carroll that the congregation had elected

John Charles Helbron, and they requested his "concurrence"

in appointing Helbron as their pastor.[38]   The word

"concurrence" was significant; it implied the united action

of two parties--the Germans of Holy Trinity and Carroll,

with the latter merely approving the choice of the congre-

gation.   The trustees regarded the election by the congre-

gation as decisive, and Carroll's approbation of their

choice as a formality.[39]

---

[37]Fecher, German National Parishes, pp. 127-270, argued that the idea of jus patronatus was an important factor in giving rise to the "trustee" movement at Holy Trinity.   Robert F. McNamara, "Trusteeism in the Atlantic States 1785-1863," Catholic Historical Review, XXX (July, 1944), 153-54, challenges this interpretation. McNamara does not believe that "trusteeism" was ". . . inspired by any foreign ideology or practice." He maintained that there was no clear evidence that ". . . these foreign practices were the real models for trusteeist action. Instead they seem to have been used only as ex post facto arguments in favor of a viewpoint actually indigenous to this country." The "sincerity" of the trustees at Holy Trinity may never be known. The fact is, however, that they did refer constantly to their rights of patronage-- and, as such, the concept of jus patronatus should be considered as one of the several (though least important) factors in the rise of trusteeism.

[38]Trustees of Holy Trinity to Carroll, March 22, 1789. AAB, Case 11B-Q3.

[39]Fecher, German National Parishes, pp. 121-22.

When Carroll denied the Germans' claim to the *jus*
patronatus, Helbron came to the defense of the congregation. He reminded Carroll of the practice and teachings of
the Church which stated that anyone who built a church
with the consent of the diocesan bishop acquired the right
of patronage. Since this was the case with the Germans of
Holy Trinity, it followed that they have ". . . acquired
the *jus* *patronatus* and hence the right of presenting any
ecclesiastic, providing he be able and capable." Furthermore, ". . . the ordinary *should* *appoint* [italics mine]
the person legitimately presented, when the latter is
found capable and otherwise not legally impeded."[40] Later,
when Helbron had made his submission to Carroll who then
appointed him pastor of Holy Trinity, he asked the trustees,
for the sake of peace, to renounce their right of presentation. The trustees and the congregation (before whom they
brought the issue) replied unanimously that they could
". . . *not* upon any consideration cede those rights so
graciously granted by our Dear Mother the Holy Catholic

---

[40]Helbron to Carroll, July 15, 1789. As quoted by
Fecher, *German National Parishes*, pp. 122, 266.

Church for our true endeavours in promoting religion in particular in this country."[41]

The Germans at St. John the Evangelist held to a similar position. Reuter, in speaking for them, informed Rome: "The Bishop again appealed to the _jus patronatus_ but I denied that it belonged to him and asserted that it was the community's, appealing to the law of the Church and the Council of Trent."[42]

Carroll refused to accept the Germans' assertion that they possessed the right of patronage. He denied categorically their arguments that civil and ecclesiastical law supported their claim: "I must own, that I not only question, but, am convinced, you are not entitled to it by either ecclesiastical, or civil law, and especially by the former, in which I am most conversant."[43] Neale ridiculed the Germans of Holy Trinity for being misled by ignorant leaders into thinking that they possessed the _jus patronatus_:

---

[41]Statement of the Trustees of Holy Trinity Church, December 23, 1789. AAB, Case 11B-S9. From this position they did not deviate. Ten years later they were still maintaining their right of presentation. Elling to Carroll, December 1, 1801. AAB, Case 11B-W9.

[42]As quoted by Fecher, _German National Parishes_, p. 131.

[43]Carroll to Trustees of Trinity Church, October 11, 1789. AAB, Case 9A-H1.

"The truth is, you have no _jus_ _patronatus._ You can have

none, because your church has no fixed, permanent and

unalienable fund for the support of a pastor. Such is the

doctrine of the Council of Trent. . . ." Besides, even if

he were to admit that they possessed the right of patronage,

it only meant the right to present, and not to appoint or

discharge a pastor. The latter prerogative belonged only

to the bishop; to maintain the opposite would be

"schismatical and heretical."[44]

* * * * * * * * * *

There was no single cause for trusteeism. American

law made it possible--the Protestant tradition of lay

control, the idea of democracy, the principle of national-

ity, the concept of _jus_ _patronatus_ made it real. One last

point, however, should be considered. While not a factor

in bringing about the rise of the trustee movement, class

and racial animosities may have played a provacative role

in intensifying such disturbances once they began.

The difficulties at St. Mary's between Egan and the

Haroldites had, in addition to other factors, a class

---

[44]Neale's Address to the German Roman Catholics
Frequenting Trinity Church, December 8, 1796. Printed
copy. AAB, Case 10-U2.

basis. Egan and his supporters said that the Haroldites were from the lower class.[45] And, the bishop's board of trustees was called "tory."[46] At St. Mary's Church in Albany, a power struggle evidently broke out between the pastor and the trustees for control of the church. In this case the pastor turned to the "lower class" members of the congregation for support against the trustees.[47]

In Charleston, S.C., many of the Catholics who opposed LeMercier and supported Gallagher did so because they considered his presence as an infringement on their right to name their pastor. However, an added reason may have been that LeMercier favored certain undesirable groups in the parish. A Mrs. McDonald, who supported Gallagher, complained to Carroll that if LeMercier continued to rule the church it would be dominated by "Creoles and Mulattoes."[48]

---

[45] Egan to Carroll, April 27, 1813. AAB, Case 11-D19; J. Carrell to Carroll, May 5, 1813. AAB, Case 11-D20.

[46] Egan to Carroll, August 15, 1813. AAB, Case 11-O13. It is not certain whether this was Egan's description of the board or of his critics. In any case, the term tory was used, and this would denote upper-class.

[47] Trustees of St. Mary's, Albany, to Carroll, November 30, 1802. AAB, Case 10-A2.

[48] McDonald to Carroll, February 27, 1804. AAB, Case 5-C14.

* * * * * * * * * *

Dignan, an authority on the trustee movement, did
not think that Carroll would have adopted the trustee
approach had the general situation been different.[49]
Perhaps, for American law allowed more lay control than
Carroll preferred to grant. Still, those closer to
Carroll in point of time felt that the first Bishop of
Baltimore may have allowed the trustee system to develop
as a way of bringing Catholic Church government--at least
as it applied to the administration of Church government--
more in line with the liberal traditions of this country.[50]
But, by the end of his episcopacy, Carroll had decidedly
turned against a system that made it possible for laymen
to abuse their authority by interfering in purely spiritual
affairs.[51]

---

[49]Dignan, Legal Incorporation of Catholic Church
Property, pp. 51-52.

[50]Maréchal, "Maréchal's Report to Propaganda," in
Ellis, Documents of American Catholic History, p. 216;
John Hughes, Complete Works of the Most Rev. John Hughes,
ed. by Lawrence Kehoe (2 vols.; New York: Lawrence Kehoe,
1865), pp. 11, 550-51.

[51]Melville, John Carroll, pp. 280-81. Maréchal,
"Maréchal's Report to Propaganda," in Ellis, Documents of
American Catholic History, p. 216.

Throughout his episcopacy Carroll had insistently upheld the right of the religious superior to control the ecclesiastical affairs of the Church. In this area he would not allow for lay participation, much less control. When he died in 1815 "trusteeism" was far from over. It was to plague his immediate successors. Eventually, the trustee movement was crushed. In its place came strong episcopal control, and a lasting suspicion of "too active a lay participation in church management."[52]

[52]James J. Hennesey, "The American Experience of the Roman Catholic Church," Catholic Mind, LXIII (November, 1965), 30; Daniel Callahan, The Mind of the Catholic Layman (New York: Charles Scribner's Sons, 1963), pp. 23-25.

PART III

THE SPOKEN WORD: AN AMERICAN STYLE

CHAPTER VI

THE USE OF VERNACULAR IN THE

LITURGY

In the late eighteenth century the liturgical
practices of the Catholic Church in the United States were
the same as those followed in the "old world." Foreign
and local commentators noted this fact. Grassi, an Italian
Jesuit, remarked: "I shall say nothing of the [religious]
services in city churches, because they are the same as in
Europe, so far as the number of priests will permit. . . ."[1]
Mathias Ignatius O'Conway wrote his wife from Baltimore
that: "If you were here you would see everything carried
on precisely as you have seen in the Catholic countries.
You would hear the heavenly music and the High Mass performed in a manner that would raise your soul above the
thoughts of this world. . . ."[2] There was also little, if
any, basic change on the frontier, where Catholic priests,

---

[1] John Grassi, "The Catholic Religion in the United
States in 1818," Researches, VIII (1891), 105.

[2] O'Conway to his wife Rebecca, December 9, 1808.
As quoted by Sara Trainer Smith, "Philadelphia's First
Nun: Cecilia Maria O'Conway," Records, V (December,
1894), 421-22.

most of them born and educated in Europe, instructed the
faithful in old world liturgical practices.[3] And, to see
that future priests carried on the traditional forms of
the liturgy--especially on the frontier were new conditions
forced changes in the traditional ways--John Baptist Mary
David, the superior of St. Thomas Seminary, trained his
students to follow carefully the ceremonies and rites as
detailed by the Roman Congregation of Rites.[4]

The liturgy, while not as integral to Catholicism
as its theology and sacraments, was nevertheless an
essential part that went into making up the Roman Catholic
way. Catholic priests in America, then, perpetuated the
proscribed forms of the liturgy. In one area, however,
Carroll gave serious thought to changing it--and that was
to substitute vernacular for Latin in the wording of the
liturgy.

Ever since the fourth century Latin had been the
predominant language in the Roman liturgy; the use of the

---

[3]Mattingly, Catholic Church on the Kentucky
Frontier, Chap. V, "Catholic Life on the Frontier," pp. 104-
41, offers many examples to demonstrate the validity of
this point.

[4]Martin J. Spalding, Sketches of the Early Catholic
Missions of Kentucky (Baltimore: John Murphy, 1844), p. 248.
(Hereinafter referred to as Catholic Missions of Kentucky.)

vernacular was generally by way of exception from the rule. The most serious attack on Latin as a "cult" language came during the Reformation when the reformers insisted on the sole use of the vernacular in the liturgy. The Council of Trent resisted this course of action, and condemned those who argued that the mass must be celebrated only in the vernacular. The Council proscribed the use of Latin in the liturgy of the western church for three major reasons: (1) that it represented a "common" language appropriate to a universal church, (2) that it allowed for the "mystery" of the mass to be preserved, which the vernacular would not, and (3) that it was a "safe" language since the use of vernacular in the post-reformation period would allow for possible theological "errors" to find their way into the liturgy.[5]

While Carroll may have agreed with the Council of Trent's decision in the sixteenth century to retain the use of Latin in the liturgy he no longer felt the compelling need to do so in the eighteenth. Its retention was of no advantage to the religious life of Catholics in America.

[5]Angelus A. DeMarco, Rome and the Vernacular (Westminister, Md.: Newman Press, 1961), pp. 93-94, 101-34.

He said as much in 1787 to Joseph Berington, a well-known English Catholic author. Carroll stated to Berington that one of the principal obstacles ". . . to Christians of other denominations to a thorough union with us, or at least to a much more general diffusion of our religion, particularly in North America," was the use of Latin in the liturgy. With respect to this point, Carroll exclaimed:

> . . . I cannot help thinking that the alteration of the Church discipline ought not only to be solicited, but insisted on, as essential to the service of God and benefit to mankind. Can there be anything more preposterious, than for a small district containing in extent no more than Mount Libanus and a trifling territory at the foot of it, to say nothing of the Greeks, Armenians, Coptics, etc. to have a liturgy in their proper idiom, and on the other hand for an immense extent of countries, containing G.B. Ireland, all North America, the W. Indies, etc. to be obliged to perform divine service in an unknown tongue. In spite of all evasions, the Latin is an unknown tongue, and in this country, either for want of books, or inability to read, the great part of the congregations must be utterly ignorant of the meaning and sense of the publick offices of the Church. It may have been prudent, for aught I know, to refuse a compliance in this instance, with the insulting and reproachful demands of the first reformers; but to continue the practice of the Latin liturgy in the present state of things must be owing either to chimerical fears of innovation or to

the indolence or inattention in the first
pastors of the national churches in not
joining to solicit, or indeed ordain the
necessary alteration.[6]

Several English Catholics criticized Carroll's
views on the liturgy which became known when Berington
published the letter to support his own position against
Bishop John Douglass, Vicar-Apostolic of London. Carroll
replied to one of his critics, Arthur O'Leary. He
defended the reasonableness of his request that English-
speaking Catholics should celebrate the liturgy in their
own language, especially when Rome has granted such permission to other national churches, much smaller in size and
number. His reasons for desiring the liturgy in the
vernacular were twofold: first, because ". . . one of the
most popular prejudices against us [in America] is that
our public prayers are unintelligible to our hearers"; and,
secondly, "many of the poor people, and the Negroes generally
not being able to read, have no technical help to confine
their attention."[7]

In November, 1791, Carroll presided over the first
diocesan Synod of the Clergy which set down the basic

[6]Carroll to Berington, 1787. AAB, Special Case
C-C1.

[7]Carroll to O'Leary, no date. AAB, Special Case
C-C3.

regulations governing the religious life of the Catholic Church in the United States. It was Carroll's first opportunity to implement his earlier ideas concerning liturgy in the vernacular. The question of religious services was discussed in the Fourth Session on November 8, 1791, and the finished statement represented little change from the traditional position of the Catholic Church. Latin was retained as the basic language of the liturgy. The Synod declared Latin as the language of the mass, with the Gospel and the prayers at the end--the Our Father, Hail Mary, Apostle's Creed, and the acts of faith, hope and charity--said in the vernacular. In the afternoon services, the Synod insisted that the singing of the vespers continue in the Latin, though it allowed the vernacular language for some hymns and prayers.[8]

The decree of the Synod on the liturgy remained in force until 1810, when the bishops of the Catholic Church-- Neale, Cheverus, Egan, Flaget--met, under Archbishop Carroll's leadership, to issue a new regulation. A still more stringent pronouncement was made in favor of retaining

[8]Statutes of the Diocesan Synod of the Clergy, November 7-8, 1791. AAB, Case 9A-L; the statutes were printed in Concilia Provincialia Baltimore Habita ab Anno 1829, usque ad Annum 1840 (Baltimore: John Murphy Co., 1842).

Latin as the cult language. The bishops expressed their concern that there existed ". . . a difference of opinion and practice among some of the clergy . . . concerning the use of the vernacular language in any part of the public service, and in the administration of the Sacraments. . . ." All priests were therefore obliged

> . . . not only to celebrate the whole Mass in the Latin language, but likewise when they administer baptism, the holy Eucharist, Penance, and Extreme Unction, to express the necessary and essential form of those Sacraments in the same tongue, according to the Roman ritual; but it does not appear to be contrary to the injunctions of the Church to say in the vernacular language the prayers previous and subsequent to the sacred forms. . . ."[9]

* * * * * * * * * *

The liberal position of Carroll on the use of the vernacular in the liturgy, as expressed to Berington and O'Leary in the late 1780's, was not implemented by the Synod of 1791 or the Bishop's Meeting of 1810. The bishops' statement in 1810, which decided in favor of tradition over innovation, clearly indicated that Carroll

[9]Regulations given by Archbishop Carroll and the other Bishops, November 19, 1810. AAB, Case 11-I2.

had moved some distance away from his earlier and more
advanced position.[10]   What had happened?

Did Carroll make a serious effort to have his
ideas on the liturgy accepted by his fellow clergy and
bishops at either of these two meetings? Unfortunately,
the evidence does not speak to this question. In any case,
even if the American clergy approved the contemplated
change, Carroll knew that a solitary bishop (or even the
five American bishops in 1810) did not possess the
authority to change the liturgical language of the Church.
Actually, he would not have had it any other way. As early
as 1787 he had told Plowden that vernacular could not be
used in place of Latin in the liturgy without the approval
of the Holy See and the Church. When Carroll learnt that
many priests in London (perhaps influenced by his own
remarks to Berington, which the latter published) openly
espoused the vernacular in liturgy, he asked of Plowden:
"Is it really true, that any are so bold as to . . . assert
that any Single Bishop may alter the language of the
liturgy without the approbation of the Holy See, and a

[10]John Tracy Ellis, "Archbishop Carroll and the
Liturgy in the Vernacular," Worship, XXVI (November, 1952),
550-52.

general concurrence of at least other national bishops?

I should be indeed sorry, if the few words of my letter to

Berington should be tortured to such a meaning."[11] He

reiterated his position to another correspondent:

> If the Holy See and pastors of the Church
> should find cause to allow either generally,
> or in such a country as this, where so many
> poor people and Negroes cannot hold their
> attention by reading, liberty to have the
> divine office in a language generally under-
> stood, I should feel a satisfaction in it;
> but till they alter that point of discipline
> I should think any single Bishop or
> Ecclesiastical Superior to blame for making
> such an innovation.[12]

Perhaps Carroll discussed his ideas with his

fellow-priests, only to find many of them unreceptive.

Without their support he could not begin to act. When

Berington led others to believe that Carroll would change

the liturgy, he explained to O'Leary that: ". . . Berington'

brilliant imagination attributes to me projects, which far

exceed my powers, and in which I should find no cooperation

from my clerical brethren in America, were I rash enough

to attempt their introduction upon my own authority."[13] Of

[11]Carroll to Plowden, June 4, 1787. Maryland
Province Archives, Box 202-B15.

[12]Carroll to _____, June 13, 1787. AAB, Case
9-K2.

[13]Carroll to O'Leary, no date. AAB, Special Case
C-C3.

the few clerics who considered the question of the liturgical language, most were against change. Carroll may have known of their sentiments.

Egan, the Bishop of Philadelphia, was probably sympathetic. He supported the request of the congregation of St. Mary's to chant the vespers in the English language:

> One good effect it is hoped will result from
> this mode, it will be an incitement to the
> congregation to be more punctual at evening
> prayers than they have been heretofore, as
> they may all then join in singing praise to
> God in a language they understand.[14]

Badin, Gallitzin, and Valinière favored the retention of Latin in the liturgy, and they all used similar arguments in its defense. They considered Latin as a universal language, which allowed for uniformity in public worship throughout the Catholic world. Latin, as a "dead" language, was not subject to the perpetual fluctuations of modern languages, and therefore it preserved uncorrupted the traditional faith. Its retention was not detrimental to Catholic religious life, since the laity

---

[14]Egan to Carroll, January 21, 1805. Notre Dame Archives, Transcript. Griffin, Egan's biographer and a close student of Catholicism in Philadelphia, does not think that Carroll granted permission for this to be done Griffin, Egan, pp. 18-19.

had the mass prayers translated in their prayerbooks.[15]

In 1810 Carroll was seventy-five years old. An old man, he had had a difficult episcopacy. There were numerous practical problems to overcome--a vast diocese to be governed, churches to be built, priests to be found to serve the growing number of Catholics. There was so little time to strike out in new directions, when all one's energy was being exhausted in establishing the bare essentials. Besides, he was having severe difficulties with dissident priests and laymen. In a land where liberty was rampant, where authority was so often and so easily challenged, change should not be entered into so lightly. Perhaps this was not the time to innovate, at least not until the ecclesiastical authorities could absolutely control the processes of change. And so he retreated from his earlier position which would have made the Catholic Church so much more at home in America--back to the Roman liturgy, to the old world, to the Roman Catholic way.

---

[15]Stephen T. Badin, Summary Proofs of the Catholic Doctrine from Scripture (Baltimore: Bernard Dornin, 1810), pp. 11-12; Gallitzin, "A Letter to a Protestant Friend," Gallitzin's Letters: A Collection of the Polemical Works, pp. 205-06; Pierre Huet de la Valinière, Curious and Interesting Dialogue (New York: Greenleaf, 1790), p. 67. Valiniere also argued against replacing Latin because it was ". . . the language Jesus spoke himself."

CHAPTER VII

THE NEED FOR GOOD PREACHING

In Roman Catholicism the mass constitutes the central focus of worship, the climax of which is the sacrificial offering by the priest of Christ's body and blood. The "altar" and not the "pulpit" (contrary to Protestant practice)"constituted the architectural, theological and liturgical center" for Catholicism.[1]

Despite this fact American Catholics during the episcopacy of John Carroll were very much concerned about good preaching from the pulpit. Carroll well understood the need for elegant preachers who, versed in the American idiom, could compete in a Protestant America so fond of orators. Speaking of Ralph Smith and Felix Daugherty, two young boys studying for the priesthood in Rome, Carroll instructed Antonelli that:

> . . . they [should] also be thoroughly schooled
> in their vernacular and cultivate acquaintance
> with the approved authors. In this way they
> will be much better prepared for work in their

[1] Edwin Scott Gaustad, A Religious History of America (New York: Harper and Row, 1966), pp. 288-89.

land of birth. For, as the heretics cultivate
elegant diction and delivery, the pastors of
souls must make an effort that men be drawn
to truth and piety through the pleasure of
hearing them.[2]

Carroll's incisive comment to Antonelli represented

the thoughts of many other Catholics. When Cheverus sought

a priest for a new church erected at Damariscotta, Maine--a

congregation composed mostly of converts from the Protestant

faith--he expressed a preference for one who could speak

well and whose native tongue was English.[3] The Abbé Louis

Sibourd complained to Carroll that he felt most uncom-

fortable and unqualified as pastor of St. Peter's Church,

New York, a position he wished to resign. "My endeavours

to bring about some good," he lamented to Carroll, "are

ineffectual. I am deficient in abilities for the pulpit,

the language I speak, is not familiar to me, and I am too

old, to improve."[4] In Boston the Abbé de la Poterie

referred disparagingly of his successor, the Abbé Louis

Rouselet as ". . . this wordy and tedious Rooselet [sic],

this very poor orator and bad preacher, not able to

---

[2]Carroll to Antonelli, July 2, 1787. AAB, Case
9A-A1.

[3]Cheverus to Carroll, July 30, 1808. AAB, Case
2-01.

[4]Sibourd to Carroll, January 7, 1808. AAB, Case
7-Q11.

persuade a single proselyte, but made to scare everyone

by his rough speech and insupportable accent. . . ."[5]

Mastery of English was not alone sufficient to

make one a good preacher; in addition, a priest must be

learned and eloquent. Most of the established Protestant

sects--Anglican, Presbyterian, Congregational--and many

teachers of homiletics considered learning an important

qualification of the good pulpit orator.[6] Catholics also

desired "learned" preachers.

The trustees of St. Mary's Church, Albany, com-

plained to Carroll that their pastor--Father Cornelius

Mahoney--was neither a learned nor eloquent preacher:

> My Lord, this city is in the centre of a
> flourishing State and many people of different
> persuasions come to hear our Sermons, being
> taught to believe that the ministers of our
> Church are learned and well-informed men; but
> in the present case we are sorry to say that
> they find themselves disappointed.[7]

---

[5] Robert H. Lord, John E. Sexton and Edward J.
Harrington, History of the Archdiocese of Boston: In the
Various Stages of Its Development, 1604 to 1943 (3 vols.;
New York: Sheed and Ward, 1944), I, 418. (Hereinafter
referred to as History of the Archdiocese of Boston.)

[6] Floyd Wesley Lambertson, "A Survey and Analysis
of American Homiletics Prior to 1860" (2 vols.; unpublished
Ph.D. dissertation, State University of Iowa, 1930), I,
110-11, 163.

[7] Trustees of St. Mary's, Albany, to Carroll,
November 30, 1802. AAB, Case 10-A2.

And, when Carroll sent the eloquent Dominican, Father
Matthew O'Brien, to serve as pastor of the church in
Norfolk, Virginia, he pointed out to the trustees that
O'Brien was ". . . a gentleman of pleasing manners ,
[possessing] a very considerable stock of literature, not
only on sacred but on general subjects, and who has enjoyed
a distinguished character for preaching. . . ."[8]

Above all, a preacher must be eloquent, capable of
using the language in such a way that he moved his audience
by the sheer power of his words. Father Ferdinand Farmer
lamented the infatuation of some Catholics for beautiful
oratory. He complained to Carroll that the Catholics of
New York were waiting for ". . . one J. Jones, who is
said to be a great preacher (which, alas! is all what some
want who never frequent the H. Sacraments)."[9] The Catholics
of distant Natchez, territory of Mississippi, spoke for
many Catholic congregations when they petitioned Carroll

---

[8]Carroll to the Trustees of the Church in Norfolk,
April 18, 1815. As quoted by Peter Keenan Guilday, The
Catholic Church in Virginia 1815-1822 (New York: United
States Catholic Historical Society, 1924), pp. xxxii-
xxxiii, xxv.

[9]Farmer to Carroll, November 8, 1784. AAB, Case
3-P5.

for a priest who was ". . . not only a good man, but a
<u>graceful</u> [italics mine] preacher and orator."[10]

What constituted good preaching for American
Catholics? If they followed the majority of Protestant
teachers of homiletics--and no American Catholic of this
period composed a manual on preaching--they first wrote a
well-structured sermon which they then read from the
pulpit.[11] Carroll made a practice of writing out his
sermons, and presumably read them from the pulpit. Father
Robert Molyneux, pastor of St. Mary's, Philadelphia, read

---

[10]William Vousdan to Carroll, May 24, 1801. As
quoted by Shea, <u>John</u> <u>Carroll</u>, pp. 505-06. Carroll quoted
this passage to Matthew O'Brien, perhaps trying to convince this distinguished preacher to go and serve the
Catholics at Natchez. Carroll to O'Brien, September 23,
1799. AAB, Case 9A-C3.

[11]Prior to 1800 a majority of teachers on homiletics
favored sermon reading or memoriter preaching, and only a
few spoke in favor of extemporaneous preaching. After 1800
there was a decided move away from the written to the
unwritten sermon, from reading sermons to extemporaneous
preaching. A breakdown of the major Protestant sects would
show the following: Episcopalians, Congregationalists and
Unitarians read their sermons; Dutch Reformed favored
memoriter preaching; Methodists and Baptists long approved
of extemporaneous preaching; and the Presbyterians used all
three approaches. Lamberton, "A Survey and Analysis of
American Homiletics Prior to 1860," I, 111-13, 158-60,
164, 166-71; Fred Jackson Barton, "Modes of Delivery in
American Homiletic Theory in the Eighteenth and Nineteenth
Century" (2 vols.; unpublished Ph.D. dissertation, State
University of Iowa, 1949), I, 146-48, 160.

his sermons. The changing complexion of his congregation,
however (from German to Irish) caused him some concern.
He complained to Carroll: "I wish I had the talent of
doing it _ex tempore_. To preach with a paper does not suit
this place so well, and now from want of time and habit, I
should find it difficult to speak without."[12] Evidently,
Sibourd also read his sermons. In a letter to Carroll, in
which he admitted his deficiency as a preacher, he noted
that part of the problem was his sight which ". . . grows
worse and worse everyday. . . ."[13] Sibourd, then, must
have had difficulties reading his prepared sermon; age and
a poor knowledge of English probably prevented him from
either memorizing the sermon beforehand or speaking
extemporaneously.

Most American teachers of homiletics in the late
eighteenth century favored a plain and natural style free
from either extreme or artificial embellishments or
roughness.[14] Irish preachers were an exception to some

---

[12]Molyneux to Carroll, 1785. AAB, Case 5-K9;
Philip S. Hurley, "Father Robert Molyneux, 1738-1808,"
Woodstock Letters, LXVII (October, 1938), 274.

[13]Sibourd to Carroll, January 7, 1808. AAB,
Case 7-Q11.

[14]Lambertson, "A Survey and Analysis of American
Homiletics Prior to 1860," I, 98-102, 104, 148-51; Barton,
"Modes of Delivery in American Homiletic Theory in the
Eighteenth and Nineteenth Century," I, 163.

of the standards established by these teachers of
homiletics. They were emotional in their delivery, and
rich in the use of ". . . imagery and splendid metaphors."[15]

Catholic congregations noticed the presence or
absence of those qualities which made for eloquence. The
Germans of Philadelphia were prepared to build their own
church so as to obtain the services of Father John Charles
Helbron, who was German, talented, and eloquent.[16] At
St. Mary's, Philadelphia, the trustees petitioned Carroll
to appoint Father Micheal Egan, whom they considered a
gifted preacher.[17] Cheverus' sermons were admired by his
congregation and, for that matter, by all Boston, because
he possessed, in the words of his friend, Father J.S.
Tisserant, an eloquence that was "brilliant, agreeable, full
of unction, and captivating."[18]

---

[15]Carroll to Plowden, November 11, 1813. AAB,
Case 9-S3; Frederick R. Webber, A History of Preaching in
Britain and America (3 vols.; Milwaukee: Northwestern
Publishing House, 1952-1957), II, 621.

[16]Fecher, German National Parishes, p. 6.

[17]Trustees of St. Mary's to Carroll, February 6,
1803. AAB, Case 11-J2; Kirlin, Catholicity in Philadelphia,
p. 179.

[18]As quoted by Lord, Sexton, and Harrington, The
History of the Archdiocese of Boston, I, 604-05.

Those who lacked the special gifts which made for
good preaching often lost favor with their congregation.
Whelan, a good priest, was forced out from the pastorate
at St. Peter's Church, New York, in part because he was not
". . . eloquent when speaking in public. . . ."[19] Mr.
E. Lynch, a member of the congregation at St. Mary's,
Charleston, informed Carroll that the supporters of
Gallagher opposed the coming of LeMercier (whom they had
never met) because they supposed ". . . he cannot
preach. . . ."[20] Did the Irish think that LeMercier, as a
Frenchman, lacked the richness of speech which they
expected to find in a good speaker? The trustees of
St. Mary's, Albany, rejected the terms of a Father
Fitzsimmons, who wanted to serve as their pastor, as
". . . an exorbitant sum for a man that is no preacher."[21]

The call for distinguished preachers was universal
among Catholic congregations, regardless of their location
or ethnic composition. Catholics, like Protestants,
appreciated an eloquent and moving sermon. There were,

---

[19] Farmer to Carroll, May 10, 1785. AAB, Case 3-P9.

[20] Lynch to Carroll, September 9, 1803. AAB, Case
5-B9.

[21] Trustees of St. Mary's, Albany, to Carroll,
August 16, 1806. AAB, Case 10-A4.

however, two external reasons for demanding good preachers
and preaching--the influence of the Protestant churches
and the question of prestige which was especially important
for a minority church like the Catholic.

As Carroll made clear to Antonelli the two young
men studying in Rome must master the art of public speaking
if they were to be successful in a Protestant America that
valued good preaching.[22] He was more specific on this
point with regard to the case of Whelan in New York. In
his opinion the Catholics of New York had adopted the
practice of the Protestant sects in judging the worth of a
priest on the basis of his ability to preach. As he told
Plowden, this worked against Whelan who was no preacher:

> The Capuchin [Whelan] is a zealous, pious, and
> I think, humble man: he is not indeed so learned
> or good a preacher, as I could wish, which
> mortifies his congregation, as at N. York, and
> most other places of America, the different
> sectaries have scarce any other test to judge of
> a clergyman, than his talents for preaching:
> and our Irish Cong--, such as N. York, follow
> the same rule.[23]

An equally important force at work was the desire
of Catholic congregations to impress their Protestant

---

[22]Carroll to Antonelli, July 2, 1787. AAB, Case
9A-A1.

[23]Carroll to Plowden, December 15, 1785. Maryland
Province Archives, Box 202-B10.

neighbors. As members of a minority and often despised church this was important. Since Protestants appreciated good preaching, it would be a point of attraction and admiration for a Catholic Church to possess an eloquent preacher.

The trustees of a Catholic Church in Augusta, Georgia, petitioned Carroll for a good preacher: "We are instructed to request he may be such as will in point of talent and conduct do credit to himself and us. It would be mortifying in the extreme, should he suffer by comparison with the other clergy here."[24] The trustees of St. Mary's, Albany, as already indicated, complained to Carroll that their pastor was neither learned nor eloquent, a real loss in a city that served as the capital . . . of a flourishing state and [where] many people of different persuasions come to hear our sermons. . . ."[25] At St. Mary's, Philadelphia, the Catholics wanted a good preacher since ". . . St. Mary's, being one of the oldest of our

[24]Trustees of the Catholic Church in Augusta, Georgia, to Carroll, July 19, 1805. AAB, Case 10-A6.

[25]Trustees of St. Mary's, Albany, to Carroll, November 30, 1802. AAB, Case 10-A2.

churches and in our most populous city, should have some
of the ablest preachers."[26]

Carroll tried hard to satisfy the petitions that
poured in from so many Catholic congregations. He
recognized the importance for good preaching in a Protestant
America which placed such value on the spoken word. It was
for this reason that he encouraged those students studying
for the priesthood to master the art of public speaking.[27]
A good preacher, trained in the American style, would
edify the faithful, make converts among non-Catholics, and
enhance the prestige of the Catholic Church. The call for
good preaching, then, on the part of Carroll and his
co-religionists, was one more way in which the Church took
on the color of its surroundings--one more way in which the
Church could be made more acceptable to America.

---

[26]John Carrell, a trustee of St. Mary's, to Carroll,
March 10, 1802. As quoted by Griffin, Egan, pp. 6-7.

[27]Carroll to Grassi, March 8, 1813. Maryland
Province Archives, Box 204-28; Carroll to Gallagher,
August 23, 1808. Propaganda Archives. Scritture Riferite
nei Congressi, America Centrale, Vol. III, Fol. 23.
Guilday Transcripts. Catholic University of America
Archives.

PART IV

CATHOLIC-PROTESTANT RELATIONSHIPS

CHAPTER VIII

ECUMENISM--LIVING SIDE BY SIDE

In 1790, the year John Carroll became Bishop of Baltimore, the Catholic population in the United States numbered less than 40,000--a very distinct minority in a population of nearly 4,000,000, many of whom were Protestants.[1] Catholics were surrounded on all sides by Protestants, and contact with them, which occurred in a hundred different ways, was unavoidable.

Carroll viewed such contact with mixed feelings. He realized that only by establishing ties with their fellow Protestants could Catholicism and Catholics become better known and long held prejudices against Catholics be put aside; yet, the established relationships must not become so close that Catholics fall prey to the errors of Protestant thought. Carroll stated the dilemma to Cardinal Hyacinthe Gigismond Gerdil, Prefect of the Congregation of Propaganda. This frequent intercourse in

[1]Gerald Shaughnessy, Has the Immigrant Kept the Faith? A Study of Immigration and Catholic Church Growth in the United States 1790-1920 (New York: Macmillan Co., 1925), pp. 36-38.

public and private life, between Catholics and Protestants,

Carroll told Gerdil, posed special problems for pastors in

the United States:

> They must be on guard lest the faithful be
> gradually infected with the so-called prevail-
> ing indifference of this country; but they
> must likewise take care lest unnecessary
> withdrawals from non-Catholics alienate them
> from our doctrines and rites, for, as they
> outnumber us and are more influential, they
> may, at some time, be inclined to renew the
> iniquitous laws against us.[2]

Fortunately, Protestant opinion of Catholics

gradually improved throughout the post-revolutionary period.

The American Revolution had made a significant impact on

the position of Catholics in the United States. American

Catholics had proven their loyalty during the long struggle

for independence, and further assistance had come in

generous measure from Catholic France. The spirit of the

Declaration of Independence, with its stress on the natural

rights of all men, had, to some extent, a liberating effect

in the area of religious freedom. Furthermore, this was

an era of nation building, and in such times the allegiance

of all citizens, regardless of their religion, was a

[2]Carroll to Gerdil, December, 1795. John Carroll
Papers, Transcript. Catholic University of America
Archives.

necessary factor for success. As a result of these forces

Catholics were everywhere allowed the free and public

exercise of their religion. Several of the states even

went so far as to also remove all political disabilities,

thereby granting full citizenship to Catholics. In the

remaining states, however, old prejudices remained, and

Catholics still suffered from laws which barred them,

because of their religious beliefs, from voting and

officeholding.[3]

All this did not cause any significant change in

the American attitude towards Roman Catholicism as a

religion (for which there still existed considerable hatred

and suspicion); but, there was no denying that, in practice,

America had grown more tolerant of the "Catholic" as a

person and a citizen. The word "Catholic" no longer

connoted all that was bad, and Americans had to grudgingly

admit ". . . that a Roman Catholic, in spite of, not

---

[3]A good brief introduction to this period can be
found in Ray Allen Billington, The Protestant Crusade
1800-1860: A Study of the Origin of American Nativism,
Quadrangle Paperback (Chicago: Quadrangle Books, 1964),
Chap. I, "The Roots of Anti-Catholic Prejudice," pp. 1-31;
Ray, American Opinion of Roman Catholicism, Chaps. VIII,
"The Revolution," pp. 310-50, and IX, "Making the
Constitutions," pp. 350-94.

because of, his religion, might be a desirable neighbor, a devoted friend, a loyal citizen."[4]

American public opinion of Roman Catholics, then, had changed, if ever so slightly. If much of the old prejudice remained, a good deal had disappeared. John Carroll was to find out, to his pleasant surprise, how much had changed, even in that bastion of anti-Catholicism, Puritan New England.

Carroll visited Boston in the early summer of 1791. Many Bostonians gave him a warm welcome, and they invited him to several large functions. Carroll attended a dinner in honor of the Ancient and Honorable Artillery Company (June 6, 1791), where he gave "thanks" at the banquet at Faneuil Hall.[5] He celebrated mass in the Catholic church on the second Sunday of his stay, and prominent Bostonians--among whom was Governor John Hancock--

---

[4]Ray, American Opinion of Roman Catholicism, pp. 310, 348-49.

[5]Rev. John Eliot noted in his interleaved almanac for that day--"An elegant entertainment at the hall, where a clergyman of the C. of England (Rev. Dr. Parker) and a Romish Bp. acted as Chaplains. How would our Fathers have stared! Tempora mutantur etc., and much to the credit of modern times." As quoted in Percival Merritt, "Sketches of the Three Earliest Roman Catholic Priests in Boston," The Colonial Society of Massachusetts, Publications, XXV (1923), 205-06.

attended out of respect for him. He wrote enthusiastically to his friend Plowden: "It is wonderful to tell, what great civilities have been done to me in this town, where a few years ago a popish priest was thought to be the greatest monster in the creation."[6] The warm reception given to Carroll, however, was out of respect for his person and not for the religion which he represented. Rev. Jeremy Belknap made this point clear to his correspondent Hazard: "Bishop Carroll is here yet, and I assure you is treated with the greatest attention and respect by most of our distinguished characters; but the cause which he meant to serve is not the foundation of this respect: it is wholly owing to his personal character."[7]

---

[6]Carroll to Plowden, June 11, 1791. Maryland Province Archives, Box 202-B36. Twenty-four years after Carroll's visit to Boston, Joseph-Octave Plessis, Bishop of Quebec, passed through the city. "Who could have said," Plessis commented, "thirty years ago, that the true faith would be known and respected in Boston, the city the most opposed to Catholicism in all English America. . . ." He concluded, prematurely it would seem, that the practice of religion liberty caused Americans to lose ". . . that spirit of persecution and fanaticism to which they had formerly yielded." Joseph Octave Plessis, "Pastoral Visitation of Bishop Plessis of Quebec 1815," trans. and ed. by Lionel Lindsay, Records, XV (December, 1904), 380-81.

[7]Belknap to Hazard, June 11, 1791, as quoted in Lord, Sexton, and Harrington, History of the Archdiocese of Boston, I, 457.

Carroll was perceptive enough to realize that despite the fine reception he had received in Boston the prejudice against his religion and its adherents was so deep-rooted that it would take a long time before it disappeared.[8]

Events in New England later demonstrated the accuracy of this observation. In the town of Newcastle, District of Maine, James Kavanagh and Matthew Cottrell, two respectable merchants, maintained a chapel for Catholic worship. They decided in 1799, along with Father Francis Anthony Matignon, Pastor of the Church of the Holy Cross in Boston, to challenge the Massachusetts State Constitution of 1785 and subsequent laws of the General Court, which compelled Catholics to support with their taxes Congregational churches and ministers. Matignon, who entered suit against the town of Newcastle, maintained in court that taxes paid by Kavanagh and Cottrell should be used to support the Catholic Church and its priests. The case was taken all the way to the State Supreme Court

[8]Thomas O'Brien Hanley, "The Emergence of Pluralism in the United States," Theological Studies, XXIII (June, 1962), 229.

which ruled against Matignon.[9] According to Father

Cheverus, Matignon's assistant at Holy Cross, the judges

lectured Matignon on the proper place of Catholics in

New England: '"The Constitution (of Massachusetts),"'

said they, '"obliges everyone to contribute for the

support of Protestant Ministers and them alone. Papists

are only tolerated and as long as their ministers behave

well, we shall not disturb them. But let them expect no

more than that."'[10]

From New England to frontier Kentucky was a long

way in time and distance, but not in similarity of senti-

ment towards Catholics. Benedict Joseph Flaget, Bishop of

Bardstown, wrote with some satisfaction to his friend

Father Simon William Gabriel Bruté that the Protestants

around Lexington ". . . do not seem to have prejudices

against Catholics, which is a great [italics mine] deal in

this section." At Danville, Flaget said mass which some

---

[9]For a full account of this incident see Matignon's
letter to Carroll, March 16, 1801, AAB, Case 5-H4. This
letter, along with several others of Matignon, was printed
under the title "Letters From the Archdiocesan Archives at
Baltimore, 1797-1807," Records, XX (June, 1909), 202-04. A
good secondary account of this controversy is William Leo
Lucey, Edward Kavanagh: Catholic, Statesman, Diplomat
from Maine 1795-1844 (Francestown, N.H.: Marshall Jones
Co., 1947), pp. 3-38.

[10]Cheverus to Carroll, March 10, 1801. AAB,
Case 2-N3.

Protestants attended. "I do not know," he told Bruté,
"the impression that my exhortation made on their spirits,
but from the coldness that I observed on most of their
faces, I have good reason to believe that their hearts
were no warmer."[11] A serious case of anti-Catholic prejudice involved Father Charles Maurice Whelan, the first
Catholic priest to serve in Kentucky, who was sued for
slander by some of his parishioners. The jury found him
guilty, and fined him 500 pounds with imprisonment until
paid. Fortunately, one of Whelan's "detractors" stood
bail, and the priest did not go to jail. Later, Father
Stephen Theodore Badin, pioneer missionary to Kentucky
Catholics, spent a night with a man named Ferguson who had
served on that jury. Ferguson, not knowing Badin was a
priest, said to him of that case: ". . . they [the jurors]
had tried very hard to have the priest hanged, but were
sorry that they could find no law for it."[12]

A bitter tirades against Roman Catholicism came
from a Mr. Ogden, who tried to persuade his sister-in-law,

---

[11]Flaget to Bruté, October 28, 1811. Notre Dame
Archives, Schauinger Transcripts.

[12]Spalding, Catholic Missions of Kentucky, p. 47.
Cf. also, pp. 26, fn., 119-20 of this work for further
incidents of anti-Catholicism.

Harriet Seton (Mother Seton's step-sister), away from
conversion to the Catholic Church. Ogden was stunned that
Miss Seton should ignore the teachings of Protestant
divines:

> . . . who have pronounced the Catholic faith
> (as now used and emanating from the Pope) not
> orthodox, and bordering on profanation and
> idolatry. . . . You must then perceive the
> immense difference between worshiping an
> Invisible and Infinite Trinity in spirit and
> in holiness, and the senseless addresses to
> wooden images or imaginary saints. The for-
> mer is in union with our rational and estab-
> lished religion, the latter with superstition,
> ignorance, misguided zeal, and degenerate
> Catholicism.[13]

Despite these continuing signs of animosity,
Catholics did not isolate themselves from their Protestant
neighbors. This would not only have been impractical in a
society composed largely of non-Catholics, but also highly
undesirable. There was no other way for the Church, her
doctrines, rites, and her followers, to become known and
understood except by Catholics involving themselves in
Protestant society. Hopefully, a better understanding of
Catholicism and Catholics would diminish prejudice. So,

[13]Mr. Ogden to Harriet Seton, November 27, 1809,
as printed in Robert Seton, comp. and ed., Memoirs, Letters,
and Journal of Elizabeth Seton (2 vols.; New York:
P. O'Shea, 1869), 11, 66-67.

in countless ways, in private and public life, Catholics

and Protestants touched each other along life's way.

* * * * * * * * * *

The small number of Catholics scattered throughout

Protestant America, the scarcity of religious buildings,

and the shortage of priests often led to novel situations.

Catholic priests frequently celebrated religious services

in Protestant churches or homes. Carroll described to

Plowden one approach to preaching the Gospel, which some

of the clergy were compelled to adopt:

> To pass thro' a village, where a Roman
> Catholic clergyman was never seen before, to
> borrow of the parson the use of his meeting
> house, or church, in order to preach a sermon;
> to go or send about the village, giving notice
> at every house, that a priest is to preach at
> a certain hour, and there to enlarge on the
> doctrines of the Church. . . .[14]

Father John Thayer celebrated the first mass in Salem,

Massachusetts, in the home of Reverend William Bentley,

pastor of the town's Unitarian Church.[15] In Boston, the

---

[14]Carroll to Plowden, April 30, 1792. Maryland
Province Archives, Box 202-B42.

[15]William Bentley, The Diary of William Bentley
(4 vols.; Salem Mass.: Essex Institute, 1905-1914), I,
161-62, 165-66. Bentley was a generous and tolerant
person. He assisted Thayer in finding the few Catholics
that lived in Salem. When no Catholic family could be
found to maintain Thayer while in the town, Bentley offered
his own house for the visiting priest. Bentley was not
personally impressed or pleased with Thayer whom he found
lacking in humility and gratitude.

relatives of the deceased M. Breckvelt de Larive chose to
have an Episcopal minister, Reverend Samuel Parker, perform
the funeral services at Trinity Church, rather than avail
themselves of the services of Thayer, leader of the Irish
"faction" in the Catholic Church of the Holy Cross. When
the French priest Louis Rousselet returned from missionary
work, he requested and obtained permission from Parker to
celebrate a Requiem Mass at Trinity Church for the
deceased.[16] And, in the western regions, Badin remarked
that for want of chapels Catholic priests preached in
Protestant churches.[17]

Sometimes, the shortage of priests and facilities
led Catholics to participate in Protestant services.
Bruté said that the Catholics at Emmitsburg, Maryland,
sometimes attended the religious meetings of the Presbyterians, which were held in the open fields.[18] Thayer
wrote Carroll that he had to reproach a Mr. Barry, a
Catholic living in Albany, New York, ". . . for paying for

---

[16]Merritt, "Sketches of the Three Earliest Roman
Catholic Priests in Boston," pp. 199-202.

[17]Stephen Theodore Badin, "Origin and Progress of
the Missions of Kentucky," Catholic World, XXI (September,
1875), 830-31.

[18]Simon William Gabriel Bruté, "Bishop Bruté's
Account of Religion at Emmitsburg, Md," Researches, XV
(January, 1898), 89.

a pew in the Protestant Church and for bringing up all his family in that religion. . . ."[19] Barry was evidently not the only Catholic in Albany to frequent a Protestant Church. The trustees of the Catholic Church in this city lamented to Carroll that the failure to provide a resident pastor had a harmful effect, since several members of the priestless congregation attended Protestant churches.[20]

Protestants returned the visits of their Catholic neighbors by frequently participating in Catholic religious services. They often attended Catholic mass (either out of curiosity or sincere interest), and this was as true on the frontier as in the urban churches of the east. When the Trappist fathers built a chapel in the Casey Creek Settlement in Kentucky, several Protestant families attended mass on Sundays and feastdays.[21] Bishop Flaget, making a trip to Baltimore, noted the several occasions when Protestants came to hear mass, which he celebrated in

---

[19]Thayer to Carroll, October 4, 1797. AAB, Case 8B-I6.

[20]Trustees of the Catholic Church in Albany to Carroll, April 26, 1802. AAB, Case 11A-A5.

[21]Joseph Durand, "Epistle or Diary of the Reverend Marie Joseph Durand, " trans. by Ella M.E. Flick, Records, XXVI (December, 1915), 331; Lawrence Flick, "The French Refugee Trappists in the United States," Records, I (1884-1886), 101, 112.

private homes.[22] When Flaget visited Vincennes, Indiana,
in 1814, and preached in English, many Protestant settlers
were present at the service.[23] In Boston, Protestants
were attracted to Sunday services at the Church of the
Holy Cross by the eloquent sermons of the learned
Cheverus.[24] Father Anthony Kohlmann, the Jesuit pastor of
St. Peter's Church, in New York City, expressed his pleasure
that non-Catholics came to Sunday mass.[25] Further south,
at St. Peter's Church in Baltimore, Protestants came to
see John Carroll celebrate his first mass as Bishop upon
his return from England where he had gone for his
consecration.[26]

On one occasion Protestants were more than mere
spectators. In Detroit, Gabriel Richard allowed Protestants to participate in the procession of the Corpus Christi

---

[22]Benedict Joseph Flaget, "Bishop Flaget's Diary,'
trans. by William J. Howlett, Records, XXIX (September,
1918), 240, 244.

[23]Thomas T. McAvoy, The Catholic Church in Indiana
1789-1834 (New York: Columbia University Press, 1940),
p. 128.

[24]Anthony Filicchi to Elizabeth Bayley Seton,
October 8, 1804. As printed in Seton, Memoirs, Letters,
and Journal of Elizabeth Seton, I, 200-01.

[25]Francis X. Curran, "The Jesuit Colony in New York
1808-1817," pp. 58-59.

[26]Guilday, John Carroll, p. 384.

by holding the ribbons of the canopy under which the

Blessed Sacrament was carried. Joseph-Octave Plessis,

Bishop of Quebec, who recorded this event on his visit to

Detroit, observed that not all of Richard's parishioners

approved of this step. "The Abbé Richard," Plessis added,

"justifies his conduct by what the Bishop of Baltimore has

given as a principle to his clergy: to do towards

Protestants all that might draw them to the Catholic Church,

an excellent principle as long as it does not violate the

essential rules."[27]

It must sometimes have come as a surprise to those

Protestants visiting a Catholic church to hear the choir

singing Protestant hymns, or to see hanging on the walls

religious pictures painted by non-Catholics. John Aitken,

a Protestant, published the first compilation of sacred

songs for use in Catholic Churches in the United States.[28]

Aitken included a considerable number of Protestant-composed

songs in his collection.[29] Benjamin Carr, an Episcopalian,

---

[27] As quoted in Sister M. Dolorita Mast, Always the
Priest: The Life of Gabriel Richard (Baltimore: Helicon
Press, 1965), p. 144. (Hereinafter referred to as Richard.)

[28] John Aitken, A Compilation of the Litanies and
Vespers, Hymns and Anthems, as they are Sung in the Catholic
Church (Philadelphia: By the Author, 1787).

[29] Erwin Esser Nemmers, Twenty Centuries of Catholic
Church Music (Milwaukee: The Bruce Publishing Co., 1948),
p. 166; H.T. Henry, "A Philadelphia Choir Book of 1787,"
Records, XXVI (September, 1915), 219-21.

published another collection of sacred songs for use in

Catholic Churches--a work which he dedicated to Bishop

Carroll.[30] Carr also included Protestant hymns in this

work.[31] For a number of years he served as organist and

choirmaster at St. Mary's and St. Augustine's Churches in

Philadelphia.[32]

As for non-Catholic paintings in the churches,

Father John Grassi, an Italian Jesuit who was President of

Georgetown from 1812-1817 and ecclesiastical Superior of

the Society of Jesus in America during this same period,

made this revealing remark:

> The good impression produced upon the people
> by sacred pictures cannot be sufficiently
> described. . . . But unfortunately, paintings
> are rare and of little artistic merit, the
> production generally of non-Catholic pencils:
> I make particular mention of this circumstance,

---

[30]Benjamin Carr, Masses, Vespers, Litanies, Hymns, Psalms, Anthems, & Motets, Composed, Selected and Arranged for the Use of the Catholic Churches in the United States of America (Philadelphia, 1808).

[31]Nemmers, Twenty Centuries of Catholic Church Music, p. 168; Jane Campbell, "Notes on a Few Old Catholic Hymnbooks," Records, XXXI (June, 1920), 132-33. Campbell pointed out that Carr's hymnbook was used in the choirs at St. Mary's and St. Augustine's Churches, Philadelphia. Copies of Carr's work were purchased by Bishops Carroll and Egan, and by Father William DuBourg, President of Mount St. Mary's College, at Emmitsburg, Maryland.

[32]Kirlin, Catholicity in Philadelphia, pp. 191-92.

because the observation has been made by many,
that non-Catholic painters do not succeed in
imparting to their works that air of piety
which helps so much to excite devotion.[33]

Protestants did more than come to Catholic churches

for mass or sermons. They sometimes, especially in the

more remote areas, called upon the priest to perform a

religious service. Flaget noted that he heard the

"confession" of several Protestant women.[34] On another

occasion he baptized three children of a Protestant.[35] In

New Orleans, where there was no Episcopalian ministry,

several couples requested Father Lewis Sibourd to bless

their marriages.[36] Closer to home, in St. Mary's County,

Maryland, Father James Van Huffel married several Pro-

testant couples who did not want to go before the Methodist

minister.[37]

Since Protestants often contributed their money,

land, and labor to the establishing of Catholic churches,

they may not have felt so strange entering a Catholic

[33]Grassi, "The Catholic Religion in the United
States in 1818," p. 105.

[34]Flaget, "Bishop Flaget's Diary," pp. 46, 48.

[35]Ibid., p. 160.

[36]Sibourd to Carroll, February 12, 1812. AAB,
Case 7-R4

[37]VanHuffel to Carroll, February 18, 1811. AAB,
Case 8-P7.

church, or calling upon the services of a priest. In
Boston, non-Catholics contributed $3,453 towards the
building of Holy Cross Church. It was, accordingly, only
appropriate for them to attend the dedication ceremony of
the new church performed by Bishop Carroll on September 29,
1803.[38] When Whelan made plans to build a Catholic church
in New York City he appealed successfully to the Protestants
for funds.[39] The Catholics of Alexandria, Virginia, turned
to the Protestants for financial assistance in building
their church;[40] and so did the Catholics of rural
Chambersburg, Pennsylvania.[41] Kentucky Catholics were
equally indepted to their Protestant neighbors for money
to build their churches. Badin built the churches of
St. Peter's in Lexington and St. Louis in Louisville, with
generous assistance from non-Catholics. In the building

---

[38]Lord, Sexton, and Harrington, History of the
Archdiocese of Boston, I, 581-83, 584; Arthur J. Connolly,
"Rev. Frances A. Matignon, First Pastor of the Church of
the Holy Cross, Boston, Massachusetts," United States
Catholic Historical Magazine, III (1890), 143.

[39]Farmer to Carroll, May 10, 1785. AAB, Case 3-P9.

[40]Trustees of Catholic Church in Alexandria to
Carroll, June 20, 1810. AAB, Case 10-A5.

[41]Patrick Campbell to Mathew Carey, August 8, 1812.
Chambersburg. As printed in "Selections from the
Correspondence of the Deceased Mathew Carey, Writer,
Printer, Publisher," p. 345.

of St. Peter's, two of Badin's close Protestant friends
helped to circulate the list; as for the building of
St. Louis, Badin remarked that nine-tenths of the sub-
scribers were non-Catholics.[42] The most magnificent
church structure in Kentucky was the bishop's Cathedral at
Bardstown. Protestants contributed nearly ten thousand
dollars for the building of the Cathedral, and three non-
Catholics served on the Board of Directors to oversee the
work.[43] The Protestants of Bardstown may have assisted in
the building of the Cathedral by a desire to have an
impressive edifice grace their town. David told Bruté
that the Protestants ". . . have said openly that if it
were a question of a small church, they would not contribute
willingly, but that if we wanted to build a good, large
substantial church, they would contribute generously. . . ."[44]

---

[42]Mattingly, Catholic Church on the Kentucky
Frontier, pp. 89, 92.

[43]Flaget to Plessis, June 18, 1816. As printed in
Lionel Lindsay, trans. and ed., "Correspondence between
Bishop Plessis of Quebec, Canada and Bishop Flaget of
Bardstown, Ky. 1811-1833," Records, XVIII (March, 1907),
24; Sister M. Columba Fox, The Life of the Right Reverend
John Baptist Mary David 1761-1841 (New York: United
States Catholic Historical Society, 1925), p. 85.
(Hereinafter referred to as David.)

[44]David to Bruté, July 18, 1811. Notre Dame
Archives. Schauinger Transcripts.

In some cases Protestants offered land and services for the building of Catholic churches. Several churches in Kentucky were established on land donated by non-Catholics.[45] And, when ground was broken on March 31, 1788 for the building of Holy Trinity Church, Philadelphia (a German-Catholic parish), the German Protestants of the city contributed their time, labor, and materials, all free of charge.[46]

Having contributed so much in time, land, and money for the building of Catholic churches, it almost seemed natural for Protestants to become members of the Board of Trustees, which governed the temporal concerns of the church. This actually happened. The Church of St. Louis in Louisville, Kentucky, built largely with the support of non-Catholics, contained two Protestants on its Board of Trustees.[47] As Badin told Carroll these two Protestant Trustees were his friends:

> I received this day a letter of Mr. Fairbairn
> giving his assent that the Church of St. Louis
> be built on his lots: but some of the trustees

---

[45]Mattingly, Catholic Church on the Kentucky Frontier, pp. 96, 98-99, 101.

[46]Hertkorn, Holy Trinity Parish, pp. 29-30.

[47]Mattingly, Catholic Church on the Kentucky Frontier, p. 92; Schauinger, Badin, p. 148.

who are Protestants (mirabile diety) want to
procure a five acres lot, that a Priest may
also be accomodated. If all the Catholics
are not my friends, I am amply compensated by
the friendship of many non-Catholics of
respectability.[48]

In some cases, especially on the frontier,

Protestants gave money and land for the building of Catholic

churches for speculative reasons. After informing his

relatives in Belgium that non-Catholics often gave land to

Catholic priests for their churches, Nerinckx explained the

reason why this was done: "These people know that the

Catholics follow their priests, and that by those they

would gain settlers and have a chance to sell the public

lands."[49] Grassi supported Nerinckx's analysis that land

was often given for speculative purposes:

The settlers in newly opened sections are most
anxious to have churches and missionaries; many
landholders also, even Protestants, offer
hundreds of acres gratis for this purpose, not
through any special zeal for religion, but simply
as a matter of speculation. For people prefer
to settle in places where they can easily procure
the helps of religion, and hence the land
increase in value.[50]

---

[48]Badin to Carroll, October 3, 1810. AAB, Case
1-J10.

[49]Nerinckx to relatives in Belgium, September,
1805. As quoted in Howlett, Nerinckx, p. 119.

[50]Grassi, "The Catholic Religion in the United
States in 1818," p. 103.

Whatever the reasons--piety or speculation--
Protestants contributed to the building of Catholic churches,
but there are few, if any incidents, where Catholics
reciprocated. According to Édouard de Mondésir, a French
Sulpician, who came to America in 1791, ". . . nos frèrer
de l'Eglise romaine r'en auraient pas fait autant en faveur
des dissidents . . . Jamais un romain ne contribuait a
l'erection d'un prêche hérétigue."[51]

Catholics and Protestants attended each others
schools. The fewness of, or dissatisfaction with, existing Catholic schools, forced Catholics to attend non-
Catholic schools. John Lee, the son of the Catholic
Governor of Maryland, went to Harvard, much to the regret
of Matignon who feared for the boy's religion.[52] When
Georgetown suffered a decline in the early 1800's, many
parents withdrew their children and sent them to Protestant
schools.[53] The same thing happened at the New York Literary
Institution, founded by the Jesuits in 1808, where the

---

[51]Édouard de Mondésir, Souvenir d'Édouard de
Mondésir (Baltimore: Johns Hopkins Press, 1942), p. 48.

[52]Lord, Sexton, and Harrington, History of the
Archdiocese of Boston, I, 603-04.

[53]Charles Sewall to Nicholas Sewall, July 29, 1803.
As printed in Hughes, Documents, I, Part ii, 798-99.

severity of one member of the staff turned away young boys

who probably went on to Protestant schools.[54]

Protestants, in turn, attended most of the Catholic

schools. Within the first years of their existence the

New York Literary Institution,[55] Georgetown,[56] and

St. Mary's College, Baltimore,[57] admitted Protestant boys.

Likewise, St. Joseph's Academy at Emmitsburg, Maryland

(founded by Mother Seton),[58] the Ursuline Convent School

in New York City,[59] and the school founded by the Sisters

of Loretto in Kentucky,[60] admitted Protestant girls. The

general rule in such cases was that Protestant students

---

[54]Wallace to Grassi, September 21, 1812. Maryland Province Archives, Box 203-C16.

[55]Kohlmann to William Strickland, November 28, 1810. Maryland Province Archives, Box 4-S2; Kohlmann to Grassi, July 26, 1809. Maryland Province Archives, Box 203-N4.

[56]Ms. Brother John McElroy, Diary. Vol. I, January 1, 1813 to September 4, 1815, pp. 2, 59-60. Georgetown University Archives, Box 521-9.

[57]Joseph William Ruane, The Beginning of the Society of St. Sulpice in the United States 1791-1829 (Washington: Catholic University of America Press, 1935), pp. 121-22. (Hereinafter referred to as St. Sulpice.)

[58]Annabelle M. Melville, Elizabeth Bayley Seton 1774-1821 (New York: Charles Scribner's Sons, 1951), p. 221. (Hereinafter referred to as Seton.)

[59]Kohlmann to Grassi, May 18, 1813. Maryland Province Archives, Box 204-Z16.

[60]Howlett, Nerinckx, p. 267.

were subject to the moral discipline of the college,
except that they were free to attend their own places of
worship and instruction.[61]

Not all Catholic educators favored the idea of
having Protestants attend Catholic schools. Mr. Thomas
Kelly tried to persuade Elizabeth Bayley Seton from sending
her children to St. Mary's because there were too many
Protestant students there, which might have an adverse
effect on the religious life of her boys.[62] Father John
Dubois, a teacher at Mount St. Mary's, advised Mother
Seton not to admit Protestant girls into her school, but
St. Joseph's did not adopt this policy.[64] Wallace
regretted that the debt-burdened New York Literary
Institution had to take in Protestants, for ". . . they are a

---

[61]Copy of a Proposal for Establishing an Academy
at Georgetown, 1788. Maryland Province Archives, Box
56-Zl. At St. Mary's College, in Baltimore, which had a
considerable number of Protestant students, non-Catholics
were not required to attend religious services. This is
the reply of the Catholic writer, "Pliny the Younger,"
to charges made by the Protestant author, "Quintilian,
Jr.," that discipline of St. Mary's was not congenial with
the civil and religious freedom practiced in America. The
controversy can be followed in Strictures on the
Establishment of Colleges, Particular that of St. Mary's
(Baltimore, 1806).

[62]Kelly to Seton, April 8, 1806. As printed in
Seton, Memoir, Letters, and Journal of Elizabeth Seton, I,
244-46.

[63]Melville, Seton, p. 221.

curse to any Catholic Institution."[64] The Sulpicians
looked with disfavor on DuBourg for accepting Protestants
at St. Mary's College. Father Jacques-André Emery,
Superior of the Society of St. Sulpice, wrote DuBourg that
he could not approve of this practice. He had taken up
the matter with Pius VII who ". . . gave a sign of
disapprobation by turning his head." Antonelli, with whom
he also consulted, disapproved even more strenuously.[65]
Emery eventually changed his position, and accepted
St. Mary's as a Sulpician institution. He did so, in great
part, to satisfy Carroll, who did not object to the
admission of Protestants into the college.[66] In fact, as
Carroll told Plowden, ". . . I believe that the general
effect will be beneficial."[67]

Frequent contact between Catholics and Protestants
often led to fast bonds of friendship for many of the
clergy. Father Peter Helbron, financially pressed and

[64]Wallace to Grassi, September 21, 1812. Maryland
Province Archives, Box 203–C16; Wallace to Grassi, July 1,
1813. Maryland Province Archives, Box 204-W1.

[65]Emery to DuBourg, February 26, 1804. As quoted
in Ruane, St. Sulpice, pp. 121-22.

[66]Ibid., p. 123.

[67]Carroll to Plowden, January 10, 1808. As printed
in Hughes, Documents, I, Part ii, 799.

persecuted by several prominent Catholics of Philadelphia, turned to a Protestant friend who loaned him $50.[68] When certain Catholics accused Gallitzin of appropriating a sum of money for his own personal use, many of his Protestant neighbors, with whom he was friendly, ". . . shewed as much indignation at the base, malicious and foul steps that are a taking, as some of the most zealous Catholics. . . ."[69] In Kentucky, Badin numbered among his friends laymen, such as Colonel Joe H. Daviess (for whom he composed a Latin poem on his friend's death in the War of 1812), and clergymen, like the Presbyterian minister, Mr. Moore.[70] And, in Boston, the generous and warm Matignon and Cheverus counted innumerable Protestants--clerical and lay--as their good friends.[71]

The Catholic laity were free to carry their relationships with Protestants beyond the bounds of mere friendship. In many cases Catholics married Protestants--and

---

[68]Helbron to Carroll, April 19, 1800. AAB, Case 4-E2.

[69]Gallitzen to Carroll, May 11, 1807. AAB, Case 8A-06.

[70]Badin to Carroll, March 2, 1797. AAB, Case 1-E7; Schauinger, Badin, p. 79.

[71]Lord, Sexton, and Harrington, History of the Archdiocese of Boston, I, 763, 765, 767; Annabelle M. Melville, Jean Lefebvre de Cheverus 1768-1836 (Milwaukee: Burce Publishing Co., 1958), pp. 135-36, 140-42. (Hereinafter referred to as Cheverus.)

this was only to be expected in a land where Catholics were far outnumbered by those of different faiths. Carroll explained to Plowden the situation as it existed in America:

> Here our Catholics are so mixed with Protestants
> in all the intercourse of civil society, and
> business public and private, that the abuse of
> intermarriage is almost universal; and it sur-
> passes my ability to design any effective bar
> against it--No general prohibition can be
> enacted, without reducing many of the faithful
> to live in a state of celibacy, as in sundry
> places there would be no choice for them of
> Catholic matches.[72]

As some members of the clergy understood, there simply were not enough Catholic young men or women available--and often Catholics had to look outside the fold for suitable partners.[73]

Carroll knew the problem first hand, for several of his own relatives had married non-Catholics, often to the detriment of their faith.[74] Many of the children of Dominick Lynch, a prominent Catholic resident of New York

---

[72]Carroll to Plowden, February 12, 1803. Stony-hurst Archives. Guilday Collection, Catholic University of America Archives.

[73]Carroll to James Barry, April 8, 1806. AAB, Case 9-C6; Matignon to Carroll, March 19, 1801. AAB, Case 5-H5.

[74]Bishop Carroll to Charles Carroll, July 15, 1800. AAB, Case 9-F2; Carroll to James Barry, April 8, 1806. AAB, Case 9-C6.

City, married Protestants, and few of their children

remained Catholic.[75] Father Joseph Pierre Picot de

Clorivière complained to Carroll that the coldness of the

Trustees of St. Mary's Church, Charleston, resulted from

their being married to Protestants.[76] James Patrick Oeller,

a son of the leading Trustee of Holy Trinity Church,

Philadelphia, married a Baptist woman, and left the

Church.[77] Two daughters of Mrs. Lancaster, an influential

Kentucky Catholic, married two brothers, both Presbyterian.[78]

If mixed-marriages were unavoidable in the United

States, they were nontheless undesirable, and condemned as

such by the clergy as detrimental to the faith of the

Catholic partner and the children. In a "Sermon on

Marriage" Carroll defined the ends of marriage as three-

fold: (1) to find companionship in life, (2) to have

children, (3) to avoid carnal temptation. These ends were

best reached when both partners in the marriage were

Catholics. In Carroll's opinion, to deviate from this

---

[75] Thomas F. Meehan, "Some Pioneer Catholic Laymen in New York--Dominick Lynch and Cornelus Heeney," Historical Records and Studies, IV (October, 1906), 285, 290-91.

[76] Clorivière to Carroll, November 2, 1813. AAB, Case 2-Q6.

[77] Griffin, Egan, p. 29.

[78] Badin to Carroll, February 20, 1799. AAB, Case 1-E12.

rule usually endangered the happiness--temporal and
spiritual--of oneself and one's children.[79] While Carroll
admitted that sometimes some good resulted from these
marriages, more often than not, the Catholic partner grew
cool towards his faith, and the children ". . . thro the
discordancy of the religious sentiments of [the] parents
. . . grow up without attachment to any, and become an
easy prey to infidelity or indifferentism. . . ."[80]
Carroll's fears were shared by Grassi, who considered
mixed-marriages as troublesome to religion, for
". . . sometimes the husband hinders his wife from frequenting the Sacraments, sometimes the wife does not allow
the children to be reared in the faith. . . ."[81]

The problem of mixed-marriage was viewed as so
serious to religion that Carroll and the clergy took up
the question at the first Diocesan Synod of the Clergy,

---

[79]Carroll's "Sermon on Marriage," January 17, 1802.
Notre Dame Archives. John Carroll Papers, Transcript.
Catholic University of America Archives. Daniel Brent,
Biographical Sketch of the Most Rev. John Carroll, ed. by
John Carroll Brent (Baltimore: John Murphy, 1843),
pp. 301-23, printed the entire sermon.

[80]Carroll to Plowden, February 12, 1803. Stonyhurst Archives. Guilday Collection, Catholic University
of America Archives; Carroll to James Barry, April 8,
1806. AAB, Case 9-C6.

[81]Grassi, "The Catholic Religion in the United
States," p. 107.

meeting in Baltimore, November 7-11, 1791. The Synod
urged priests to try to prevent Catholics from marrying
non-Catholics, but since this appeared unlikely because of
conditions prevailing in America, the Synod established
the following regulations to guide priests in questions of
mixed-marriages: (a) admonish Catholics of the dangers
resulting from such unions, (b) inquire whether the non-
Catholic party will promise ". . . not to put any
obstacles to having all the children from the marriage
educated in the true Religion," (c) if the priest forsees
that by not performing the ceremony the couple would go
before a non-Catholic minister then he should marry them,
(d) but these marriages ". . . may not be sanctioned with
the blessing which is prescribed in the Roman Ritual."[82]

Despite the work of the Synod, Catholics continued
to marry non-Catholics and Protestant ministers often
performed the ceremony. Such practices were a serious
breach of Catholic discipline. Marriages so contracted

[82]Synod of the Clergy, Third Session, No. 16. AAB,
Case 9A-L. The Statues of the Diocesan Synod were printed
in the Latin in Concilia Provincialia, Baltimore, Habita
ab Anno 1829, usque ad annum 1840 (Baltimore: John Murphy
Co., 1842).

were not recognized as valid by the Church.[83] Carroll

felt compelled to speak out strongly against Catholics

marrying before non-Catholic ministers. In a "Circular

Letter on Christian Marriage" he declared that those

Catholics who did so ". . . rendered themselves guilty of a

sacrilegious profanation of a most holy institution [of

marriage] . . ." Carroll instructed the clergy to inform

all those who had been (or would be) married before any

other than a priest, that they ". . . cannot be admitted

to reconciliation and the Sacraments, till they shall agree

to make public acknowledgment of their disobedience, before

the assembled congregations, and beg pardon for the scandal

they have given."[84]

Protestants did not favor mixed-marriages either.

The tradition of discouraging marriages with Catholics,

---

[83]Grassi, The Catholic Religion in the United
States in 1818, p. 107; Propaganda to Flaget, October 5,
1816. Propaganda Archives. Lettere della S.C., Vol. 297,
Fol. 280. Guilday Transcripts, Catholic University of
America Archives; Disposition of the Care of Samuel Brown.
AAB, Case 9A-N1.

[84]Carroll to Francis Beeston, Secretary to the
Diocesan Synod, November 16, 1791. AAB, Case 9-E2. Cf.
Carroll to Father Michael Levadoux, June 26, 1797. Notre
Dame Archives. John Carroll Papers, Transcript, Catholic
University of America Archives; and, Carroll to Father
Claude Florent Bouchard de la Poterie, December 24, 1788.
AAB, Case 9A-G3, in which he insists on ". . . subjecting
to a public penance" (not merely a public acknowledgment)
those who marry before a Protestant minister.

which stemmed from the Reformation, carried over into the eighteenth century.[85] Reverend William Endfield, in an oft printed treatise on marriage, considered mixed-marriages as a major factor in causing unhappy marriages and divorce.[86] Reverend Stephen West reminded his fellow Presbyterians that, according to the Westminister Confession, it was the ". . . duty of Christians to marry only in the Lord; and, therefore, such as profess the true reformed religion, should not marry with infidels, papists [italics mine], or other idolators. . . ."[87] The Methodists expelled from their society those who married with "unawakened persons." Thomas Coke and Francis Asbury, two prominent Methodists, explained what their church meant by the term "unawakened person":

> By the word unawakened . . . we mean one whom
> we could not in conscience admit into society.
> We do not prohibit our people from marrying
> persons who are not of our society, provided,

---

[85]George Elliot Howard, A History of Matrimonial Institutions (3 vols.; Chicago: University of Chicago Press, 1904), I, 391-92.

[86]William Endfield, An Essay on Marriage (Philadelphia: Zachariah Poulson, 1788), p. 5.

[87]Stephen West, The Duty and Obligations of Christians to Marry Only in the Lord (Hartford: Watson and Goodwin, 1778), p. 18; The Constitution of the Presbyterian Church in America (Philadelphia: Robert Aitken, 1797), Chap. xxiv.

such persons have the form, and are seeking the
power of godliness; but if they marry persons
who do not come up to this description, we
shall be obliged to purge our society of them.
And even in a doubtful case, the member of our
society shall be put back upon trial.[88]

Presumedly the Methodists would have designated the

Catholics, who did not subscribe to the theology of

Protestantism, as "unawakened persons."

The Catholic clergy took strong measures against

mixed-marriages which, in their opinion, invariably

weakened the faith of the Catholic partner. But even the

less intimate contact that took place between members of

the two faiths posed problems, for that could lead Catholics

to mistakenly believe that all religions were equally

pleasing and valid in the eyes of God. Despite these

dangers, Catholics were not encouraged to avoid normal

contact with their non-Catholic neighbors. A policy of

segregation would only perpetuate their minority and

suspected position in American life. The clergy hoped,

then, that the involvement of Catholics in American society

would diminish anti-Catholic prejudice and attract converts

to the church. The Catholic clergy, however, had to

[88]Thomas Coke and Francis Asbury, The Doctrines and
Discipline of the Methodist Episcopal Church in America
(10th ed.; Philadelphia: Henry Tuckniss, 1798),
pp. 156-57.

carefully instruct their congregations not to lose sight of the significant differences that separated the two religions. No amount of personal contact or friendship with Protestants could change the teachings of the Roman Catholic Church that Protestantism, as a religious system, possessed limited value and truth.

CHAPTER IX

CATHOLIC OPINION OF PROTESTANTS

AND PROTESTANTISM

John Carroll, in the first sermon he delivered to his congregation as Bishop of Baltimore, stated the fundamental position that American Catholics would take toward Protestants and their faith. He informed the members of the congregation that, as their bishop, his duty was:

> . . . to preserve their faith untainted amidst the contagion of error surrounding them on all sides: to preserve in their hearts a warm charity and forbearance toward every other denomination of Christians; and at the same time to preserve them from that fatal and prevailing indifference, which views all religions as equally acceptable to God and salutary to men.[1]

Carroll expressed a desire for Catholics to live on good terms with their fellow Americans, even though many of them belonged to different Christian churches. At the same time, however, he made it clear that it was his duty to guard

[1] Carroll's First Sermon as Bishop of Baltimore, December 12, 1790. Maryland Province Archives.

them from being tainted by the theological errors of their
non-Catholic neighbors and from falling prey to the mistaken notion that religious differences were unimportant.
Their very salvation depended on retaining, in all its
purity, their Catholic faith.

* * * * * * * * * *

Although Catholics viewed Protestantism as theo-
logically false, this did not prevent them on occasion,
from showing, as Carroll had asked in his sermon ". . . a
warm charity and forbearance toward every other denomination
of Christians." Some Catholics refrained from the harsh
epithet "heretic" when referring to Protestants. Instead,
Catholics sometimes designated Protestants as "separated
brethren," "separated fellow Christians."[2] The vulnerable
position of Catholics in America, of course, dictated such
prudence, though Catholics often refrained from using this
harsh term out of a real desire to establish good

---

[2]Flaget to his brother, March 21, 1811. Mount
St. Mary's Seminary Archives. Schauinger Transcript;
Memorial of Haroldite supporters to Carroll, March 10, 1813.
AAB, Case 11-D15; Kohlmann to Carroll, January 22, 1812.
AAB, Case 4-M7; Louis Guillaume Valentin DuBourg, St.
Mary's Seminary and Catholics at Large Vindicated Against
the Pastoral Letter of the Ministers, Bishops, and of the
Presbytery of Baltimore (Baltimore: Bernard Dornin, 1811),
p. 43; Anonymous, The Catholic Religion Vindicated (n.p.:
the author, 1813), p. 57.

relationships with Protestants. Nonetheless, the occasional use of such language, did not change for Catholics their conviction that Protestantism, as a religious system, was in fundamental error.

As Bishop of Baltimore, Carroll could exert a considerable influence on the development of Catholic thought in the United States. He could (and did on occasion) move the Catholic Church in this country in directions more acceptable to the American spirit. But, on this question--what recognition should be accorded to the Protestant faith--he could not slide over into the emerging pattern of "non-denominationalism," generalized religion without dogma. As a Roman Catholic, a member of an international organization, he had to hold to the teachings of his Church that Roman Catholicism alone was the true religion, all others false.[3]

As early as 1771, while on a tour of Europe, Carroll noted in his "Journal" the following observations.[4] Passing

---

[3]Daniel J. Boorstin, The Genius of American Politics, Phoenix Books (Chicago: University of Chicago Press, 1958), pp. 145-49; John Tracy Ellis, American Catholicism (Chicago: University of Chicago Press, 1956), pp. 153-54.

[4]Carroll's "Journal" was printed in Brent, Carroll, appendix, "Journal of a Tour in Company with the Hon. Mr. Stourton," pp. 223-76.

through Bavaria, he spoke well of his fellow Jesuits whose
labors prevented the Catholic religion of this area from
being corrupted ". . . with the pernicious tenets of the
neighboring provinces. . . ."[5] He remarked of Trent that
it was the site of the last General Council ". . . called
chiefly to stop the progress of the errors which took their
rise in Germany. . . ." While the Council did much good
for the Church ". . . it was not so fortunate, as to put
an end to the new heresies."[6] His many, and in some cases
warm, contacts with Protestants in America did not make him
change his opinion about Protestantism. This was most
clearly revealed in his correspondence with foreign church-
men. In appealing for help from the Apostolic Nuncio in
Paris, Doria-Pamphili, Carroll expressed his hope that
Pamphili would not fail to assist ". . . a weak portion of
the Church [in America] too far from the edifying examples
which enliven the faith and piety in Catholic countries,
and too exposed to the contagion of heresies. . . ."[7] In
his efforts to enlist support for the Church under his care,
he also asked Cardinal Vitaliano Borromeo to help the

[5]Ibid., p. 265.
[6]Ibid., pp. 269-70.
[7]Carroll to Doria-Pamphili, February 27, 1785.
AAB, Case 9A-F1.

American Catholics ". . . who are fighting in this very
distant region, and, if I may so speak, in this sink of all
errors."[8] And when he gave thought to the building of his
Cathedral in Baltimore, he shared his hopes with the Bishop
of New Orleans: ". . . it is a matter very near to my
heart to see such a monument erected to the honor of God,
in a country, where error and heterodoxy have usurped so
long that Superiority which ought to belong to truth only,
and to genuine Catholicity."[9] Carroll's fellow bishops--
Flaget and Cheverus--likewise viewed Protestantism as
erroneous.[10]

The most thorough statement denying the religious
validity of the Protestant faith came from Badin.[11]

---

[8]Carroll to Borromeo, April 19, 1788. AAB, Case
9A-G1.

[9]Carroll to Bishop of New Orleans, March 31, 1790.
Notre Dame Archives. John Carroll Papers, Transcript.
Catholic University of America Archives.

[10]Joseph Benedict Flaget, "Bishop Flaget's Report of
the Diocese of Bardstown to Pope Pius VII, April 10, 1815,"
ed. and trans. by Victor F. O'Daniel, Catholic Historical
Review, I (October, 1915), 317-18; Flaget to Plessis,
March 31, 1811. As printed in Lionel Lindsay, ed. and
trans., "Correspondence Between Bishop Plessis of Quebec,
Canada and Bishop Flaget of Bardstown, Ky. 1811-1833,"
Records, XVIII (March, 1907), 13-15; Jean Lefebvre de
Cheverus, "Report to Propaganda," February 7, 1817, as quoted
in Lord, Sexton, and Harrington, History of the Archdiocese
of Boston, I, 695-96.

[11]Stephen T. Badin, Summary Proofs of the Catholic
Doctrine from Scripture (Baltimore: Bernard Dornin, 1810).

"According to sacred Scripture as well as Tradition," Badin
wrote, "the true Church must be ONE, HOLY, CATHOLIC, and
APOSTOLICAL." Since the Protestant sects enjoyed none of
these marks, which distinguished solely the Church of
Rome, it followed that the latter was exclusively the true
Church. Protestantism, ever dividing into new sects,
without fixed principles, was clearly destitute of <u>unity</u>.
"Indeed," Badin thought, "it is not possible that they
should ever be brought to unity in religion since every
man's private fancy or fallible spirit is with them the
ultimate judge of Scripture and controversies. . . ." The
Protestant churches were not <u>holy</u>; in fact, their very
". . . doctrines tended to the subversion of moral
virtue. . . ." For Badin, the central tenet of Protestant-
ism--that man is justified by faith alone, without good
works--was destructive of good. How could it turn out
otherwise, when, as history demonstrated, ". . . Protestantis
was founded on pride, rebellion, lust, breach of vows,
rapine and sacrilege. . . ." The Protestant Church could
not claim to be <u>Catholic</u> or universal (which implies being

in all ages and all nations) ". . . since it had no being for fifteen ages after Christ, and none of the modern sects can be called the church of all nations." And, the Protestant churches were not apostolical, since they were not founded by any of the Apostles, nor do they have ". . . any succession of doctrine, communion, order, or lawful mission from them."[12] In short, as Badin said on several occasions, the Protestant churches were "erroneous," in "error," "heretical."[13] Badin's colleagues in Kentucky-- Charles Nerinckx, Michael Fournier, and Thomas Wilson-- shared his sentiments.[14]

Converts to Catholicism were most insistent on the truth of their new faith, and on the falsity of their old one. Thayer, concerned that those who belonged to the Protestant churches were in danger of "eternal ruin," returned

---

[12] Ibid., pp. 28-41.

[13] Badin to Carroll, June 15, 1808. AAB, Case 1-I9; Badin to Carroll, February 10, 1804. As printed in "The Church in Kentucky," Records, XXIII (September, 1912), 147; Schauinger, Badin, p. 153.

[14] Nerinckx, Einen Ooglag op den Tegenwoordigen Staet der Roomsch-Catholyke Religie in Noord-America, pp. 4, 7, 20-21; Fournier to Carroll, March 2, 1797. AAB, Case 8A-M1; Fournier to Carroll, August 28, 1797. AAB, Case 10-B4; Wilson to Carroll, July 25, 1806. AAB, Case 8B-L5; Wilson to Carroll, October 11, 1807. AAB, Case 8B-L7; Wilson to Carroll, December 5, 1809. AAB, Case 8B-L8.

from France to the United States in order to propagate the "true faith" of Catholicism.[15] Judge James Twyman, whom Badin converted to Catholicism, told the priest that the Protestants in Kentucky were so confused in their religious beliefs that a pious, judicious priest would reap a harvest of new converts to the true faith.[16]

Twyman was not the only layman interested in bringing Protestants to a knowledge of the true faith. Laymen from the congregation of St. Frances, in Scott County, Kentucky, petitioned Carroll for a resident priest who, in addition to restoring a true spirit of religion among the parishioners, could try to bring non-Catholics back to the fold, since many Protestants were ". . . weary of their own extravagances, and might . . . be disposed to seek refuge, and rest in the bosom of the true Church."[17] Ignatius Goff stayed for three months in Brownsville, Pennsylvania, at the home of a Protestant--Richard Noble. Goff told Carroll that he had a few Catholic books which he shared with Noble who ". . . begins in a great

---

[15] John Thayer, An Account of the Conversion of the Reverend John Thayer (Baltimore: William Goddard, 1788), pp. 16-25.

[16] Twyman to Badin, December 24, 1804. AAB, Case 10E

[17] Petition of Laymen from the Congregation of St. Francis to Carroll, 1808. AAB, Case 10-D7.

measure to come into the knowledge of the true church of Christ."[18]

Perhaps the most interesting and spirited exchange on this subject took place between the Jesuit Brother Joseph Mobberly and a Presbyterian merchant, Mr. Melvin.[19] In the Georgetown section of Washington a street called the Scotch Row had been "run out" by the surveyor, George Fenwick (who was a Catholic). The final direction of the street had yet to be determined. Mr. Baulch, a Presbyterian minister, wanted it to run by his house, but Fenwick warned him that this could only be done by cutting away at a hill that bordered the minister's place, with the danger that the house could topple. '"Oh! said the parson, I am founded on a Rock (alluding to the Catholic rock) and can never fall. If God had foreseen and predetermined that it shall fall, it will fall whether that hill be cut away or not."' The street went by Baulch's house, the hill was cut away, and the western wall of the house fell! Catholics laughed '"that his rock was melted down."' Several days later,

[18]Goff to Carroll, February 12, 1803. As printed in Felix Fellner, "Trials and Triumphs of Catholic Pioneers in Western Pennsylvania," Records, XXXIV (December, 1923), 302-03.

[19]MS. Joseph Mobberly, "Diary," I. Georgetown University Archives. Box 4.4 1/2.

Mobberly, feeling (as he himself said) a little zealous and
mischievous at the same time, visited Mr. Melvin, a leading
member of the Presbyterian Church, to sell him a copy of the
Douay Bible. Melvin said that he did not need one, for he
already owned three Protestant Bibles. Mobberly replied,
'"Oh, Sir, you know that Bible is corrupt--consequently
worth nothing."' Melvin replied, '"And pray, Sir, on what
infallible authority do you build the truth of your Bible?"'
'"Not, Sir,"' Mobberly answered, '"upon the infallible rock
so much boasted of by a certain gentlemen of this town a
few weeks ago, and which by the by, is melted down, but
upon the infallible authority of the Catholic Church."'
The conversation continued, and Mobberly obtained from
Melvin the following statement: '"No, sir, we don't
acknowledge any Church to be perfect."' Mobberly quickly
made use of Melvin's admission to show that the Presbyterian
Church was not a true one:

> 'Then, Sir, your Church cannot be the true
> Church of God--for St. Paul writing to the
> Ephesians concerning the Church of Christ, says:
> it is "a glorious Church, not having spot or
> wrinkle, nor any such thing, but that it should
> be holy, and without blemish." Thus you see the

Church of God is without spot or blemish--
consequently perfect--but you may say that
your Church is not perfect--therefore it
cannot be the Church of God--I thank you Mr.
Melvin for having acknowledged what I wanted
to prove--that is, that your Church is false.'[20]

* * * * * * * * * *

The denial of religious truth to Protestantism was

a sentiment shared by all Catholics. Such was not the case

with regard to how Catholics felt about Protestants as

religious persons. Some Catholics were inclined to doubt

the religious integrity, sincerity and worth of those who

belonged to heretical churches; while other Catholics were

willing to admit, that despite their religion, Protestants

were moral and good people.

Several of the clergy had harsh words for Protestant

ministers. Father Lawrence Phelan called the ministers in

western Pennsylvania ". . . the very dregs of the pretended

reformation."[21] Father Francis Bodkin complained to Carroll

that in New Orleans the ". . . Methodist rascals are

beginning their infernal mission in this city, public

preaching, etc. . . ."[22] Nerinckx doubted the commitment of

[20]Ibid., pp. 1-5.

[21]Phelan to Carroll, May 26, 1796. AAB, Case 6-G10.

[22]Bodkin to Carroll, February 2, 1804, AAB, Case
1-T9.

those Protestant ministers who were unwilling to leave family and home to engage in the arduous task, undertaken by the Catholic clergy, to bring the savages in America to Christianity.[23]

Some Catholics thought that little good could come to individuals from their association with Protestant churches and institutions. Father Edward D. Fenwick, the founder of the Dominican Order in the United States, declared that in Kentucky there was ". . . no predominant religion, but a great variety of sectaries, much ignorance, and little virtue, except [italics mine] among Catholics. . . ."[24] Kohlmann regretted that in New York City Catholic orphans had to receive their education in Protestant establishments ". . . where they lose both their morals and their religion. . . ."[25] Even Carroll, who was usually more generous to non-Catholics, attributed Catholic fondness for those undesirable pastimes of dancing, reading love

---

[23]Nerinckx, Einen Oogslag op den Tegenwoordigen Staet der Roomsch-Catholyke Religie in Noord-America, p. 21.

[24]Fenwick to Luke Concanen, first Bishop of New York, July 10, 1808. As quoted in Victor Frances O'Daniel, The Right Reverend Edward Dominic Fenwick (Washington: The Dominicana, 1920), p. 172.

[25]Kohlmann to   , September 13, 1810. This letter of Kohlmann's was printed under the title "An Unpublished Letter of Father Anthony Kohlmann," Woodstock Letters, XXXI, No. 1 (1902), 30-32.

stories, and free contact between young people of opposite sexes, to frequent association with Protestants.[26]

A few Catholics saw little value coming from the revival meetings that took place in the early nineteenth century. Badin denounced the Kentucky revival meetings in sarcastic terms: "The Baptists, etc., are now attacked with malady of nerves, called jerking, which is very unnatural . . . they appear to me to bear a strong resemblance to the possession of Devils. . . ."[27] Lay Catholics shared his sentiments. Judge Twyman doubted the long range meaning of these revivals. He pointed out to Badin that so many Protestants, ". . . who only a few years past were enthusiastically mad and fiery zealous in religion (if it deserves the name) [are] now changing from one thing to another and many to nothing at all. . . ."[28]

Some Catholics responded more favorably toward Protestants. Dilhet spoke well of some Presbyterian ministers he had met in upstate New York. He was impressed

[26]Carroll to Antonelli, March 1, 1785. Propaganda Archives. Scritture Riferite nei Congressi. America Centrale, II, Fol. 312. John Carroll Papers, Transcript. Catholic University of America Archives.

[27]Badin to Carroll, September 7, 1804. As printed in "The Church in Kentucky," pp. 153-55.

[28]Twyman to Badin, December 24, 1804. AAB, Case 10-E13.

with their labors: they gave instructions, held prayer

meetings, taught catechism, preached the gospel, repressed

evil conduct, and rooted out scandal among their people.

Dilhet asked ". . . should we not regard these men as moral

teachers and benefactors of mankind?" Considering the fact

that no Catholics lived in this area Dilhet thought it

desirable to have the settlers know about the Christian

religion until that day when priests could come ". . . to

make these Christians in good faith enlightened Catholics."[29]

Bruté was willing to grant that the "poor" Protestants at

Emmitsburg, despite living in the midst of error, possessed

a good ". . . fund of religion, and of principle. . . ."[30]

Grassi was pleasantly surprised with the character of so

many Protestants whom he found ". . . gentle in character,

[and] upright in their lives. . . ."[31] Richard was prepared

to go even further in his praise of the virtuous lives that

some Protestants led. Major Orlando B. Wilcox, a Protestant,

reported that Richard said to his mother: '"if all

[29]Dilhet, État de l'Église Catholique on Diocese des États-Unis de L'Amerique Septentrionale, pp. 83-85.

[30]Bruté, "Religion at Emmitsburg," pp. 90-91.

[31]Grassi, "The Catholic Religion in the United States in 1818," p. 110.

Catholics were as good as you, there would be no trouble in the world."'[32]

* * * * * * * * * *

Granted, then, that Protestantism was not a true religion, did it follow that its adherents could not achieve salvation? Was there no room in heaven for those outside the one true, Roman Catholic Church?

The question was placed squarely and perhaps uncomfortably before the American Catholic body in 1784 by none other than the apostate Jesuit (and relative of John Carroll), Charles Wharton. In his essay, Wharton reminded his former co-religionists that there was a time when he too took pleasure in being a Catholic:

> I daily thanked God, that I was not, like other men, heretics, schismatics, and infidels; I subscribed with unfeigned sincerity to that article of your belief: 'That the Roman Church is the mother and mistress of all churches, and that out of her communion no salvation can be obtained.'

Wharton now rejected this doctrine. While in England, where he served as pastor to the Catholics of Worcester, he lived on terms of friendship and intimacy with many Protestants.

[32]As quoted in Mast, _Richard_, pp. 102-03.

It became painful and hard for him to believe that these good Christians were in danger of losing salvation because they were outside the pale of the Roman Catholic Church. Such a cruel doctrine he dismissed with contempt and indignation. He believed, instead, that Protestants were entitled to the same grace and redemption as Catholics.[33]

John Carroll took it upon himself to reply to Wharton's charges.[34] He was reluctant to engage in debate, especially if it would ". . . disturb the harmony now subsisting among all Christians in this country, so blessed with civil and religious liberty. . . ." Yet, he felt the need to rebut Wharton's erroneous conclusions which, if not corrected, would tend to embitter Protestants against Catholics and disturb the peaceful relations that existed in the United States among all religious groups.[35]

While Carroll understood that, in the broad meaning of the term, there was no salvation outside the Church, he did not believe that this necessarily excluded baptized

---

[33] Charles Henry Wharton, A Letter to the Roman Catholics of the City of Worcester (Philadelphia: Robert Aitken, 1784), pp. 7, 9-10, 13.

[34] John Carroll, An Address to the Roman Catholics of the United States of America (Annapolis: Frederick Green, 1784).

[35] Ibid., pp. 11, 114.

non-Catholics or non-Christians from salvation. He did not
accept that extreme position of some divines that since the
Catholic Church was so absolutely necessary for salvation
that one could not be saved unless he was actually a
Catholic.[36] Nor could he accept the opposite extreme
position (that Wharton called for) which minimized the
necessity of membership in the Catholic Church to such an
extent that all it required for salvation was a formal
adhesion to any of the Christian churches. Instead,
Carroll subscribed to a school of thought which, in effect,
constituted the mainstream of Catholic thinking on the
thorny question of no salvation outside of the Church.
While theologians of this persuasion also believed that
membership in Christ's Church was necessary for salvation,
they held to a more open and generous interpretation of
what constituted the "Church" and who were its "members."
They stressed that those individuals--baptized non-
Catholics and non-Christians--who held to certain fundamental religious beliefs (e.g., a belief in God and
immortality) and lived a moral life, could be considered as

[36]Carroll to Plowden, January 22, 1787. Maryland
Province Archives, Box 202-B13.

"members" of, or "belonging" to, the Church and therefore capable of salvation.[37]

Carroll began his argument by pointing out that:

> . . . to be in the <u>communion of the Catholic Church</u>, and to be a <u>member of the Catholic Church</u> are two very different things. They are in the <u>communion of the Church</u>, who are united in the profession of her faith, and participation of her sacraments, through the ministry, and government of her lawful pastors. But the <u>members of the Catholic Church</u> are all those who with a sincere heart seek true religion, and are in an unfeigned disposition to embrace the truth, whenever they find it. Now it was never our doctrine that salvation can be obtained only by the former. . . .

It was necessary for salvation to believe in the "Catholic faith," which, as Carroll defined it, was essentially (though not exclusively) contained in the Apostles Creed, and one did <u>not</u> have to be an actual member of the Roman Catholic Church to do this. Under certain conditions, he had shown that it was possible for non-Catholic Christians to be saved. Carroll tried to strengthen his case by demonstrating that even non-Christians could be saved. Although most theologians considered baptism as necessary to bring a person into the Church, the Council of Trent had

_____

[37]Maurice Eminyan, "Extra Ecclesiam Nulla Salus," <u>New Catholic Encyclopedia</u>, V,(1967), 768; Maurice Eminyan, "Salvation, Necessity of the Church For," <u>New Catholic Encyclopedia</u>, XII (1967), 995-97.

stated '". . . that salvation may be obtained without actual baptism."' It followed, then, that ". . . we not only may, but are obliged to believe, that out of our communion salvation may be obtained."[38]

Carroll turned next to discuss the meaning of heresy. He accepted the distinction drawn by Catholic divines between those who held to false opinions through ignorance, and those who did so willfully and obstinately. The latter were heretics; the former, while in error, were not, and could be saved. Carroll expressed his position by quoting from the work of Bergier, a French theologian:

> 'First, with regard to heretics (the author
> here means those, who though not heretics in
> the rigorous sense of the word, go under that
> general denomination) who are baptized and
> believe in Jesus Christ, we are persuaded, that
> all of them, who with sincerity remain in their
> error; who through inculpable ignorance believe
> themselves to be in the way of salvation; who
> would be ready to embrace the Roman Catholic
> Church, if God were pleased to make it known
> to them, that she alone is the true Church,
> we are persuaded, that these candid and
> upright persons, from the disposition of their
> hearts, are children of the Catholic Church.'[39]

[38]Carroll, _An Address to the Roman Catholics of the United States of America,_ pp. 11, 15.

[39]_Ibid._, pp. 15-17.

Wharton was not convinced that Carroll had exoner-
ated the Catholic Church from the charge that she held to
the idea that outside of her communion there was no
salvation.[40] Still, he was pleased that Carroll had
personally made every effort to allow for salvation to
those outside the Roman Catholic Church. Carroll, however,
did not go far enough for Wharton. Wharton was distressed
that the charitable assertion of some Protestant divines--
that all the essentials of true religion are to be found in
the Roman Catholic Church--was not returned by Carroll in
saying that ". . . all the essentials of true religion may
be found also in the Protestant communion." True Christian
liberality shall be shown, Wharton declared, only when the
Pope, his councils, and divines ". . . shall declare . . .
that a person, not pretending to the plea of invincible
ignorance, may safely leave the Roman Church and become a
member of ours, because it is a safe way to salvation."[41]
Wharton was asking for that which Carroll, as a Catholic,
could not grant.

---

[40] Charles Henry Wharton, A Reply to the Address to
the Roman Catholics of the United States of America
(Philadelphia: Charles Cist, 1785), pp. 11-12, 14.
      [41] Ibid., pp. 10, 15-19.

A number of American Catholics also considered the question--can a person outside of the Church be saved? While none could go as far as Wharton hoped, a few were willing to admit (as Carroll had done) that salvation was possible for those non-Catholic Christians, who, out of invincible ignorance, did not belong to the Catholic Church. Several others would not admit even this; they chose not to allow for any exception to the statement--that out of the communion of the Catholic Church there was no salvation. Three out of the four that took this position were converts, which may help to explain their actions. Some converts often assume a harsher attitude towards their former faith that many baptized Catholics.

Charles Carroll of Carrollton, a prominent lay Catholic, admitted that non-Catholics could be saved. He wrote to Harriet Chew Carroll that: "I feel no ill will or illiberal prejudices against the sectarians which have abandon[ed] that faith [Roman Catholic]; if their lives be conformable to the duties and morals prescribed by the Gospel, I . . . hope and believe they will be rewarded with eternal happiness. . . ."[42] DuBourg conceded that many Protestants were in error only because they had never been exposed to Catholicism; he hoped that this fact would be taken into account by a merciful God to excuse their errors.[43] Brother Joseph Mobberly, who had been accused by a Protestant minister of having said that all non-Catholics would go to hell, denied having uttered such a severe statement. What he did say was that ". . . every man is bound in conscience and under pain of the eternal loss of his soul to embrace the one Religion which Jesus Christ has established wherever he finds it to be the religion of Jesus Christ." For Mobberly, the Roman Catholic Church was the Church which Christ established; therefore, ". . . no man, who knowingly, willingly and obstinately refuses to the last breath to adhere to the Church of Jesus Christ after discovering it to be such, can ever obtain salvation." Those non-Catholic Christians who lived in ignorance of the truths of Catholicism were obviously excluded from this condemnation.

---

[42] Charles Carroll to Harriet Chew Carroll, August 28, 1816. As quoted by Ellen Hart Smith, Charles Carroll of Carrollton, pp. 275-76.

[43] DuBourg, St. Mary's Seminary Vindicated, pp. 42-43

[44] MS. Joseph Mobberly, "Diary," I, 120-23. Georgetown University Archives, Box 4.41/2.

Hay's catechism, published with Carroll's approval, took a harder line, though it did not foreclose the question of salvation for those outside of the Church. After demonstrating that the Roman Catholic Church, founded by Jesus Christ, possessed an infallible authority to teach the true faith necessary for salvation, Hay stated that one of the consequences following from this observation was: "That therefore out of her communion there is no _ordinary_ [italics mine] possibility of salvation, seeing that out of the communion of the Church of Christ, that one faith, without which it is impossible to please God, is not to be found, and that those who refuse to hear the Church, are by Christ himself declared to be as heathens and publicans."[45] It would seem that the word "ordinary" was crucial, for its use by Hay implied that under certain extraordinary circumstances (i.e., invincible ignorance, or baptism by desire) salvation might be possible.

Thayer, a convert from Protestantism, offered _no_ concessions to non-Catholics. Anyone who did not accept the infallible teaching authority of the Roman Catholic

[45]Hay, An Abridgement of the Christian Doctrine, pp. 32-34.

Church, founded by Jesus Christ himself, should understand

". . . that there is no salvation out of this Church, for

this is a part of her doctrine grounded on the words of

Christ 'He who hears you, hears me, and he who despises

you, despises me.' This merits the most serious reflections,

since they who despise God are not in the way of salva-

tion."[46] Stephen Cleveland Blythe, a former Episcopalian,

declared without any reservation that outside of the

Catholic Church there was <u>no</u> salvation.[47] Gallitzin, who

came late to Catholicism, stated that ". . . out of that one

Church [Roman Catholic] salvation is not to be had." He

pleaded with a Protestant minister to understand the truth

before it is too late:

> The very garb which is at present considered
> by you as a mark of distinction and honor,
> will before the dreadful tribunal on the day
> of God's eternal vengeance, be the terror and
> despair of your soul and its everlasting
> condemnation; I mean the garb of Protestantism.
> . . . For God's sake, dear sir, if you value
> the glory of God and the salvation of your

---

[46]Thayer, <u>Controversy</u>, pp. 15, 21-25.

[47]Stephen Cleveland Blythe, <u>An Apology for the Conversion of Stephen Cleveland Blythe</u> (New York: Joseph Desmones, 1815), pp. 39-40, 64. (Hereinafter referred to as <u>Conversion</u>.)

soul, give up protesting against the
Catholic Church. In it alone you will
find salvation. . . .[48]

When the fictional character "Mr. Goodwish," in Father

Pierre Huet de la Valinière's Dialogue, asked if it was out

of charity that Catholics ". . . judge and condemn all

those who are not of their own religion?" "Doctor

Brevilog" replied, "Yes, Sir, for it is a great charity to

do all one can to save those who are in danger and ready

to perish. . . ."[49]

The Catholic position, then, may have appeared

harsh and severe, but for the Catholic qua Catholic he

could not hold to any other opinion than that his Church

was the one, true Church founded by Jesus Christ, without

which salvation was difficult, and, in some cases,

---

[48]Gallitzin, "A Defense of Catholic Principles,"
in Murphy (ed.), Gallitzin's Letters: A Collection of the
Polemical Works, pp. 96, 110. In all fairness to Gallitzin,
he does admit, pp. 101-02, that the Church ". . . charitably
supposes them [non-Catholics] honest in their errors and
therefore not guilty in the sight of God of the crime of
heresy." But he immediately qualifies this limited concession by stating that the Church still grieves because these
non-Catholics are being deprived ". . . of so many means of
salvation not to the found out of her pale."

[49]Pierre Huet de la Valinière, Curious and Interesting Dialogue (New York: Greenleaf, 1790), p. 69.

impossible to obtain. The many and warm relationships, which American Catholics had with Protestants, could not change for them the traditional teaching of their Church on this subject.

PART V

THE CATHOLIC CHURCH AND THE "AMERICAN WAY"

CHAPTER X

THE CATHOLIC CHURCH AND

AMERICANISM

The episcopacy of John Carroll coincided with a
period in American history noted as a time of nation-build-
ing and nationalism. The Revolutionary War had helped to
solidify in the minds of many Americans that they constituted
a separate "people," who possessed a different way of life
from that of the "old world." Specifically, Americans no
longer considered themselves as "Englishmen," nor England
as their "homeland." Continual attacks by Europeans on
America sustained post-war nationalism. Americans were
forced to a constant defense of their nation and nationality. Like so many other nationalists, the Americans went
beyond a mere defense of their country; they came in time
to glory in their nation, its people, and its institutions
as superior to a declining Europe. Americans considered
their country as superior to Europe because it had left

behind the old world's ignorance and injustices, and because it had developed in the new world--in a land immense and rich beyond imagination--a new and better political and social organization that allowed for freedom and dignity to man. Americans viewed their country as an asylum, as Paine called it, for "the persecuted lover of civil and religious liberty from every part of Europe." The United States would show to the world the ability of free men to govern themselves, and to create a new society and culture, which would lead the way to a brighter and better future for humanity.[1]

* * * * * * * * * *

John Carroll returned to America in 1774. He was forty years old, and had spent the last twenty-seven years living in Europe. Still, this absence did not diminish his loyalty to America. Within two years of his return he had agreed to serve his "country" in its fight with England, by accompanying a delegation from Congress in an

---

[1]The following works offer a more extended treatment of the developing idea of American nationalism during this period: Evarts Boutell Greene, The Revolutionary Generation 1763-1790 (New York: Macmillan Book Co., 1946), pp. 300-05, 416-18; John Allen Krout and Dixon Ryan Fox, The Completion of Independence 1790-1830 (New York: Macmillan Co., 1944), pp. 206-11; Russell Blaine Nye, The Cultural Life of the New Nation 1776-1830, Harper Torchbooks (New York: Harper and Row, 1960), pp. 37-49.

unsuccessful attempt to win over Canada to the American cause.

Carroll felt at home in America (as a member of an old and distinguished Maryland family he was easily accepted by other Americans), and he wanted his Church to be so also, even though, at first glance, it might seem that much in America was new to Catholic life and culture. Ever sensitive to the rising tide of nationalism, and to America's dislike of Europe and its interference in American affairs, Carroll encouraged his fellow Catholics to put aside their European connections and become wedded to their new homeland; and, wherever the faith and discipline of the Catholic Church allowed, he thought that the institutions of the Church in the United States should conform to the spirit of America. He was wise enough to understand that, in the light of post-war nationalism, the Church and its members must become "Americanized," or else they would never be accepted. For Carroll, however, this advice to his fellow Catholics was not motivated just by "politics"; he genuinely loved America, and he believed that the ideas and institutions of America (at least as he understood them) were in consonance with Catholic doctrine and practice.[2]

Carroll had high hopes for his Church in America, more so than in Europe. He looked with suspicion and disfavor on the "old world." He had been there when the Pope, pressured by the rulers of Europe, had suppressed his beloved Society of Jesus. It was a bitter experience. As he told Plowden: "I can assure you, that one of my strongest inducements to leave Europe, was to be removed not only out of sight, but even out of the hearing of those scenes of iniquity, duplicity and depredation of which I had seen and heard so much." While he thought the people of Europe irreligious and disrespectful of legitimate authority, he reserved his sharpest comments for those rulers who concentrated all power in their hands so that ". . . they may be uncontrollable in the exercise of every act of despotism.' As for the Emperor of Germany who was considered a lover of justice, as well as of innovation, Carroll said the latter point probably explained this change since ". . . it is so new a thing for crowned heads to be just. . . ." And, he

[2]Dorothy Dohen, <u>Nationalism</u> <u>and</u> <u>American</u> <u>Catholicism</u> (New York: Sheed and Ward, 1967), pp. 92-93, 105-06.

added in a significant afterthought, which showed how
typically American he had become: "You see, I have
contracted the language of a Republican."[3]

He took Plowden to task for adopting the language
of America's English critics who represented the country as
being ruled by "imperious leaders." Actually, the opposite
was true:

> . . . but, alas! our imperious leaders, by
> whom I suppose you mean the Congress, [are]
> at all times amenable to our particular
> assemblies, elected by them every year,
> often turned out of their seats, and so
> little envied, that . . . it has at all
> times been a difficult matter to get men
> disinterested and patriotic enough to accept
> the charge.[4]

In fact, rather than criticize, Plowden (and other English
Catholics) should find much to admire in America. Carroll
thought that the American principle of religious liberty
was such a significant step forward, that England could do
well to imitate it.[5]

---

[3] Carroll to Plowden, February 20, 1782. Maryland
Province Archives, Box 202-B3.

[4] Carroll to Plowden, September 26, 1783. Maryland
Province Archives, Box 202-B5.

[5] Carroll to Plowden, February 28, 1779. Maryland
Province Archives, Box 202-B1; Carroll to Lord Petrie,
August 31, 1790. AAB, Special Case C-R1.

Carroll was a proud American. The seal he adopted
for his diocese--that of the Blessed Virgin Mary surrounded
by thirteen stars--may have been an expression of his
attachment to the Church and to America. The usual representation in Christian art of Mary based on St. John's
vision in the Apocalypse (12:1-6), was that of a woman with
a crown of twelve stars on her head. Could it be that
Carroll had combined in his seal the two objects most dear
to him--the Blessed Virgin Mary and the United States?[6]

Throughout his episcopacy Carroll strove to
establish a Church free of foreign admixture. When the
congregation of Holy Cross Church in Boston split into
French and Irish factions, Carroll wrote them to put aside
their differences and live together: ". . . that since it
has pleased Divine Providence to unite all parts of the
United States under one Episcopacy, all would lay aside
national distinctions and attachments, and strive to
form not Irish, or English, or French congregations and

---

[6]I am indebted for this acute observation to John
M. Daly, Georgetown University: Origin and Early Years
(Washington: Georgetown University Press, 1957), p. 59,
Fn 60. There is a photograph copy of the seal in the
Georgetown University Archives, Folder 255-56. For a short
study of this representation of Mary in Christian art see
E.F. Siegman, "Woman Clothed with the Sun," New Catholic
Encyclopedia, XIV (1967), 1000-001.

churches, but Catholic-American congregations and churches."[7]

Catholicism and America. The two fittingly belonged together. They were not incompatible. One could be a good Catholic and a good American. As Carroll told the congregation at Holy Trinity Church, Philadelphia:

> To our country we owe allegiance, and the tender
> of our best services and property when they are
> necessary for its defense; to the Vicar of
> Christ we owe obedience in things purely
> spiritual. Happily, there is no competition
> in their respective claims on us, nor any
> difficulty in rendering to both the submission,
> which they have a right to claim.[8]

On the surface, Carroll's analysis was correct. The spiritual allegiance that a Catholic owed to his Church was not in conflict with the political allegiance that he owed to the state. Catholicism and Americanism appeared compatible. But, on a deeper level, the republican spirit of America, with its emphasis on the right of free men to control their own lives, posed a challenge to Carroll's

---

[7]Carroll to Masson and Campbell, April 30, 1790. AAB, Case 9A-H3. Thayer, a native American (whom the Irish faction supported) used Carroll's own arguments so as to gain the latter's support in his quarrel with Rousselet: "In all your letters you wish for an American, and not a French church. How can you form American churches, but by priests who speak the language of America? Thayer to Carroll, May 13, 1790. AAB, Case 8B-H2.

[8]Carroll's Address to the Trustees of Trinity Church, February 22, 1797. Printed Copy, AAB, Case 10-W2.

optimistic conclusions. The monarchial-episcopal structure of the Roman Catholic Church, founded by divine institution, demanded from the clergy and laity an obedience and submission to the bishop's authority that was at variance with republican principles. Carroll must have understood this dilemma, for he tried, at first, to accomodate the Church to its republican environment by recognizing the role of the laity in the parish church and the right of the clergy to participate in the selection of their bishops. But, the Roman tradition of episcopal rule eventually prevailed, and Carroll ended his episcopacy by opposing a meaningful role for laymen at the parish level, and by limiting the clergy to a minor role in the selection of their religious superiors. He had stifled the two movements--lay trusteeism and ecclesiastical democracy--which were valid expressions of republicanism. In short, while Carroll encouraged Catholics to accept republican America, he was not prepared to allow the republican spirit to penetrate too deeply into his Church's ecclesiastical structure.

Many of the clergy--even those who were foreign born--shared Carroll's attachment to America. When Gallitzin's federalist political philosophy was attacked as royalist and aristocratic--thereby implying less than a full acceptance of the American way--he denied the allegation and asserted his deep attachment to the country and its institutions; moreover, as he pointed out, Catholicism encouraged such devotion, for it ". . . strongly inculcates the principles of loving and serving . . . [one's] country."[9] Gallitzin was as hopeful as Carroll for the future of the Catholic Church in America. He shared his thoughts with his companion Lemcke:

> Generally speaking you cannot do much with the old rascals coming from _senile_ [italics mine] Europe. If you can manage to keep them in the faith and patiently abide the time when the young native German and Irish will intermarry, you are master of the situation; for then a new Catholic nation has come into existence that does not give offense at every turn and is not wed to secondary issues . . . but is competent to support, and to harmonize with each other, Catholicism and the American constitution, without over-straining the one and neglecting the other.[10]

[9]Gallitzin, "Letter to the Editor of the Lancaster _Federal Gazette_, September 20, 1808," in Murphy (ed.), _Gallitzin's Letters: A Collection of the Polemical Works_, pp. 294-95, 298.

[10]Lemcke, _Gallitzin_, p. 223.

Badin, too, seemed to tie together the love he felt
for his country and for his religion. He declared, late in
life: "I was an American in feeling and conviction long
before I became a naturalized citizen of this Republic. I
would now die with a devotion next to that which I owe my
God for the country of my choice."[11]

* * * * * * * * * *

Carroll's patriotism did not merely remain on the
level of personal expression. He was prepared, as with
several other members of the clergy, to use his office for
the cause of America.

In some special cases this meant that the degree of
one's loyalty to the United States could serve as a decisive
factor in the appointment to, or discharge from, an
ecclesiastical position. Carroll appointed Father Pierre
Huet de la Valinière as his vicar-general for the Illinois
territory in 1786, in part to reward the priest for the
sufferings incurred when British officials evicted him from
Canada during the revolutionary war because of his pro-
American sympathies.[12] Matignon was moved by similar

---

[11] Schauinger, Badin, pp. 259-60.

[12] Fintan Glenn Walker, The Catholic Church in the
Meeting of Two Frontiers: The Southern Illinois Territory
1763-1793 (Washington: Catholic University of America
Press, 1935), pp. 130, 134-35.

reasons to recommend to Carroll that he provide a Father
Burke with a clerical position in the United States. In
Burke's favor, Matignon pointed out that the priest
supported ". . . the principles of the federal government."[13]
In the newly-acquired territory of Louisiana, torn with
conflicting loyalties, Carroll was willing to exert his
authority to support United States' interests. He
instructed his nephew, Daniel Brent, to assure his superior,
James Madison, the Secretary of State, that any priest in
Louisiana unfriendly to the United States would be
discharged.[14]

In the Northwest Territory lived numerous Indian
tribes that opposed the United States. The government, at
Carroll's suggestion, hoped to improve its relations with
the Indians through the assistance of Catholic priests.
Carroll appointed Jean Francois Rivet, a French refugee
priest, to serve in this capacity, and for his efforts to
civilize the Indians and attach them to the interests of
the United States, the government promised to provide

[13]Matignon to Carroll, July 23, 1798. AAB, Case
5-G10.
[14]Carroll to Brent, March 3, 1807. Notre Dame
Archives, Transcript.

Rivet an annual allowance of $200.[15] Rivet's mission was

not very successful, and he confessed his failure to

William Henry Harrison, the Governor of the Indiana

Territory. Harrison conforted Rivet by pointing out that

his services among the French inhabitants were of importance

to the government; besides, in the future, there would be

further need of his assistance. "He added," Rivet informed

Carroll, "that I should therefore be satisfied, keeping my

eyes open for everything that concerns the Government and

keeping myself ready to give to the United States such

services as he might be called upon to ask of me. His

answer has completely reassured me."[16]

Opposition to the United States also existed at the

settlement of Detroit, acquired from Great Britain as a

result of the Peace Treaty of 1783. Those inhabitants who

remained friendly to the English denounced Father Michael

Levadoux for supporting the American cause. The partisans

of the English disliked Levadoux for holding religious

services in thanksgiving, as he called it, for ". . . being

---

[15]Camillus P. Maes, "John Francis Rivet," American
Ecclesiastical Review, XXXV (July, 1906), 35-36; Carroll to
Samuel Dexter, Secretary of War, September 15, 1800. AAB,
Case 9-F6.

[16]Rivet to Carroll, October 14, 1802. AAB, Case
8B-F7.

united to a free people."[17] Though his critics called him

". . . an enemy of royalty and a veritable sans-culotte . . ."

Levadoux remained undaunted. "I am not disturbed," he told

Carroll. "According to my opinion I am a citizen of the

United States, and I should be a traitor if I abandoned

their interest to sustain those of a crown from the yoke of

which they have freed themselves. I try to do my duty . . .

and I would never be so imprudent as to compromise myself

with the government."[18] Evidently, Levadoux had no regrets

in using his office to inculcate in his congregation

affection for the United States. Cheverus was prepared to

do the same in Boston. He assured Carroll that: "I shall

use my best endeavours to reconcile the people entrusted to

my care, to all the measures of the humane and liberal

government they live under. I shall on all occasions shew

myself a hearty friend to the interests of the United States

and to the Federal government."[19]

---

[17]Levadoux to Carroll, September 10, 1796. As printed in "Letters from the Archepiscopal Archives at Baltimore 1790-1814," ed. by E.I. Devitt, Records, XX (September, 1909), 261.

[18]Levadoux to Carroll, February 8, 1797. Ibid., p. 267.

[19]Cheverus to Carroll, January 26, 1797. AAB, Case 2-M9.

* * * * * * * * * *

Ever sensitive to American jealousy of all foreign
jurisdiction, Carroll was determined that the Catholic
Church in the United States would in no way give offense by
showing any undue dependence on a foreign power, civil or
ecclesiastical. He made it a major goal of his administration to limit the ecclesiastical role of Rome (especially
that of the Congregation of Propaganda) in the internal
affairs of the Catholic Church in this country lest its
presence reawaken old cries that the Church was un-American,
a foreign body. And he was no more tolerant of the meddling
of European bishops in the ecclesiastical administration of
his diocese.[20]

Equally determined that no other foreign interests
should play any role in the life of the American Church,
Carroll took strong exception to the conduct of Claude
Florent Bouchard de la Poterie, a French priest serving in
Boston. Every Sunday, at the Church of the Holy Cross,
Poterie included in his discourse the following prayer:
"We pray . . . for the King of France and other friends and

[20]See above, Part I, Chaps. I, II for a full dis-
cussion of these points.

allies of America; for all those who respect the interests of his most Christian Majesty in foreign countries."[21] Carroll sent Poterie a stern rebuke. He pointed out to Poterie that his _Pastoral_ contained ". . . many passages highly improper for publication in this country, and of a tendency to alienate from our Religion, and disgust the minds of our Protestant Brethren." Actually, Carroll considered himself partially responsible, for he should not have appointed Poterie until the latter had ". . . had time to be better acquainted with the temper and habits of thinking in America, where more caution is required in the ministers of our Religion, than perhaps in any other country. . . ." He warned Poterie against public prayers for the King of France because ". . . it will be concluded that your congregation consider him entitled to some sovereignty over them."[22]

---

[21]Claude Florent Bouchard de la Potiere, _A Pastoral Letter_ (Boston: Thomas and Andrews, 1789), p. 18.

[22]Carroll to Poterie, April 3, 1789. AAB, Case 9A-G3. Carroll later told Plowden that he had forbidden Poterie to say public prayers for the king of France because ". . . a government jealous of its independence might construe it into an undue attachment of American Roman Catholics to a foreign prince." Carroll to Plowden, July 12, 1789. Maryland Province Archives, Box 202-B22.

For similar reasons, Carroll cautioned the Catholics of Charleston, South Carolina, who were appealing to the king of Spain for funds to build a church and to support a pastor. While he would not oppose the project-- for he understood how badly the Catholics of Charleston needed a church--he expressed his wish to the congregation that their clergymen ". . . may be entirely independent of and unconnected with any foreign prince." Carroll's reservations were twofold: first, that such priests who courted the favor of monarchs were often not the most religious; and, secondly, that neither the congregation nor the ecclesiastical superior in the United States could effectually interfere in their appointment. Carroll insisted, however, that any priest designated by a foreign ruler <u>must</u> have his approval; in this way, Carroll hoped to nullify the influence of a foreign power in the affairs of the American Catholic Church.[23]

Even when religion demanded some measure of foreign involvement in the American Catholic Church Carroll was reluctant to allow it. When Carroll became Prefect-Apostolic

[23]Carroll to the Catholics of Charleston, June, 1790. AAB, Case 9-F3; Guilday, <u>John England</u>, I, 137; Hopkins, "St. Mary's Church, Charleston, S.C.," in <u>Yearbook</u>, <u>1897</u>, <u>City of Charleston</u>, <u>S.C.</u>, pp. 438-40.

the whole territory claimed by the United States fell under

his jurisdiction. Rome, however, did not change accordingly

the boundaries of the diocese of Quebec, whose bishop--

Jean-Francois Hubert--claimed the Illinois Territory as

within his jurisdiction. Hubert questioned Carroll's right

to appoint Valinière as his vicar-general for this

territory.[24] Carroll replied that he did not know that

Hubert's pastoral care extended to that region. He was

willing, however, that Hubert continue to provide spiritual

services to the Catholics there, but he expressed his

concern that the American government would take exception

to such a policy: "In such an event, my only anxiety would

be that probably the United States would not allow the

exercise of power, even of a spiritual nature, to a subject

of Great Britain."[25]

---

[24]Walker, The Catholic Church in the Meeting of Two Frontiers: The Southern Illinois Country, pp. 123-27.

[25]Carroll to Hubert, May 5, 1788. As printed in "Correspondence Between the Sees of Quebec and Baltimore, 1788-1847," trans. and ed. by Abbé St. George Lindsay, Records, XVIII (June, 1907), 156. A year earlier a similar jurisdictional clash had occurred between Carroll and Hubert--this time, further west, along the Mississippi River. Carroll notified Rome that he was willing to work out some kind of arrangement with Hubert but he feared ". . . that those in authority here would not tolerate under any condition the exercise of jurisdiction by a prelate who is a British subject." Carroll to Antonelli, January 12, 1787. AAB, Case 9A-G1.

* * * * * * * * * *

Carroll's "Americanism" extended over into Catholic institutional life as well. He wanted the Church's institutions to take on an American complexion, but never to such an extent that their basic Catholic character would be suppressed. This was true of Carroll throughout his episcopacy, as he attempted to implement his program for the Church in America, with all its internal tensions, in a number of areas: the building of a national church, the idea of ecclesiastical democracy as it applied to the clergy and laity (the trustee movement), and the principle of the liturgy in the American idiom.

The founding of Georgetown was no exception. As early as the mid-1780's he favored the creation of a Catholic college to provide a Christian education for youth, and which, at the same time, could prepare students for the ecclesiastical life.[26] An expanding Catholic population demanded more priests, and Carroll was not eager to depend so heavily on foreign clergymen. While so many who came over were outstanding and pious men, a significant

[26]Carroll to Plowden, September 26, 1783. Maryland Province Archives, Box 202-B5; Carroll to Plowden, December 15, 1785. Maryland Province Archives, Box 202-B10.

number fell short of the high standards that he thought
necessary for priests coming to live and work in
Protestant America.[27]

Carroll hoped that the founding of Georgetown in
1789--in which he played a leading part--would help put an
end to this pressing problem. He thought of Georgetown as
serving three main functions. First, as a Catholic school,
it would "preserve attention to the duties of religion and
good manners, in which other American schools are more
notoriously deficient."[28] More specifically, Georgetown
would become, for those Catholic youth who attended it,
". . . the safeguard of their faith."[29] Secondly, it would
serve as a nursery for the seminary (which Carroll considered as a necessary companion to the college), thereby
providing the Catholic population with a steady supply of
their own clergymen; no longer need they depend so heavily

---

[27]Carroll to John Troy, Archbishop of Dublin,
August 11, 1788, and November 9, 1789. As printed in
Spicilegium Ossoriense: Being a Collection of Original
Letters and Papers Illustrative of the History of the Irish
Church from the Reformation to the Year 1800, comp. and ed.
by Patrick Francis Cardinal Moran (3 vols.; Dublin: Browne
and Nolan, 1874-1884), III, 504-604.

[28]Carroll to Plowden, March 1, 1788. Maryland
Province Archives, Box 202-B17.

[29]Carroll to Apostolic Nuncio at Lisbon, April 23,
1790. AAB, Case 9A-H2.

on foreigners.[30] Thirdly, and equally important, Georgetown

was to help in the training of an <u>American</u> clergy--

". . . that is of men accustomed to our climate, and

acquainted with the temper, manners, and government of, the

people, to whom they are to dispense the ministry of

salvation."[31] Since he believed that Catholicism could

best succeed in the United States if the Church adopted

itself to the temper of America, this last point--an

American clergy--was crucial to its success.

Georgetown's subsequent history caused Carroll some

uneasy moments. Enrollment, which numbered sixty-six

students in 1792, fell to twenty by 1803. The number of

students remained under thirty for the next few years.

Carroll was discouraged, and he actually considered

temporarily closing the college.[32]

---

[30] Carroll's "First Sermon as Bishop," December 12,
1790. Maryland Province Archives; Carroll to Hubert,
January 20, 1792. Archives of the Archdiocese of Quebec,
E.U.I-2. John Carroll Papers, Transcript. Catholic
University of America Archives.

[31] Carroll's "Pastoral to the Catholics of the United
States," May 28, 1792. Maryland Province Archives. Carroll
"Pastoral" is printed in <u>The National Pastorals of the
American Hierarchy 1792-1919</u>, ed. by Peter Keenan Guilday
(Washington: National Catholic Welfare Conference, 1923),
pp. 4-5. Cf. Carroll's letter to the Apostolic Nuncio at
Lisbon, April 23, 1790. AAB, Case 9A-H2 for a similar
statement.

[32] Francis Patrick Cassidy, <u>Catholic College Foundati</u>
<u>and Development in the United States 1677-1850</u> (Washington:
Catholic University of America Press, 1924), pp. 13-17;
Daly, <u>Georgetown University</u>, pp. 73, 113-14, 135-37.

Part of the problem was caused by the severe rules established by the Neale brothers--Fathers Leonard Neale and Francis Neale--the two principal administrators of the college in the early 1800's. Though worthy men, Carroll complained to Plowden, they "deter parents from sending sons thither by some rigorous regulations, not calculated for the meridian of America. Their principles are too monastic and with a laudable view of excluding immorality, they deny that liberty, which all here will lay claim to."[33] In 1806, Father Robert Molyneux replaced Leonard Neale as President of Georgetown. Still, the situation did not noticeable improve. Carroll feared that there may have been ". . . some radical defect in its [Georgetown] constitution, so far as related to its aptitude to suit the inclinations and genius of my countrymen."[34] Carroll's fears proved unfounded. Under the capable leadership of Father John Grassi, the learned Italian Jesuit who became

---

[33]Carroll to Plowden, March 12, 1802. Stonyhurst College. Guilday Collection, Catholic University of America Archives. Father Charles Sewall thought likewise. He wrote to his brother, Father Nicholas Sewall, that bad regulations caused parents to remove their sons from the school. Charles Sewall to Nicholas Sewall, July 29, 1803. As printed in Hughes, Documents, I, Part ii, 798-99.

[34]Carroll to Molyneux, May 22, 1807. Maryland Province Archives, Box 203-R6.

President of the college in 1812, Georgetown's fortunes began to improve.[35]

Carroll considered the founding of a seminary as a companion piece to Georgetown, both of which were necessary for the training of an American clergy.[36] Georgetown was established and controlled in its early years by the American clergy; St. Mary's Seminary in Baltimore, which was founded in 1791 by the French-based Society of St. Sulpice, was not. Actually, Carroll lacked the resources to have established a seminary on his own, and when the Sulpicians expressed a willingness to open a seminary in America at their own expense, he gratefully accepted their offer.[37] Perhaps Carroll would have preferred a seminary directed by Americans, who would be more capable of training an American clergy. He did not, however, voice such sentiments, and he always spoke with praise of the work of the Sulpicians. In a country where Catholics were so few, and their resources so inadequate, desire often gave way to

---

[35]Daly, Georgetown University, p. 168.

[36]Carroll to Plowden, December 15, 1785. Maryland Province Archives, Box 202-B10.

[37]Ruane, The Beginnings of the Society of St. Sulpice in the United States, Chap. II, "Nagot and St. Mary's Seminary 1791-1810," pp. 37-94.

reality, and Carroll could only be thankful that the Sulpicians were there to train a badly needed clergy.

* * * * * * * * * *

Americanism also called for an acceptance of the political principles of the United States--republicanism and its corolary, civil liberty. Contrary to the assertions of some Protestants who argued that Catholicism was incompatible with republicanism, American Catholics found nothing in their religion to prevent them from accepting the political principles of the country.

DuBourg corrected the accusations of his Presbyterian critics--that Catholics were not attached to republican institutions--with a short historical lecture:

> As if any one could be ignorant that all the
> European republics took their birth, were
> reared and fostered in the bosom of the Catholic
> Church. . . . As if, in fine, Catholics had
> ever been behind any of the other Christian
> sects in the promotion and support of American
> independence. The fact is that the Catholic
> Church, for that great reason, that it was
> intended by its divine author to be Catholic,
> that is, universal, is, by its very consti-
> tution, adapted to every form of civil
> government. . . . Monarchs have no better
> subjects, Republics no better citizens, whose

> political creed consists in professing that
> he who resisteth the established power,
> resisteth the ordinance of God (Rom. 13.2).[38]

Blythe, a convert to Catholicism, likewise rejected the charge that Catholics were foes to civil liberty. History proved otherwise. "All the European republics, which have appeared these last six hundred years," he pointed out, "were reared and fostered in the bosom of the Catholic Church. . . ." And, he reminded the critics of the Catholic Church that the document which they considered the bulwark of English liberties--Magna Carta--"was the enterprise of Catholics."[39]

Bishop Carroll was a good republican and friend of civil liberty. He was no supporter of royalty. Very early in his career he told Plowden that the kings of Europe loved power too much, and justice too little.[40] Carroll was pleased to live under a government in which civil liberty prevailed.[41] He constantly reminded his flock that

[38]DuBourg, St. Mary's Seminary Vindicated, p. 26.

[39]Blythe, Conversion, pp. 42-43.

[40]Carroll to Plowden, February 20, 1782. Maryland Province Archives, Box 202-B3. Another mark of Carroll's republicanism was his unwillingness to accept any title of nobility. When Poterie addressed him as "Lord," Carroll remarked that such a title was ". . . very odious in America, and in no wise due to me." Carroll to Poterie, April 3, 1789. AAB, Case 9A-G3.

[41]Carroll to Plowden, September 26, 1783. Maryland Province Archives, Box 202-B5.

Catholicism was compatible with the political principles
and institutions of America.[42]   Robert Walsh, a younger
contemporary of Carroll, well summarized the venerable
archbishop of Baltimore's political principles: "He loved
republicanism; and so far preferred his own country, that if
ever he could be excited to impatience or irritated [sic],
nothing would have that effect more certainly than the
expression of the slightest preference, by any American
friend, of foreign institutions or measures."[43]

Carroll, then, was committed to the republican
institutions of America and the idea of liberty, though the
enthusiasm of Americans for the latter often tried him. He
was especially concerned that the America fondness for
liberty carry over (as the thought it was doing) into
ecclesiastical affairs.[44]   For several reasons--his family's
position in Maryland society, his Catholic background and
training, his ecclesiastical position in a hierarchically
structured church organization--Carroll spoke in favor of
the established order. Those who challenged such authority--
and, Carroll's opinion, too many Americans in the 1790's
were doing this--were overstepping the rightful bounds of
liberty; he referred to such men as the ". . . sowers of

---

[42]Cf. Carroll's Address to the Trustees of Holy
Trinity Church, February 22, 1792. AAB, Case 10-W2; Dohen,
Nationalism and American Catholicism, pp. 92-93, 105-06.

[43]As quoted by Guilday, John Carroll, p. 829.

[44]Carroll to Antonelli, April 23, 1792. AAB,
Case 9A-I.

sedition, and wild democracy."[45] Carroll was no democrat,
but an eighteenth century republican who believed in a
government founded on law and order, restraint in human
conduct, and measured liberty.

Carroll was not the only member of the clergy who
questioned America's enthusiasm for civil liberty. Flaget,
the Bishop of Bardstown, had his own reasons to complain
about the political climate in America. He was having some
difficulty with Badin, who refused to surrender to him
certain ecclesiastical property. Flaget wanted to take
disciplinary measures against Badin but, as he informed Rome,
feared doing so because:

> . . . if I punish his delinquency, I feel that
> by his stubbornness and open rebellion he will
> stir up great scandal and perhaps break out
> into schism. And such a thing is to be dreaded,
> especially in this country where the principles
> of liberty and independence are carried to such
> extremes, and where a schismatic finds support
> and protection in the very constitution of the
> Republic and has unbridled liberty to write and
> say whatever he pleases. . . .[46]

---

[45] Carroll to Plowden, September 24, 1796. Maryland
Province Archives, Box 202-B49; Cf. also Carroll to Troy,
1795. As printed in Moran, Spicilegium Ossoriense, III, 516
Carroll's "Sermon on the Death of Washington," February 22,
1800. Carmelite Convent, Baltimore. Carroll Papers,
Transcript. Catholic University of America Archives.

[46] Flaget, "Report," p. 314; Badin used America's
dislike of monarchical government against Flaget's efforts
to vest title to all ecclesiastical property in his name.
He told Maréchal of Flaget's scheme: ". . . nothing can be
more utopian or imprudent in a country where monarchical
government is so vehemently reprobated. The Legislative and
civil authorities would soon be alarmed and grow jealous, if
much eccles. property were accumulated on the head of one
clergyman, especially if a R.C. Bishop. . . ." Badin to
Maréchal, July 14, 1815. As quoted by Schauinger, Badin,
p. 179.

Father Benedict Joseph Fenwick, an American born member of
the Jesuit order, was equally critical of his fellow countrymen's excessive love of liberty. Fenwick wrote Grassi, the
Superior of the Jesuits in America, that he would not be
surprised if over half of the young men entering the novitiate
left before the completion of their studies:

> What will you do with, or can you expect from
> young hair-brained Americans: Particularly
> if they enter over young, though within the
> line marked out by the Institute which was
> drawn up for Europeans and those accustomed
> to other governments than ours and who were
> not so infatuated with the sound of liberty
> and equality.[47]

* * * * * * * * * *

Despite these limited reservations American
Catholics were deeply attached to America--to the nation
and the political principles for which she stood. They
accepted and supported republican institutions, and
showed no desire for monarchy as did many of their European
counterparts. They recognized no incompatibility, no
conflict between the obedience and loyalty which Catholics
owed to their Church and to their country. In short, good
Catholics could be good Americans.

[47]Fenwick to Grassi, February 20, 1815. Maryland
Province, Box 204-K5.

CHAPTER XI

THE CATHOLIC CHURCH AND RELIGIOUS

LIBERTY

By 1784, when Carroll became Prefect-Apostolic over
the Catholic Church in the United States, the country had
begun to move, however cautiously, in the direction of
religious freedom for all groups and the separation of
church and state. The significance of the religious changes
taking place was not lost on Carroll. "You are not ignorant,
he wrote to his agent in Rome, "that in these United States
our Religious system has undergone a revolution, if
possible, more extraordinary than our political one. In
all of them, free Toleration is allowed to Christians of
every denomination. . . ."[1]

Carroll's use of the word "toleration," however,
was appropriate, for many of the states were not prepared
to grant more than that (even though toleration was an
advance over what prevailed in the colonial period when

[1]Carroll to Roman agent, November 10, 1783. AAB,
Special Case C-A4.

many religious groups had no right to public worship). Few
of the states were willing to embark on the radical path to
complete religious liberty. The distinction, of course,
between toleration and religious liberty was a crucial one.

Toleration implies that a particular religion or
church represents a departure from an accepted ideal; that
there exists an established (or favored) church, recognized
by the state, with less than perfect equality for dissenting
groups; and that the privileges or immunities which dissenting groups enjoy are to be "regarded merely as a
revocable concession rather than as a defensible right."
Religious liberty implies, instead, that religious truth
cannot be legally known; that therefore there can be no
established church or religion, with all religious groups
enjoying perfect equality under the law; that religion is a
private affair, beyond the jurisdiction of the state; and
that the right to worship according to one's conscience is
a natural and inalienable right.[2]

While the religious history of the states during
the revolutionary period was involved and varied, two basic

---

[2]Anson Phelps Stokes, Church and State in the United
States (3 vols.; New York: Harper and Row, 1950), I, 16-17;
22; Guido de Ruggiero, "Religious Freedom," Encyclopaedia
of the Social Sciences, XIII (1934), 239-46.

patterns emerged. The states adopted, in various degrees, either a position (as defined above) of "toleration" or "religious liberty."[3] Massachusetts and Virginia can serve as models for these respective religious developments.

The religious clauses of the Massachusetts' Bill of Rights, adopted in 1780, rested upon the following basic assumptions: that religion was essential to the happiness of a people and necessary for the preservation of civil society; that proper religious truth can be known and, as such, given institutional form, recognized by the state; that the recognized institution was, within certain limits, to tolerate error; and that the privileges which dissenters enjoyed derived not from natural right but from the concessions granted by the established powers.[4]

Article II of the Massachusetts' Declaration of Rights began on a positive note. While it declared that all men in society had a right, as well as a duty, to worship God, it nevertheless assured that "no subject shall

---

[3]For a thorough study of religious developments in all the states consult Stokes, Church and State in the United States, I, 358-446.

[4]Jacob Conrad Meyer, Church and State in Massachuset From 1740 to 1833 (New York: Russell and Russell, 1968), p. 107; Stuart Gerry Brown, The First Republicans: Politica Philosophy and Public Policy in the Party of Jefferson and Madison (Syracuse: Syracuse University Press, 1954), pp. 136-37.

be hurt, molested, or restrained, in his person, liberty,
or estate, for worshipping God in the manner and season most
agreeable to the dictates of his own conscience. . . ."[5]
By this article the state of Massachusetts agreed to
tolerate the public worship of all religious groups. That
the framers of the religious clauses did not intend for this
article to serve as the prelude to religious liberty in
Massachusetts was made clear in subsequent paragraphs of
the Declaration of Rights. Article III, which represented
the classic statement of a system based on toleration and
not religious liberty, declared:

> As the happiness of a people, and the good
> order and preservation of civil government,
> essentially depend upon piety, religion, and
> morality; and as these cannot be generally
> diffused through a community but by the insti-
> tution of the public worship of GOD, and of
> public instructions in piety, religion, and
> morality; therefore, to promote their happiness,
> and to secure the good order and preservation
> of their government, the people of this common-
> wealth have a right to invest their legislature
> with power to authorize and require . . . the
> several towns, parishes, precincts, and other
> bodies politic, or religious societies, to make
> suitable provisions . . . for the institution
> of the public worship of GOD, and for the
> support and maintenance of public Protestant

[5]Francis Newton Thorpe, The Federal and State
Constitutions (7 vols.; Washington: Government Printing
Office, 1909), III, 1889.

[italics mine] teachers of piety, religion, and morality, in all cases where such provisions shall not be made voluntarily.

And the people of this commonwealth have also a right to, and do, invest their legislature with authority to enjoin upon all the subjects an attendance upon the instructions of the public teachers . . . if there be any on whose instructions they can conscientiously and conveniently attend.

. . . .

And all moneys paid by the subject to the support of public worship, and of the public teachers aforesaid, shall, if he require it, be uniformly applied to the support of the public teacher or teachers of his own religious sect or denomination, provided there be any on whose instruction he attends; otherwise it may be paid towards the support of the teacher or teachers [Congregational] of the parish or precinct in which the said moneys are raised.[6]

In effect, this article established "Protestantism" as the religion of Massachusetts, with the Congregational Church retaining its privileged position. Furthermore, since the Protestant religion was necessary to civil society the state had an obligation to promote it, even to the point that it ordered its citizens to support their churches and attend to the instructions of their religious teachers. Those outside the designated "Protestant" faith--Catholics, Jews, and non-believers--were required to support Protestant

[6]Ibid., III, 1889-1890.

churches and teachers, in clear violation of the right of
conscience.

Chapter VI of the Massachusetts' Constitution was
another affront to religious freedom since it punished men
for their beliefs. Article I, in this section, was so
framed that it excluded Catholics from officeholding for
it demanded that every person, before assuming state office,
take the following oath:

> I do renounce and abjure all allegiance,
> subjection, and obedience . . . to every . . .
> foreign power whatsoever; and that no foreign
> prince, person, prelate, state, or potentate,
> hath, or ought to have, any jurisdiction,
> superiority, pre-eminence, authority, dis-
> pensing or other power, in any matter, civil,
> ecclesiastical, or spiritual, within this
> commonwealth. . . .[7]

No conscientious Catholic could take an oath which, in
effect, denied the spiritual authority of Rome.

Many of the states followed Massachusetts' lead.
The majority of Americans still considered "religion"
necessary to the maintenance of civil society, and they
favored state support of religion. Most Protestant Americans
did not approve of a policy of religious liberty. They came

[7] _Ibid._, III, 1908.

238

to adopt a policy of toleration out of necessity, for they

understood that there could be no national (and in some

case no state) establishment, because of so many different

denominations. Since it was no longer possible to maintain

religious uniformity (which was what most desired),

toleration, perhaps with some kind of establishment--

Protestantism, Christianity--was the best alternative.

Better that than religious liberty, which constituted such

a radical departure from the colonial religious tradition.

In the light of this, the accomplishment of Virginia--the

first state to achieve complete religious freedom--was all

the more remarkable.[8]

In the opinion of Stuart Gerry Brown, the political

achievement of those Virginians who fought for religious

liberty was to replace the underlying assumptions that

prevailed in Massachusetts with an entirely different set:

> that ultimate truth is not in any legal sense
> known. If it is not so known, it cannot be
> institutionalized, and there can be no agency
> to tolerate error. Thus religion is to be
> disengaged from the civil power, and toleration
> disappears in favor of freedom of conscience
> and thought, limited only by the secular wel-
> fare of the people.[9]

[8]Sidney E. Mead, The Lively Experiment: The Shaping
of Christianity in America (New York: Harper and Row, 1963)
pp. 19-20, 35-37, 59-60.

[9]Brown, The First Republicans, p. 137.

The implementation of their philosophy took ten long years in Virginia. The sequence of events began with the drafting by George Mason of the sixteenth article of the Virginia Declaration of Rights in 1776. In the original draft of this article, which concerned itself with the right of worship, Mason had said that ". . . all men should enjoy the fullest Toleration in the exercise of religion, according to the dictates of conscience. . . ." James Madison, a member of the committee which framed Virginia's Declaration of Rights, succeeded in having struck the word "toleration" and having substituted the following words: ". . . that all men are equally entitled to enjoy the free exercise of religion, according to the dictates of conscience."[10] The article, as finally accepted by the Virginia Convention, read:

> That religion, or the duty which we owe to
> our Creator, and the manner of discharging it,
> can be directed only by reason and conviction,
> not by force or violence; and therefore all
> men are equally entitled to the free exercise
> of religion, according to the dictates of
> conscience; and that it is the mutual duty of
> all to practice Christian forbearance, love,
> and charity towards each other.[11]

[10]William T. Hutchinson and William M.E. Rachal (eds.), The Papers of James Madison (Chicago: University of Chicago Press, 1962), I, 170-80.

[11]Thorpe, Federal and State Constitutions, VII, 3814.

By eliminating the word "toleration" and substituting for it the "free exercise of religion," Madison made ". . . religious freedom a natural right growing out of the liberty of conscience, instead of a concession from the ruling church. . . ."[12]

The Virginia Assembly then implemented the religious article of the Declaration of Rights by enacting into law a bill drafted by Mason. Though Mason's bill established the Episcopal Church, for its members only, it in no way nullified the principles established in article sixteen. Religious dissenters were completely exempted from any obligation to support the Episcopal Church or its ministers. Mason had based this exemption on the principles of reason and justice which demanded that no man should support a church that his conscience would not permit him to join. And, significantly for the future, the bill even suspended-- for one year--the obligatory support which Episcopalians owed to their church.[13] Actually, no taxes for religious purposes were ever collected after January 1, 1777, and, in 1779, the payment of salaries to Episcopalian clergymen as

[12] Irving Brant, James Madison: The Virginia Revolutionist (New York: Bobbs-Merrill Co., 1941), Chap. XII, "Proclaiming the Right of Man," pp. 234-50.

[13] Stokes, Church and State in the United States, I, 304-05.

a matter of general state authorization was finally dis-
continued by legislative action.[14] For all practical

purposes, the disestablishment of the Episcopal Church--

which Madison and Jefferson had called for in 1776--was

accomplished.[15]

In the mid 1780's a reaction set in. Episcopalians,

Methodists, and even some Presbyterians pressed for a

general assessment to revive, what they considered, the

fallen state of religion in Virginia. The assessment bill,

as originally proposed, would have levied a general tax on

the people of Virginia ". . . for the support of the

Christian religion, or of some Christian church . . . or of

some form of Christian worship." In the face of some

opposition the bill was later modified to simply provide

for the laying of a general tax to support the "teachers of

the Christian religion."[16] In any form, Madison was

strongly opposed to the whole idea of assessment. He spoke

warmly against the measure in the Assembly, and then drafted

---

[14] Ibid., I, 383.

[15] Brant, James Madison: The Virginia Revolutionist,
pp. 245-46; Dumas Malone, Jefferson and His Time, Vol. I:
Jefferson the Virginian (Boston: Little, Brown and Co.,
1948), . 237.

[16] Stokes, Church and State in the United States, I,
387-92.

his justly famous _Memorial_ _and_ _Remonstrance_ _Against_

Religious _Assessments_, one of the best defenses of the

American doctrine of the free conscience.[17] Madison's main

argument against laying an obligatory tax for religion--

that it violated the right of every man to follow his own

conscience in religious matters, and that religion was

exempt from the cognizance of civil authority--was well

stated in the first article of the _Remonstrance_:

> Because we hold it for a fundamental and
> undeniable truth 'that Religion or the duty
> we owe to our Creator and the Manner of
> discharging it, can be directed only by reason
> and conviction, not by force or violence.'
> The Religion then of every man must be left
> to the conviction and conscience of every
> man; and it is the right of every man to
> exercise it as these may dictate. This right
> is in its nature an unalienable right. . . .
> We maintain therefore that in matter of
> Religion, no man's right is abridged by the
> institution of Civil Society, and that Religion
> is wholly exempt from its cognizance.[18]

Madison's _Remonstrance_, as summarized by Brown, ". . . reject

entirely the idea of toleration, rested the freedom of

religion upon natural law, and limited the state to exclu-

sively secular functions."[19]

---

[17] Brown, _The_ _First_ _Republicans_, pp. 143-46; Irving
Brant, _James_ _Madison_: _The_ _Nationalist_, _1780-1787_ (New York:
Bobbs-Merrill Co., 1948), Chap. XXII, "Freedom of Religion,"
pp. 343-55.

[18] Gaillard Hunt (ed.), _The_ _Writings_ _of_ _James_ _Madison_
(9 vols.; New York: G.P. Putnam's Sons, 1900-1910), II, 183

[19] Brown, _The_ _First_ _Republicans_, pp. 144-46.

The Virginia Assembly rejected the assessment bill. Elated, Madison resurrected Jefferson's Bill for Religious Freedom, which the Assembly had tabled when it was presented to that body in 1779. Madison presented it to the Assembly in 1785 and, to his joy, it was accepted. Jefferson's Bill for Religious Freedom represented the climax of ten long years of struggle in Virginia for a system of religious liberty. The bill's enactment clause declared that:

> We the General Assembly of Virginia do enact that no man shall be compelled to frequent or support any religious worship, place, or ministry whatsoever, nor shall be enforced, restrained, molested, or burthened in his body or goods, nor shall otherwise suffer, on account of his religious opinions or belief; but that all men shall be free to profess, and by argument to maintain, their opinions in matters of religion, and that the same shall in no wise diminish, enlarge, or affect their civil capacities.
> And though we well know that this Assembly . . . have no power to restrain the acts of succeeding Assemblies, constituted with powers equal to our own, and that therefore to declare this act irrevocable would be of no effect in law; yet we are free to declare, and do declare, that the rights hereby asserted are of the natural rights of mankind, and that if any act shall be hereafter passed to repeal the present

or to narrow its operation, such act will be
an infringement of natural right.[20]

American Catholics would work out their position on religious

liberty and separation of church and state within the

confines of the patterns that developed in Maryland and

Virginia.

* * * * * * * * * *

The American Revolution made a significant impact

on the position of Catholics in the United States. Every-

where they were allowed the free and public exercise of

their religion, a right they had not enjoyed earlier.

Several of the states--Pennsylvania, Rhode Island, Maryland,

Delaware, and Virginia--went so far as to remove all the

political disabilities which had disfranchised Catholics

during the colonial era, thereby granting full citizenship

to Catholics.[21]   Such a state of affairs, Carroll remarked,

". . . is a blessing and advantage, which it is our duty to

preserve and improve. . . ."[22]   Improvement, however, was

_____

[20]Julian P. Boyd (ed.), The Papers of Thomas
Jefferson (Princeton, N.J.: Princeton University Press,
1950-   ), II, 545-47.

[21]Ray, American Opinion of Roman Catholicism, Chaps.
VII, "The Tradition in the Pre-Revolutionary Decade,"
pp. 263-310; VIII, "The Revolution," pp. 310-50; IX, "Making
the Constitutions," pp. 350-94.

[22]Carroll to Roman agent, November 10, 1783. AAB,
Special Case C-A4.

certainly in order, for several of the states--either by
constitutional provision, test oath, or legislative decree--
still denied Catholics their full political and civil
rights.

Catholics protested against their second-class
citizenship. They considered it an act of injustice to
deny to them basic political and civil rights, especially
since they had sacrified, as well as any, their lives and
fortunes to obtain independence and liberty in the revolutionary struggle. In their congratulatory "Address" to
George Washington, upon his assuming office as President of
the United States, the signatories (who spoke for the Roman
Catholics in America) made this very point: ". . . whilst
our country preserves her freedom and independence, we shall
have a well founded title to claim from her justice, the
equal rights of citizenship, as the price of our blood
spilt under your eyes, and of our common exertions for her
defense. . . ."[23]

---

[23]The "Address from the Roman Catholics of America
to George Washington, President of the United States," was
signed by John Carroll for the clergy, and Charles Carroll,
Daniel Carroll, Dominick Lynch, and Thomas Fitzsimons for
the laity. Shea, John Carroll, pp. 348-50, printed the
"Address."

Carroll had already developed this argument in
defense of Catholic claims for religious equality. In the
summer of 1787 an attack against the Catholic faith
appeared in the Columbian Magazine; Carroll felt obliged to
reply. In his letter to the editor of the magazine he
praised those states which had justly granted to all
Christian sects equal privileges. He argued that such a
position was only right since "Freedom and independence,
acquired by the united efforts, and cemented with the
mingled blood of Protestant and Catholic fellow-citizens,
should be equally enjoyed by all."[24] Carroll made the same
point a few years later, in answer to an article that
appeared in the Gazette of the United States (May 9, 1789),
which called for preference to the Protestant religion.
Carroll spoke against the author's attempt to revive "an
odious system of religious intolerance," against the members
of a denomination whose ". . . blood flowed as freely . . .
to cement the fabric of independence, as that of their
fellow-citizens."[25] Badin also expressed his surprise that

---

[24] A Reader [John Carroll], "A Letter to the Editor,"
The Columbian Magazine, I (December, 1787), Supplement,
881-82.

[25] E.C., "The Importance of the Protestant Religion
Politically Considered," Gazette of the United States (New
York), May 9, 1789, p. 29; Pacificus [John Carroll], "A
Letter to the Editor," Ibid., June 10, 1789, p. 65.

some of the states denied the basic rights of citizenship to Catholics. He asked: "Is this consistent with the principles of the Federal constitution? Was not the blood of American Catholics shed in defense of those states?"[26]

Badin had introduced still another argument in support of the Catholic demand for religious equality-- that it was consistent with the political constitutions of the United States and of some of the states. When Maryland retained a law which forbade Catholics from acting as guardians to Protestant children, John Carroll wrote to his cousin, Charles Carroll, a member of the state legislature: "As this clause is inconsistent with the perfect equality of rights, which by our Constitution is secured to all Religions, I make no doubt but you will be able to obtain a general repeal of this and all other laws . . . enacting any partial regards to one denomination to the prejudice of others."[27] In the first years of his episcopacy an anonymous critic, who signed his name "Liberal," took exception to Carroll for signing a pastoral as "John, Bishop of Baltimore." Liberal remarked that he did not recognize Carroll's claim

[26]Badin, Real Principles of Roman Catholics, p. 39, fn.

[27]John Carroll to Charles Carroll, November 11, 1783. Maryland Historical Society. John Carroll Papers, Transcript. Catholic University of America Archives.

as the bishop of Baltimore, nor, for that matter, episcopacy itself. Carroll published his reply, "An Answer to Strictures on an Extraordinary Signature," in which he willingly recognized "Liberal's" constitutional right to reject both; but he equally insisted upon the same right to freely sign his pastorals to the Catholics according to the usages of his Church--a right which he presumed the constitution allowed him.[28]

* * * * * * * * * *

During the episcopacy of John Carroll, Catholics supported the "American way"--the separation of church and state and religious freedom. None was a warmer friend to these principles than Carroll himself.[29]

It is important, however, at this point, to understand how Carroll (and many Catholics) defined these principles. Separation of church and state did not imply for Carroll, as it did for Madison and Jefferson, a secular (or neutral) state, unconcerned and unconnected with religion. Carroll could no more accept this idea of the

---

[28]Carroll, "An Answer to Strictures of an Extraordinary Signature," November 21, 1792. Printed copy. AAB, Case 10-Y4; Brent, John Carroll, pp. 129-35, printed Carroll's reply to "Liberal."

[29]Melville, John Carroll, p. 86; Stokes, Church and State in the United States, I, 325, 333.

state than the majority of his fellow-Catholics, or, for
that matter, Rome itself. By separation he meant that the
state should not establish or favor one particular church
over others; he did not oppose the idea that the state
should encourage and promote religion--even a particular
religion (e.g., Christianity). As for religious freedom he
meant that every person had the right to free and public
worship. On this point, he was prepared to move beyond the
grounds of mere expediency and to point out that the denial
of this right would be an affront to the sacred right of
conscience--a position remarkable close to that argued by
Madison. (That Carroll may not have fully understood the
full implications of his advanced position on religious
freedom, however, will be discussed later.) Carroll's
acceptance of religious freedom did not imply (as it may
have for some others) an indifference to religion or
doctrinal relativism. He believed religion essential to the
happiness of man and the social order--and he never doubted
that "true religion" resided in the Catholic faith. Still,
religion should not be imposed, and men must arrive at the

truth by their own search. Hence the need for religious freedom--the right to follow one's conscience.

Carroll took pride in the advance America was making in this area. He expressed a hope to his English friends--Charles Plowden and Lord Petrie--that England would imitate her former colonies on this point, by granting toleration to all groups.[30] Carroll even defended the American system against Rome herself. In the papal brief, Ex hac apostolicae, which established the See of Baltimore, the Pope urged Catholics not to be carried away by every wind of doctrine, ". . . but, grounded on the authority of divine revelation, should reject the new and varying doctrines of men, which disturb the tranquility of government. . . ."[31] Carroll was disturbed by this passage. He told Plowden that he wanted it omitted when Coghlan published the English translation of the brief. Carroll felt that Rome's statement--that a state cannot be safe, in which new and various doctrines were permitted to range-- would not go well in America, for such a philosophy was

---

[30]Carroll to Plowden, February 28, 1779. Maryland Province Archives, Box 202-Bl; Carroll to Lord Petrie, August 31, 1790. AAB, Special Case C-Rl.

[31]A Short Account of the Establishment of the New See of Baltimore (Philadelphia: Carey, Stewart and Co., 1791), p. 12.

"contrary to the maxim of our policy, and of our experience in America."[32]

While Carroll praised the American way, it was not without problems for the Church. The absence of state support meant that the Church had to resolve its problems internally, without being able to appeal to the state for assistance. When Carroll heard that Rome had granted certain powers to Father Caesarius Reuter that would have made him, in some areas, independent of episcopal authority, he complained to Rome that this would weaken ecclesiastical discipline and disturb the government of the diocese. He explained why these results would follow if the bishop's authority were weakened:

> For we live among hostile sects of non-Catholics, so that there is no hope of gaining assistance from the civil magistracy or the secular arm to reduce stubborn men to order. Thus, it seems to me, that the spiritual jurisdiction of bishops should be confirmed rather than lessened by exemption. . . . If this jurisdiction should fail there will be no bridle left to control the conduct either of the clergy or of the laity.[33]

---

[32]Carroll to Plowden, September, 1790. Stonyhurst Archives, Guilday Collection, Catholic University of America Archives.

[33]Carroll to Prefect of Propaganda, August 20, 1799. Propaganda Archives. Scritture Riferite nei Congressi, America Centrale. Vol. III, Fol. 66. Guilday Transcripts. Catholic University of America Archives.

Despite this difficulty, Carroll would not have favored an alliance, or even too close a relationship, between the Catholic Church and the state. His knowledge of the English experience convinced him that by such arrangements the Church often surrendered to the state ". . . the independence it derives from God, and the nature of its destination."[34]

Several Catholic priests expressed appreciation for the religious system prevailing in America. Fleming praised the United States government which, by its enlightened views, has helped to ". . . unite as good fellow citizens, men of every religious persuasion." He noted with satisfaction that "under the happy government of America, conscience suffers no constraint from penal statues, nor is hypocrisy encouraged by any religious establishment."[35] Gallitzin voiced respect for the United States constitution which ". . . pries into no man's conscience, but leaves it to every one's choice to make the sign of the cross or not to make it, to read the Bible in Latin or in English, to go

---

[34]Carroll to Plowden, September 3, 1800. Stonyhurst Archives. Guilday Collection. Catholic University of America Archives.

[35]Fleming, Calumnies of Verus, pp. 39, 47.

to mass or to meeting. . . ."[36] Grassi preferred the

American way over that prevailing in Europe. "The truth

can be proclaimed freely and can triumph in America," he

explained, "since it has not there to contend with one of

the greatest obstacles which elsewhere hinders the propaga-

tion of the Christian faith, namely, religious intolerance

and the persecution of idolatrous governments."[37] Maréchal

spoke with favor of the system of religious liberty pre-

vailing in America. He reported to Rome that it protected

and helped to foster the growth of the Church in this

country.[38]

Several distinguished lay Catholics played a role

in securing the religious system which the Catholic clergy

so prized. Daniel Carroll, a brother of Bishop Carroll,

served as a member of the Constitutional Convention and the

House of Representatives in the first Congress. He signed

the constitution and, in so doing, supported Article VI

[36]Gallitzin, "Letter to Editor of the Lancaster Federal Gazette, September 20, 1808," in Murphy (ed.), Gallitzin's Letters: A Collection of the Polemical Works, p. 299.

[37]Grassi, "The Catholic Religion in the United States in 1818," p. 110; cf. Grassi, "The Memoirs of Father John Anthony Grassi," ed. by Arthur J. Arrieri, Historical Records and Studies, XLVII (1959), 204.

[38]Maréchal, "Maréchal's Report to Propaganda," in Ellis, Documents of American Catholic History, p. 213.

which contained the provision that at the national level

". . . no religious Test shall ever be required as a

Qualification to any Office or public Trust under the

United States."[39] He also supported the first amendment to

the Constitution which declared that "Congress shall make

no law respecting an establishment of religion, or pro-

hibiting the free exercise thereof." He gave a short speech

in the House of Representatives in favor of the amendment

which demonstrated his opposition to the interference of

government with the rights of conscience.[40]

The only other Catholic signer of the Constitution

was Thomas Fitzsimons, delegate from Pennsylvania.

Fitzsimons voted in favor of Article VI, but (like Daniel

Carroll) he did not speak in the Convention to this proposal.

---

[39]Evidently, Daniel Carroll did not speak in the
Convention to this particular point, for there is no mention
of his having done so in Max Farrand, The Records of the
Federal Convention of 1787. Revised edition (4 vols.;
New Haven: Yale University Press, 1937), II, 468. Daniel
Carroll's biographer, Sister Mary Virginia Geiger, makes no
mention of his having done so either. Sister Mary Virginia
Geiger, Daniel Carroll: A Framer of the Constitution
(Washington: Catholic University of America Press, 1943),
Chap. V, "In the Federal Convention," pp. 120-46.

[40]Joseph Gales (comp.), Debates and Proceedings in
the Congress of the United States (Washington: Gales and
Seaton, 1834), I, 757-58.

[41]Richard J. Purcell, "Thomas Fitzsimons: Framer
of the American Constitution," Studies, XXVII (June, 1938),
283-84; Farrand, Records of the Federal Convention, II, 468.

As a member of the House of Representatives, Fitzsimons voted for the first amendment, but he played no part in the debate that preceded its adoption.[42]

Charles Carroll, the only Catholic signer of the Declaration of Independence, was a cousin of Daniel Carroll. He served in the first United States Senate, and as a member of this body he supported the first amendment.[43] It was not surprising that Charles Carroll should have favored this amendment. He had long spoken against religious intolerance and persecution, and for religious liberty.[44] Indeed, Charles Carroll stated late in his life that the desire for religious liberty was one of the reasons why he supported the revolution:

> When I signed the Declaration of Independence
> I had in view not only our independence but
> the toleration of all sects, professing the
> Christian religion, and communicating to them
> all great rights.

---

[42] Gales, Debates and Proceedings in the Congress of the United States, I, 757-78.

[43] Stokes, Church and State in the United States, I, 546-48.

[44] Charles Carroll to Edmund Jennings, October 14, 1766 and August 13, 1767. As printed in the Unpublished Letters of Charles Carroll of Carrolltown, compiled and edited by Thomas Meagher Field (New York: United States Catholic Historical Society, 1902), pp. 134-43.

Happily, for America, he concluded, religious liberty was
made secure by the revolution, thereby "eradicating
religious feuds and persecutions, and become a useful
lesson to all governments. . . ."[45]

* * * * * * * * * *

American Catholics had accepted the separation of
church and state and the principle of religious toleration.
Their reasons were twofold in nature: first, because it was
the best way to maintain civil peace in a society where
there existed such a diversity of religious sects; and,
secondly, the rights of conscience had to be respected.

When Carroll expressed to Lord Petrie his hope that
England would take up the American system of toleration,
he stressed the daily political advantages--harmony in

---

[45]Charles Carroll to George Washington Parke Custis,
February 20, 1829. As quoted by Ellen Hart Smith, Charles
Carroll of Carrolltown (Cambridge: Harvard University Press,
1942), p. 274. Catholic historians have debated this oft-
quoted passage. Guilday, John Carroll, pp. 82, 86-87,
declared: "One is at liberty to suspect that the great
Catholic patriot was reading this laudable motive into his
part in the Revolution a half century before; it is the
only statement of this kind to be found in his writings."
Theodore Maynard, The Story of American Catholicism, Image
Books (2 vols.; New York: Doubleday and Co., 1960), I, 153,
took issue with Guilday, and saw no reason to be skeptical
about Carroll's motives. What both historians overlook,
however, was the significance of Carroll's statements--that
he favored toleration for all Christian sects. Why not all
sects? For an analysis of this limited expression see
infra, pp. 259-266.

society--that arose from such a policy.[46] Furthermore,

Carroll believed that a general and equal toleration could

lead people to religious truth, for ". . . by giving a free

circulation to fair argument, [it] is the most effectual

method to bring all denominations of Christians to an unity

of faith."[47] Gallitzin remarked that Catholics agreed with

Protestants in considering civil toleration an invaluable

blessing, ". . . especially in a country like ours where

there were so many different denominations at the time its

constitution was formed."[48]

Catholics did not rest their defense of toleration

merely on the grounds that it was necessary to maintain

civil peace. They were prepared to admit that independent

of this consideration there existed higher reasons for

supporting religious toleration--that it was consistent with

simple justice, natural rights, and the sacred rights of

conscience.

Carroll often made use of the natural rights argu-

ment in his attack against religious intolerance. Protesting

[46]Carroll to Lord Petrie, August 31, 1790. AAB,
Special Case C-R1.

[47]John Carroll, An Address to the Roman Catholics of
the United States, p. 114.

[48]Gallitzin, "A Defense of Catholic Principles,"
in Murphy (ed.), Gallitzin's Letters: A Collection of the
Polemical Works, p. 96.

against an article in the Gazette of the United States

which called for preference to the Protestant religion, he

remarked that such a policy would deny to his co-religionists

"the common rights of nature." He further regretted that

the ". . . constitutions of some of the states continue

still to entrench on the sacred rights of conscience."[49]

Carroll stated the right of conscience to worship freely

most clearly in a letter to a Col. William Vousdan: "As

far as civil toleration goes and an allowance to every

denomination freely to pursue their mode of worship, no one

has fuller persuasion than myself of its consonancy with

the laws of God. . . ."[50]

Fleming argued that interference by government in

the affairs of religion would be extremely noxious. He

considered the American principle that every man could

worship freely as ". . . a right founded on the unalterable

nature of truth."[51] Gallitzin likewise denied the right of

civil government to control "the consciences of men."[52]

[49]Pacificus [John Carroll], "A Letter to the Editor," Gazette of the United States (New York), June 10, 1789, p. 6

[50]Carroll to Vousdan, September 10, 1801. Shea Collection. Georgetown University Archives. Folder 255.4.

[51]Fleming, Calumnies of Verus, pp. iv, 47.

[52]Gallitzin, "A Defense of Catholic Principles," in Murphy (ed.), Gallitzin's Letters: A Collection of the Polemical Works, p. 96.

When the State Supreme Court of Massachusetts decided that the Catholics of Newcastle, District of Maine, were not exempt from paying a tax for the support of the Protestant church in that town, Matignon declared the decision ". . . an outrage against liberty of conscience."[53] And, when Poterie informed the residents of Boston that he would conduct classes in foreign languages opened to all, he added that at no time would he

> . . . divulge any religious questions or dogmas, unless expressly requested . . . intending in his civil, political and individual instructions, (except in the holy church and in the chair of truth) never to enjoin any creed which may affect liberty of conscience, and the spirit of christian toleration, which is the most dear and favorite principle of his heart.[54]

* * * * * * * * * *

Though Catholics called for a general and equal toleration to all religious groups, they were not always thorough or consistent in maintaining this position. John Carroll, for instance, in his letter to the editor of the Columbian Magazine, seemed to limit the full enjoyment of religious equality to Christians. He praised those states

[53]Matignon to Carroll, March 16, 1801. As printed in "Letters from the Archdiocesan Archives at Baltimore 1797-1807," Records, XX (June, 1909), 202-04.

[54]Poterie, To the Public (Boston, January 29, 1789), p. 1.

which have ". . . done justice to every denomination of

Christians [italics mine], . . . [by] placing them on the

same footing of citizenship, and conferring an equal right

of participation in national privileges.[55] Charles Carroll,

in that oft-quoted letter as to why he supported the

revolution, said he did so to gain ". . . the toleration of

all sects, professing the Christian [italics mine] religion."

Such expressions seemed to imply a willingness to substitute

the broader term "Christian" for "Protestant," which, in

effect, would allow Catholics to share equal privileges with

other Christian sects, but exclude those not of this faith.

Such a state of affairs existed in Maryland. The

Declaration of Rights, a part of the state constitution of

1776, which, interestingly enough, Charles Carroll helped

to draft, specifically excluded non-Christians from office-

holding. At no time during the debates in the Maryland

Convention (August, 1776) on the proposed Declaration of

Rights, did Charles Carroll speak against Article XXXV

---

[55]"A Reader" [John Carroll], "A Letter to the
Editor," The Columbian Magazine, I (December, 1787),
Supplement, 881-82.

[56]Charles Carroll to George Washington Parke Custis,
February 20, 1829. As quoted by Smith, Charles Carroll,
p. 274.

which excluded non-Christians from officeholding.[57]

Ironically, only two years earlier, Charles Carroll, who had been excluded from Maryland politics because of his religion, wrote critically to a friend against religious tests: "Designing and selfish men invented religious tests to exclude from posts of profit and trust their weaker or more conscientious fellow subjects, thus to secure to themselves all ye emoluments of Government."[58]

There is also no evidence that John Carroll ever lodged a specific condemnation against Maryland's discriminatory policy toward non-Christians. He, too, had once voiced public opposition to religious tests as inconsistent with justice, natural rights, and the purposes for which Americans joined in a national union.[59] And, in a letter to Charles Carroll, he recommended that all laws

---

[57] Proceedings of the Convention of the Province of Maryland (Annapolis, 1776). Serious debate on the Declaration of Rights began in the Convention on October 31, 1776. The role Charles Carroll played in drafting the Declaration of Rights has been studied by Kate Mason Rowland, The Life of Charles Carroll of Carrolltown 1737-1832 (2 vols.; New York: G.P. Putnam's, 1898), I, 186-90.

[58] Charles Carroll to William Graves, August 15, 1774. As quoted by Smith, Charles Carroll, p. 122.

[59] Pacificus [John Carroll], "A Letter to the Editor," Gazette of the United States (New York), June 10, 1789, p. 65.

which gave preference to one denomination over another should be repealed.[60] Still, such a suggestion would not have removed the civil penalties against non-Christians, since their exclusion rested not on legislative laws but the state constitution itself. Unless John Carroll worked for a change in the state constitution, the position of non-Christians would not improve--and there is again no evidence that he moved in this direction.[61]

John Carroll's apparent reluctance to have the state encourage, even indirectly, non-Christian religions showed when the Maryland Assembly proposed in 1785 a bill which would ". . . lay a general tax for the support of the ministers of the gospel of all societies of christians in the state." The bill further declared that every taxable inhabitant of the state was to pay a tax to some designated Christian body of his choice, with the exception of those

---

[60]John Carroll to Charles Carroll, November 11, 1783. Maryland Historical Society. John Carroll Papers, Transcript. Catholic University of America Archives.

[61]E. Milton Altfeld, The Jew's Struggle for Religious and Civil Liberty in Maryland (Baltimore: M. Curlander, 1924), pp. 8, 52-53, holds that Catholics later supported Thomas Kennedy, a member of the Maryland Assembly, in his struggle to repeal Maryland's offensive constitutiona' provision which prevented Jews from holding positions of trust and honor in the state. Roger Taney, for instance, spoke in the Maryland Senate in favor of abolishing test oaths which would have, in effect, enfranchised Jews.

who stated that they were a Jew, Mohammedan, or non-
believer in the Christian religion. This qualification
obviously disturbed John Carroll. In his personal copy of
the bill, Carroll marked off with brackets the objectionable
passage, and wrote disparagingly underneath it: "A bill
for the encouragement of Infidelity, Judaism, and Mahometism."[62]

The proposed bill never passed the Maryland legislature. Carroll had joined with dissenting Protestant groups
in opposing a bill which they thought favored the previously
established Episcopal Church. Furthermore, Catholic clergy,
supported by their property holdings, were not in need of
state money.[63] Besides, as indicated earlier, Carroll was
suspicious of state support for it often led to a loss of
the Church's independence. In opposing the bill, however,
Carroll did not advance the argument (which Madison did in
Virginia) that the state had no right to support or encourage
religion.

---

[62]A copy of the proposed bill, with John Carroll's
marginal notes can be found in AAB, Special Case C-A9.

[63]Thomas O'Brien Hanley, "The Impact of the American
Revolution on Religion in Maryland 1776-1800," (unpublished
Ph.D. dissertation, Georgetown University, 1961), pp. 104-09;
Thomas O'Brien Hanley, "The Emergence of Pluralism in the
United States," Theological Studies, XXIII (June, 1962),
227; cf. Carroll to Plowden, February 27, 1785. Maryland
Province Archives, Box 202-B5.

Fortunately for the Catholic side, William Gaston of North Carolina saw the incongruity between believing in the principle of religious liberty and then penalizing a person in the civil order because of his religious expression. Gaston supported Jacob Henry, a Jew, in his effort to retain his seat in the North Carolina House of Commons, contrary to that provision of the state's Constitution which restricted officeholding to Protestants. Gaston, in his defense of Henry, pleaded for religious liberty and tolerance. Actually, as a Catholic member of the legislature, Gaston was also pleading his own case (though his seat was not being challenged), for technically he should not have been there either.[64]

There were other Catholic clergy (in addition to John Carroll) who could not yet accept a policy of religious liberty. Badin and Nerinckx could not give unqualified acceptance to certain parts of Kentucky's Bill of Rights, which had been drafted by Jefferson.[65] Article XII,

---

[64]Joseph Herman Schauinger, William Gaston: Carolinian (Milwaukee: Bruce Publishing Co., 1949), p. 54; Morris U. Schapper (ed.), A Documentary History of the Jews in the United States, 1654-1875 (New York: The Citadel Press, 1950), pp. 122-25.

[65]Stokes, Church and State in the United States, I, 445-46.

Section 3 of the Bill of Rights, as Badin told John Carroll,
". . . sounds ill . . . [and] gives place to scruples." He
quoted for Carroll's benefit that part of the state constitution which disturbed him:

> Art. X: That the general, great and essential
> principles of liberty and free government may
> be recognized and established, we declare . . .
> Sec. 3: That all men have a natural and
> indefeasible right to worship Alm. God
> according to the dictates of their own con-
> science; that no man shall be compelled to
> attend, erect, or support any place of worship,
> or to maintain any ministry against his con-
> sent; that no human authority ought, in any
> case whatever, to control or interfere with
> the rights of conscience; and that no prefer-
> ence shall ever be given by law to any religious
> societies or mode of worship.[66]

Badin, however, supported (with some reservations) the state
constitution of Kentucky, and he urged Nerinckx to do likewise. He feared that failure to do so ". . . could tend to
our detriment, if there were any suspicion about the
scruples of priests concerning the civil constitution."
Besides, he pointed out, the constitution ". . . seems to
favor rather than to harm religion. For while Catholics in
some United States of America lack certain common rights,
we are established on equal grounds with other

[66]Badin to Carroll, December 4, 1809. AAB, Case
1-J6.

religionists. . . ."[67] Evidently, Badin was prepared for

certain practical reasons to accept the state's constitu-

tion--that it treated the Catholic Church as an equal with

other denominations and that failure to support it would

brand Catholics as unfaithful citizens. He may even have

realized that the religious principles which the state

constitution expounded were necessary in a society with so

many different religions; but, he was not willing to

consider these principles as good and desirable in them-

selves independent of the practical considerations already

mentioned. He was, then, opposed to Kentucky's policy of

religious liberty which implied that religious truth

cannot be legally known, nor recognized or encouraged in

any way by the state. Carroll's reply to Badin (if there

was any) does not exist.

* * * * * * * * * *

Despite these limited reservations, Catholics

accepted earlier, and with more enthusiasm, the principles

of religious freedom and separation of church and state (as

already defined), than was traditional for their

[67]Ibid.

co-religionists in Europe.[68] There were several reasons

for this remarkable turn of events.

First, Catholics in the United States had long been

denied their basic political and religious rights. As a

persecuted minority the only wise and practical course for

them to follow was to support the idea of toleration and

the separation of church and state. The adoption of such a

position, at first taken for reasons of expediency became,

in time, accepted as a matter of principle. As Edward

Frank Humphrey observed, the Catholic fight for existence

in the colonies ". . . imbued them with the American ideal

of separation of church and state as a political theory."[69]

Actually, American Catholics need not have found the

transition--from practical reasons to principle--difficult,

for there existed a Catholic tradition of religious tolera-

tion that stretched back to colonial Maryland--a historical,

native tradition that was known and accepted by the Carrolls

and most American Catholics.[70]

---

[68]Stokes, Church and State in the United States, I,
454.

[69]Edward Frank Humphrey, Nationalism and Religion in
America 1774-1789 (New York: Russell and Russell, 1965),
p. 234.

[70]Thomas O'Brien Hanley, "The Catholic Tradition of
Freedom in America," American Ecclesiastical Review, CXLV
(November, 1961), 310-13.

Secondly, American Catholics were not immune from
the spirit of the age. The very language which they
adopted illustrated their indebtedness to the natural rights
school of thought, so much a part of the eighteenth century.
Some Catholics, like Charles Carroll, were well acquainted
with the secular writers of the Enlightenment;[71] clerics,
like John Carroll, Fleming, and Gallitzin--all of whom
spoke to the question of religious freedom--made use of
liberal English-Catholic authors. The English-Catholic
writers most often read by American Catholics were Joseph
Berington, John Fletcher, and Arthur O'Leary.[72] Having long
suffered for their religion in a country dominated by a
hostile and suspicious Protestant majority, Berington,
Fletcher, and O'Leary were forced to develop arguments in
behalf of religious liberty that could secure for their
co-religionists political and religious freedom in England.
While their motives may have been pragmatic, their developed

---

[71]Nuesse, The Social Thought of American Catholics,
p. 61.

[72]Joseph Berington, The State and Behaviour of
English Catholics From the Reformation to the Year 1780
(London: R. Faulder, 1780); John Fletcher, Reflections on
the Spirit of Religious Controversy (New York: Bernard
Dornin, 1808); Arthur O'Leary, An Essay on Toleration
(Philadelphia: Kline and Reynold, 1785).

position took on the language of their era in defining

religious freedom as a right founded on nature itself.

O'Leary made the most forceful case for freedom of

worship. He considered, in the Lockean tradition, life,

liberty, and estate as natural rights which no state (or

church) could deny. Since God gave man free will to decide

for himself, man must be free to follow his conscience; no

mortal authority--state or church--can coerce him to do

otherwise. Error should be converted to truth by the word

of the Gospel, and not by the sword.[73] Berington opened his

work by praising Edmund Burke who, by pleading for a greater

measure of freedom for Catholics, ". . . had supported the

rights of human nature." He held that liberty of thought

was essential to human nature. Man's intellect--that which

distinguished him from the animal--must be free; religion,

then, was an affair of conscience, between man and God, with

which no earthly authority, state or church, could interfere.[74]

While Fletcher admitted (as did O'Leary and Berington) the

Church's right to censure or excommunicate, he noted that

this power, being spiritual, could in no way affect the

[73]O'Leary, An Essay on Toleration, pp. 13, 16-18,
23-24, 26-29, 31, 34.

[74]Berington, The State and Behaviour of English
Catholics, pp. x-xii, 139-41.

basic rights of man to "life, liberty and property."
Persecution of any kind, for reason of religious expression,
was contrary to the rights of humanity.[75]

Living under similar conditions, American Catholics
found the ideas of these English-Catholic authors attractive.
O'Leary, Berington and Fletcher raised the debate for
religious liberty above that of self interest to that of
principle, and American Catholics were impressed and influenced to do the same. Carroll read all three authors with
interest, though he was most impressed by Fletcher, whose
book he had reprinted in America.[76] Fleming and Gallitzin
referred their critics to O'Leary's work.[77]

Thirdly, Catholics could accept the idea of
religious liberty and separation of church and state in
America because it did not imply (as it sometimes did in

---

[75]Fletcher, Reflections on the Spirit of Religious
Controversy, pp. 222-25.

[76]Carroll to Plowden, December 5, 1808. Stonyhurst
Archives, Guilday Collection; Carroll to Plowden, June 29,
1785. Maryland Province Archives, Box 202-B9.

[77]Fleming, Calumnies of Verus, p. 11; Gallitzin,
"A Letter to a Protestant Friend," in Murphy (ed.),
Gallitzin's Letters: A Collection of the Polemical Works,
p. 204.

Europe) religious indifference or hostility between church and state.[78]

The separation of church and state at the national level was not a blow aimed at religion. Article VI, Section 3 of the Constitution, which prohibited religious tests for officeholding, and the first amendment were not anti-Christian measures designed to set up a secular state (in the European sense); they represented, instead, a realistic attempt to preserve civil and religious harmony in a society possessing many different denominations.[79]

Religion, then, was left the responsibility of the states. And, while many of the states disestablished a particular church, they often "established" Christianity in its place. A review of the state constitutions supports

---

[78]James J. Hennesey, "The American Experience of the Roman Catholic Church," Catholic Mind, LXIII (November, 1965), 31. When Alexis de Tocqueville visited the United States in the early 1830's he made the same observation: "The religious atmosphere of the country was the first thing that struck me on arrival in the United States. . . . In France I had seen the spirits of religion and of freedom almost always marching in opposite directions. In America I found them intimately linked together in joint reign over the same land." Alexis de Tocqueville, Democracy in America, ed. by J.P. Mayer, Anchor Books (New York: Doubleday and Co., 1969), p. 295.

[79]Stokes, Church and State in the United States, I, 555-56.

Humphrey's observation: "It appears that in the various colonial governments, toleration, when secured, had meant only the separation of some particular sect of Christians, not Christianity itself, from the civil institutions."[80] Most Americans, of all faiths, would not have had it otherwise, for they considered Christianity in particular, and religion in general, as the necessary foundation for living and the maintenance of republican institutions.[81]

Maryland's Constitution of 1776, which John Carroll knew so well, was a case in point. Although the Episcopal Church was disestablished, Maryland remained a Christian state. Article XXXIII of the Declaration of Rights declared that ". . . all persons, professing the Christian religion, are equally entitled to protection in their religious liberty"; and Article XXXV specifically stated that no person could assume office in the state unless he gave ". . . a declaration of belief in the Christian religion."[82]

---

[80] Humphrey, *Nationalism and Religion in America*, p. 489.

[81] After studying the acts and utterances regarding religion of the leading figures of post-revolutionary America, Stokes concluded that these men recognized the value of religion in producing moral men, so necessary in the social and civil order. Stokes, *Church and State in the United States*, I, 514-17; Nuesse, *The Social Thought of American Catholics*, pp. 99-100.

[82] *A Declaration of Rights and the Constitution and Form of Government* (Annapolis: Frederick Green, 1776), pp. 11-13.

The value of Christianity for civil society was evident in

the Clergy Bill of 1785 which proposed to lay a general tax

for the support of the Christian churches because, in the

opinion of the Legislature,

> . . . the happiness of a people, and the good
> order and preservation of civil government,
> essentially depend upon morality, religion,
> and piety, and these cannot be generally
> diffused through a community but by the
> institution of the public worship of Almighty
> God. . . .[83]

In the light of these religious developments Thomas O'Brien

Hanley remarked that Maryland retained ". . . not only a

religious character, but a precisely Christian one. . . ."[84]

The separation of church and state in Maryland must

be seen in this light, so as to understand why Catholics

accepted it. Catholic leaders realized that their legis-

lators and fellow citizens understood the need for

Christianity--or religion in general--to produce a moral

order so necessary for civil society.[85] There would be,

then, no hostility between state and church in Maryland,

---

[83] "An Act to lay a general tax for the support of
the ministers of the gospel of all societies of christians
within this state," Maryland House of Delegates, December 31,
1784. Printed copy, AAB, Special Case C-A9.

[84] Hanley, "The Impact of the American Revolution on
Religion in Maryland 1776-1800," pp. 59-60.

[85] Ibid., pp. 64-66, 69, 73-74, 77-79.

Basically, Maryland--and most of the states--stood
closer to the Massachusetts' tradition of religious
toleration than to the Virginia tradition of religious
liberty. Carroll, and his co-religionists, in siding with
the more conservative majority, were not then ready to
accept what has since become the prevailing religious view
in the United States--religious liberty.

CONCLUSIONS

In reviewing the life and accomplishments of John Carroll, in so many ways the most significant figure in the development of the American Catholic Church, James Cardinal Gibbons summarized the guiding philosophy of the first Bishop of Baltimore:

> . . . the dominant idea in the mind of Bishop Carroll, who was as great a statesman as he was a churchman, an idea that has remained the inspiration of the Church, and has dictated all her policy of the last century . . . was absolute loyalty to the letter and the spirit of the Constitution of the United States.

> Bishop Carroll did not wish to see the Church vegetate as a delicate exotic plant. He wished it to become a sturdy tree, deep rooted in the soil, to grow with the growth and bloom with the development of the country, inured to its climate, braving its storms, invigorated by them and yielding abundantly the fruits of sanctification. His aim was that the clergy and people should be thoroughly identified with the land in which their lot is cast; that they should study its laws and political constitution, and be in harmony with its spirit.[1]

_____

[1] James Cardinal Gibbons, A Retrospect of Fifty Years (2 vols.; Baltimore: John Murphy Co., 1916), I, 248-49.

Such an assessment could be applied as well to those
inumerable Catholics--cleric and lay--who, like Carroll,
were equally intent on making the Catholic Church American
in spirit and constitution. Carroll and his fellow
co-religionists understood that the very survival and
growth of the Catholic Church in the United States
depended upon its ability to accept, and become a part of
the American way of life. In many ways Catholics labored
to create an American Catholic Church.

Ever sensitive to the charge that they were too
dependent on a foreign power (which was what most Protestant
Americans thought Rome to be), and concerned lest such an
indictment revive anti-Catholic legislation, Catholics
wanted their Church to be independent of all foreign
jurisdiction save the spiritual authority of the Holy See.
It was for this reason that they opted for the establishment
of the more autonomous diocesan bishopric, the position to
be filled by an American elected by the clergy in this
country, rather than have Rome appoint a vicar-apostolic
who would be too dependent on the Congregation of Propaganda.

This goal achieved, the American clergy--and later the bishops--tried to assert their control over the future selection of the American hierarchy. They were unsuccessful, but the attempt indicated their commitment to the idea of a national church.

In their ideas on the power of the Pope, a sensitive topic to Protestants, American Catholics developed a position which denied any claims--direct or indirect--Rome may have ever made to temporal power. And, most Catholics in this period were equally prepared to deny that Papal Infallibility was a part of the Catholic faith.

Most Catholics, and none more so than John Carroll, favored the creation of an American, not an immigrant, Church. This demanded a willing acceptance of the political and religious systems of the United States, which Catholics were prepared to give for they saw no incompatibility between the ideas and institutions of America with Catholicism. American Catholics expressed their loyalty to republican government, civil liberty, and democracy. Carroll, for instance, was willing to admit some measure of

ecclesiastical and lay democracy even into the Church:
the first, by having the clergy participate in the selection
of the hierarchy; the second, by having the laity participate
in the affairs of the parish church--both measures he considered desirable in republican America.

Catholics so accepted the principle of religious
toleration and separation of church and state that they
made it a fundamental cornerstone of the American Catholic
Church. Nothing demonstrates better the peculiar quality
of the Catholic Church in the United States and distinguishes
it from her European counterpart, than this early and ready
acceptance of religious ideas that came so late and hard to
the Catholic Church in Europe.[2]

American Catholics developed good relationships with
their Protestant neighbors. Actually, they had little

---

[2]Of course, the political climate in Europe that
surrounded the question of separation was different than in
America. In the "old world" separation was often (though
not exclusively) pushed by anti-clerical and anti-Christian
forces. Separation, then, and religious liberty, were often
viewed by Rome as caused by, and leading to, state hostility
and religious indifference. Catholic opposition in Europe
to these religious ideas must be seen in this context.
Since these same religious principles were not advocated in
America by forces hostile to religion, Catholics more easily
accepted them. This line of argument was developed by
Desmond Fennell, "Continental and Oceanic Catholicism,"
America, XCII (March, 1955), 669-70.

choice but to do so, considering their minority status in an overwhelmingly Protestant society. Catholics could only hope that such contact would diminish misunderstandings and prejudices against their religion. From the inumerable exchanges that took place between members of the two religious bodies, some Catholics came away with sympathetic feelings toward their "separated-brethren" who, leading good lives, could also be in the way of salvation.

In order to make their Church more at home in America--and perhaps closer in appearance to that of the Protestant churches--Catholics called for preachers trained in the American idiom and mass in the vernacular.

American Catholicism, then, in certain respects, was influenced by its Protestant, republican, new world environment. As Thomas T. McAvoy stated it, American Catholicism's ". . . chief and peculiar characteristics are the product of American conditions which began to form the spirit of our Catholic minority almost from the very day the United States became a nation."[3] It was equally important that the leadership of the Catholic Church in

[3]Thomas T. McAvoy, "The Catholic Minority in the United States 1789-1821," Historical Records and Studies, XXXIX-XL (1952), 33.

this crucial period rested in the hands of John Carroll, a member of an old and patriotic house who understood so well the temper of America. As Andrew M. Greeley remarked ". . . United States Catholicism was born American. . . ." because of this fact.[4]

* * * * * * * * * *

Still, Gibbons' quotation, and the tendency of Church historians to stress the "Americanism" of the Catholic Church, slight an equally important side of American Catholicism--its Roman tradition. The failure to understand the significance of the Roman influence on the development of the Catholic Church in this country, can only result in a limited and inadequate picture of the nature of American Catholicism.

Neither John Carroll nor his co-religionists ever forgot that the Catholic Church in America was part of a

---

[4]Andrew M. Greeley, The Catholic Experience: An Interpretation of the History of American Catholicism, Image Books (New York: Doubleday and Co., Inc., 1969), pp. 46-47. Henry J. Browne referred more generally to the English Catholic experience in the New World, especially as it worked out in Maryland (of which John Carroll was a part) as being ". . . the most important in forming the American Catholic tradition and in pointing its directions for the future." Henry J. Browne, "Catholicism in the United States," The Shaping of American Religion, ed. by James Ward Smith and A. Leland Jamison (Princeton: Princeton University Press, 1961), p. 74.

universal, ancient, highly structured religious body whose center was Rome. And, their understanding of this obvious but profound fact prevented them from ever creating (even though they may have desired it) a truly national, American Catholic Church.

For John Carroll any change that took place in the Catholic Church in America could only be done within the confines of Roman Catholic doctrines and practices. This was a basic guideline from which he seldom deviated, though there were times when American conditions compelled him to adopt positions--the acceptance of republicanism, religious liberty, separation of church and state--for which Rome was not then prepared to accept. In doing so, however, Carroll did not feel that he had adopted ideas contrary to the faith of his Church; for such ideas were more political, than religious, in nature, and the belief in them was therefore not essential to Catholicism. Faced with the call for change in things spiritual, things essential (in his opinion) to the faith and practices of Catholicism--such as doctrine and ecclesiastical structure--Carroll could only stay with the Roman tradition, which, for him, was identical to the true faith. He had no choice; to do otherwise would take the American Catholic Church outside the Roman fold, a completely unacceptable consequence. McAvoy, who more than most Catholic Church historians, was conscious of the American influence on the Catholic Church in this country, nonetheless understood the tenacious hold of the Roman tradition. He argued that the "frontier" had little influence in changing certain aspects of the Catholic Church. Since Catholics everywhere accepted the "teaching magisterium" of the Church, as revealed by Pope and priest, it followed that on the frontier "Catholic theology and sacraments . . . remained essentially those of Rome. There was only one choice for him [the Catholic]: he must be Catholic or not be--he could not change the nature of Catholicism."[5]

While Carroll and the clergy wanted the American Catholic Church free from all temporal foreign jurisdiction, they never intended the Church in America to be removed from the spiritual authority of Rome, the center of

[5]Thomas T. McAvoy, "Americanism and Frontier Catholicism," Review of Politics, V (July, 1943), 294.

ecclesiastical unity and the faith itself. Furthermore,
recognizing as he must the spiritual primacy of the Holy
See over the whole Church, Carroll was compelled to accept
(though with reluctance) Rome's right to appoint episcopal
candidates to American bishoprics. And, it was this sense
of belonging to a universal church, under Rome's leadership, that ultimately prevented Carroll from changing the
liturgy from the Latin to the vernacular, a change he
earnestly desired.

At the local level Carroll was willing to accept
(though with some reservation), the system of lay trustees
managing the temporal concerns of the parish church, but
he could never tolerate their using this power to challenge
the spiritual authority of the pastor or the bishop. Such
authority was basic to the very nature of the Catholic
Church. In a similar manner he could not admit of the
lower clergy playing a continuing, meaningful, democratic
role in the selection of the hierarchy--as they had done in
his own election--for this was a function preserved
primarily for the bishops themselves.

While willing to work and live in peace with Protestants, Carroll and his co-religionists, as Catholics, could not grant Protestantism any theological validity; there was only one true church, the Roman Catholic, and no amount of contact or friendship with Protestants could alter that inescapable truth.

* * * * * * * * * *

Carroll was, like most Catholics, caught between two cultures--the American and the Roman. Often the latter took precedence, thereby preventing the Church in this country during Carroll's episcopate from ever becoming totally American. In its theology, ecclesiastical structure (both in relationship to Rome and internally), and finally even in the liturgy, the American Church remained Roman--a point whose significance has been overlooked. To the extent that the Church in the United States remained Roman, it could not become fully Americanized. It could not be a national church independent of all outside authority; it could not accept the developing latitudinarian spirit of the day; it could not really allow the democratic spirit of the country

into the Church structure, which was basically hierarchical.
Of all the major American churches that of the Catholic
was perhaps least influenced by the American "frontier."
As J.J. Mol observed, in his study of change in certain
eighteenth century Protestant churches, a clergy which
stressed ". . . the traditional doctrines, forms, and
rituals of the institutional church would be less inclined
to adjust to a new situation."[6] Mol's conclusions would be
applicable to the Catholic clergy, and explain why, in
certain areas, the Catholic Church could not become fully
Americanized.

But, in its desire to break connections with the
"old world" (save the spiritual authority of Rome), in
its willingness to live and believe in peaceful co-existence
with other faiths, in accepting without serious reservation
the principles of religious toleration and separation of
church and state, and in upholding republican government
(the spirit of which, in small measure, was admitted into
the Church structure itself), the Church under Carroll's
leadership demonstrated its Americanism. Carroll's was a

[6]J.J. Mol, "The Breaking of Traditions: Theological
Convictions in Colonial America (Berkeley: The Blendessary
Press, 1968), pp. 12-13.

difficult and delicate task--to make the Church American
and yet faithful to its Roman traditions. He succeeded in
doing just that, and therein lies the significance of
John Carroll, the first Bishop of Baltimore, the founder
of the American Catholic Church.

A SELECTED BIBLIOGRAPHY

A NOTE ON THE JOHN CARROLL PAPERS

The most indispensable collection for this study was the John Carroll Papers. In 1951 the Executive Council of the American Catholic Historical Association appointed a Committee on the John Carroll Papers, whose task it was to collect, for purposes of publication, the letters, sermons, and other writings of the first bishop of Baltimore. Monsignor John Tracy Ellis served as Chairman; Father Henry J. Browne, who acted as secretary to the committee, was responsible for collecting the materials; Father Charles H. Metzger and Annabelle M. Melville were to translate the Latin and French letters of John Carroll. The major part of the collection was gathered from 1952 to 1955 by Browne. Eventually, over seven hundred items--letters, sermons, and various writings--were obtained. For the most part these materials were facsimile copies in photostat form or on film. The largest and most important group of materials came from the following archives: the Archdiocese of Baltimore; the Maryland Province Archives of the Society of Jesus in Baltimore, Maryland; the Sacred Congregation of Propaganda Fide in Rome; and the Jesuit college in Stonyhurst, England. (The committee also made important use of Peter Guilday's collection of Carroll's letters in facsimile from Stonyhurst College and transcripts of the correspondence that passed between Carroll and high Roman officials in the Congregation of Propaganda.) Smaller groups of Carroll material came from the following archives: Archdiocese of Quebec; Georgetown University; University of Notre Dame; Carmelite Convent, in Baltimore, Maryland; St. Mary's Seminary, in Baltimore, Maryland; and the Maryland Historical Society. This significant collection was placed on microfilm and photostat, and deposited in the archives at the Catholic University of America. Father Thomas O'Brien Hanley, S.J., the editor of the John Carroll Papers, is preparing the materials for publication.

PRIMARY SOURCES

A. MANUSCRIPTS

Archives of the Archdiocese of Baltimore.

Outgoing letters and writings of Archbishop
John Carroll

Incoming letters to Archbishop John Carroll:[**]

Father Stephen Theodore Badin
Father Joseph Berington
Bishop Jean Louis Ann Magdalen Lefebvre de Cheverus
Father Joseph Pierre Picot de Cloriviere
Bishop Michael Egan
Father William Elling
Father Ferdinand Farmer
Father Simon Felix Gallagher
Father Demetrius Augustine Gallitzin
Father John Grassi
Father William Vincent Harold
Father Anthony Kohlmann
Father Lemercier
Father Michael Levadoux
Dr. Edward Lynch
Mrs. J.E. McDonald
Father Francis Anthony Matignon
Father Robert Molyneux
Archbishop Leondard Neale
Father Charles Plowden
Father Gabriel Richard
Father Jean Francois Rivet
Father John Rosseter
Father Louis Sibourd
Father John Thayer
Father John Thorpe
Judge James Twyman

[**] Names listed are only of those persons whose
letters to Carroll were significant in terms of numbers
and/or content.

Archives of the Congregation of Propaganda Fide.
Guilday Collection, Transcripts. Catholic University
of America Archives.

Letters of John Carroll and members of the American
clergy to Pope Pius VI, Pope Pius VII, and to the
Cardinal-Prefect of the Congregation of Propaganda
Fide.

John Carroll's Report to the Cardinal-Prefect of
the Congregation of Propaganda Fide--"Relation of
the State of Religion in the United States 1785."

Letters of the Cardinal-Prefect of the Congregation
of Propaganda Fide to John Carroll and to several
members of the American clergy--Lawrence Graessel,
Michael Egan, Robert Molyneux, and Leonard Neale.

Summary Reports of the annual transactions of the
Congregation of Propaganda Fide (Acta).

Maryland Province Archives of the Society of Jesus.
Baltimore, Maryland.

Letters and sermons of Archbishop John Carroll.

Letters of Bishop Benedict Joseph Fenwick
          Father John Grassi
          Father Anthony Kohlmann
          Father James Wallace

Proceedings of the meetings of the General Chapter
of the Clergy for the years 1783 and 1786.

Stonyhurst College, England. Guilday Collection,
Microfilm. Catholic University of America Archives.

Letters of Archbishop John Carroll

Georgetown University.

Shea Collection. Transcripts of Archbishop John
Carroll's letters.

Mss. Diary of Brother Joseph Mobberly.
Mss. Diary of Father John McElroy.

University of Notre Dame. John Carroll Papers,
Microfilm. Catholic University of America Archives.

Letters and sermons of Archbishop John Carroll.

Transcript letters:

Bishop John Carroll to Daniel Brent, March 3, 1807
Father Jean Baptist Mary David to Father Simon
William Gabriel Bruté, July 18, 1811
Father Michael Egan to Bishop John Carroll,
January 21, 1805
Bishop Benedict Joseph Flaget to Father Simon
William Gabriel Bruté, February 5, 1812

Carmelite Convent. Baltimore, Maryland. John Carroll
Papers, Microfilm. Catholic University of America
Archives.

Letters of Archbishop John Carroll to the
Mother-Superior.

John Carroll's "Eulogy on the death of George
Washington"--February 22, 1800.

Archives of the Archdiocese of Quebec. John Carroll
Papers, Microfilm. Catholic University of America
Archives.

Letters of Archbishop John Carroll to Jean Francois
Hubert, Bishop of Quebec.

Joseph Herman Schauinger Collection (private), 1671
Berkeley Avenue, St. Paul, Minnesota.

Translated copies of the letters of
Father Stephen T. Badin
Father Jean Baptist Mary David
Bishop Benedict Joseph Flaget
Father Charles Nerinckx

B. PUBLIC DOCUMENTS

Farrand, Max, ed. The Records of the Federal Convention
of 1787. Revised edition. 4 vols. New Haven:
Yale University Press, 1937.

Gales, Joseph, comp. Debates and Proceedings in the Congress
of the United States. Washington: Gales and
Seaton, 1834.

Maryland. Proceedings of the Convention of the Province of
Maryland. Annapolis, 1776.

Maryland. A Declaration of Rights and the Constitution and
Form of Government. Annapolis: Frederick Green,
1776.

New York. Laws of the State of New York 1777-1784.
Albany: Weed, Parsons & Company, 1886.

Thorpe, Francis Newton, ed. The Federal and State
Constitutions, Colonial Charters, and other
Organic Laws of the States, Territories, and
Colonies. 7 vols. Washington: Government
Printing Office, 1909.

C. PRINTED WORKS: CATHOLIC

Aitken, John, ed. A Compilation of the Litanies and
    Vespers, Hymns and Anthems, as they are sung in the
    Catholic Church. Philadelphia: By the Author,
    1787.

Badin, Father Stephen Theodore. The Real Principles of
    Roman Catholics, In Reference to God and Country.
    Bardstown: F. Peniston, 1805.

_____. Summary Proofs of the Catholic Doctrine from
    Scripture. Baltimore: Bernard Dornin, 1810.

_____. "Origin and Progress of the Mission of Kentucky."
    Catholic World, XXI (September, 1875), 825-835.

_____. "The Church in Kentucky." Records of the American
    Catholic Historical Society of Philadelphia, XXIII
    (September, 1912), 141-174.

_____. "Letters from the Baltimore Archives--From the
    Reverend Stephen Theodore Badin, 1797-1799." Records
    of the American Catholic Historical Society of
    Philadelphia, XIX (December, 1908), 455-482.

Berington, Father Joseph. The State and Behaviour of
    English Catholics From the Reformation to the Year
    1780. London: R. Faulder, 1780.

Blythe, Stephen Cleveland. An Apology for the Conversion
    of Stephen Cleveland Blythe, to the Faith of the
    Catholic, Apostolic and Roman Church. New York:
    Joseph Desmones, 1815.

Bruté, Bishop Simon William Gabriel. "Bishop Bruté's
    Account of Religion at Emmitsburg, Md." American
    Catholic Historical Society of Philadelphia
    Researches, XV (January, 1898), 88-95.

Carey, Mathew. Autobiography. N.p.: Research Classics, 1942.

Carr, Benjamin, ed. A New Edition, with an Appendix of Masses, Vespers, Litanies, Hymns, Psalms, Anthems & Motetts, Composed, Selected and Arranged for the use of the Catholic Churches in the United States of America. Philadelphia, 1808.

Carroll, Charles. Unpublished Letters of Charles Carroll of Carrollton, and of His Father, Charles Carroll of Doughoregan. Compiled and edited by Thomas Meagher Field. New York: United States Catholic Historical Society, 1902.

Carroll, Archbishop John. An Address to the Roman Catholics of the United States of America. Annapolis: Frederick Green, 1784.

_____. A Discourse on General Washington. Baltimore: Warner and Hanna, 1800.

_____. "Unpublished Reply of Rev. John Carroll, 1788, to the Rev. Patrick Smyth's account 'The Present State of the Catholic Missions Conducted by the Ex-Jesuits in North America.'" American Catholic Historical Society of Philadelphia Researches, XXII (July, 1905), 193-206.

The Catholic Religion vindicated, Being an answer to a sermon preached by the Rev. Mr. Cuyler in Poughkeepsie on the 30th. day of July, 1812, the day set apart for fasting and prayer in the state of New York: in which sermon the religion of the Catholics was so illiberally misrepresented as to require a vindication. N.p.: By the Author, 1813.

Concilia Provincialia, Baltimori, Habita ab Anno 1829 usque
    ad annum 1849. Baltimore: John Murphy Company,
    1851.

Devitt, Father Edward I., ed. "Propaganda Documents:
    Appointment of the First Bishop of Baltimore."
    Records of the American Catholic Historical
    Society of Philadelphia, XXI (December, 1910),
    185-235.

_____. "Letters from the Archiepiscopal Archives at
    Baltimore 1790-1814." Records of the American
    Catholic Historical Society of Philadelphia, XX
    (September, 1909), 250-289.

Dilhet, Father Jean. État de l'Église Catholique ou
    Diocese des États-Unis de L'Amérique Septentrionale.
    Translated and annotated by Patrick W. Browne.
    Washington: Salve Regina Press, 1922.

DuBourg, Bishop Louis Guillaume Valentin. St. Mary's
    Seminary and Catholics at large Vindicated against
    the Pastoral Letter of the Ministers, Bishops, &
    of the Presbytery of Baltimore. Baltimore: Bernard
    Dornin, 1811.

Durand, Father Marie Joseph. "Epistle or Diary of the Rev.
    Marie Joseph Durand." Translated by Ella M.E.
    Flick. Records of the American Catholic Historical
    Society of Philadelphia, XXVI (December, 1915),
    328-345; XXVII (March, 1916), 45-64.

Ellis, Monsignor John Tracy, ed. Documents of American
    Catholic History. 2nd ed., revised. Milwaukee:
    Bruce Publishing Company, 1962.

Flaget, Bishop Benedict Joseph. "Bishop Flaget's Report of the Diocese of Bardstown to Pope Pius VII, April 10, 1815." Translated and edited by Victor F. O'Daniel. Catholic Historical Review, I (October, 1915), 305-319.

_____. "Bishop Flaget's Diary." Translated by William J. Howlett. Records of the American Catholic Historical Society of Philadelphia, XXIX (March, 1918), 37-59; XXIX (June, 1918), 153-169; XXIX (September, 1918), 231-249.

Fleming, Father Francis Anthony, and Carey, Matthew. The Calumnies of Verus. Philadelphia: Johnston and Justice, 1792.

Fletcher, Father John. Reflections on the Spirit. New York: Bernard Dornin, 1808.

Gallitzin, Father Demetrius Augustine. Gallitzin's Letters: A Collection of the Polemical Works. Edited by Grace Murphy. Loretto, Pennsylvania: Angelmodde Press, 1940.

Grassi, Father John. "The Catholic Religion in the United States in 1818." American Catholic Historical Society of Philadelphia Researches, VIII (1891), 98-111.

_____. "Memoirs on the Reestablished Society of Jesus in the United States of North America from 1810 to 1817." Translated and edited by Arthur J. Arrieri. Historical Records and Studies, XLVII (1959), 196-234.

Guilday, Father Peter, ed. The National Pastorals of the American Hierarchy, 1792-1919. Washington: National Catholic Welfare Conference, 1923.

Hay, Bishop John. An Abridgement of the Christian Doctrine. Baltimore: Bernard Dornin, 1809.

Hughes, Father Thomas. History of the Society of Jesus in North America, Colonial and Federal. Documents, 1605-1838. New York: Longmans, Green and Company, 1910.

Kenny, Father Patrick. "Extracts from the Diary of Rev. Patrick Kenny." Edited by Martin I.J. Griffin. Records of the American Catholic Historical Society of Philadelphia, VII (March, 1896), 94-137.

Kohlmann, Father Anthony. The Catholic Question in America. New York: Edward Gillespy, 1813.

La Valinière, Father Pierre Huet de. Curious and Interesting Dialogue, between Mr. Goodwish and Doctor Brevilog, French and English: in which everyone is furnished with arguments to defend his religion against all false assertions whatever. New York: Greenleaf, 1790.

Lindsay, Abbé Lionel St. George, ed. "Correspondence between Bishop Plessis of Quebec, Canada, and Bishop Flaget of Bardstown, Ky., 1811-1833." Records of the American Catholic Historical Society of Philadelphia, XVIII (March, 1907), 8-43.

_____. "Correspondence between the Sees of Quebec and Baltimore, 1788-1847." Records of the American Catholic Historical Society of Philadelphia, XVIII (June, 1907), 155-189.

Matignon, Father Francis. "Letters from the Archdiocesan Archives at Baltimore, 1797-1807." Records of the American Catholic Historical Society of Philadelphia, XX (June, 1909), 193-208.

Maréchal, Archbishop Ambrose. "The Diocese of Baltimore in 1818; Archbishop Maréchal's Account to Propaganda, October 16, 1818." Documents of American Catholic History. Edited by John Tracy Ellis. Milwaukee: Bruce Publishing Company, 1962.

Middleton, Father Thomas C., trans. "Documents Relating to the Appointment of Rev. Laurence Graessel as Coadjutor to the Right Rev. John Carroll, First Bishop of Baltimore." American Catholic Historical Society of Philadelphia Researches, XXI (April, 1904), 59-64.

Mondésir, Father Édouard de. Souvenir d'Édouard de Mondésir. Baltimore: Johns Hopkins Press, 1942.

Moran, Patrick Francis, Cardinal, ed. Spicilegium Ossoriense: Being a Collection of Original Letters and Papers illustrative of the History of the Irish Church from the Reformation to the year 1800. 3 vols. Dublin: Browne and Nolan, 1874-1884.

Nerinckx, Father Charles. Eenen Oogslag op den Tegenwoordigen Staet der Roomsch-Catholyke Religie in Noord-America. Louvain: F. Michel, 1816.

O'Leary, Father Arthur. An Essay on Toleration. Philadelphia: Kline and Reynolds, 1785.

Paul, Father Vincent de. "Some Account of What Befel Father Vincent de Paul, With Observations Made by Him when in America." American Catholic Historical Society of Philadelphia Researches, XXII (October, 1905), 360-367.

Plessis, Bishop Joseph Octave. "Pastoral Visitation of Bishop Plessis of Quebec, 1815." Translated and edited by Lionel St. George Lindsay. Records of the American Catholic Historical Society of Philadelphia, XV (December, 1904), 337-402.

Poterie, Father Claude Florent Bouchard de la. A Pastoral
    Letter. Boston: Thomas & Andrews, 1789.

_____. To the Public. Boston, 1789.

_____. "An Abridged Formula of the Priest's Discourse
    Made Every Sunday, in the Church of the Holy Cross,
    at Boston." American Catholic Historical Society
    of Philadelphia Researches, VI (January, 1889),
    12-15.

Rosseter, Father John. "Letters of John Rosseter to Bishop
    Carroll, 1799-1808." Compiled by Francis E.
    Tourscher. Records of the American Catholic
    Historical Society of Philadelphia, XLIII (December,
    1932), 360-382; XLIV (March, 1933), 70-96; XLIV
    (June, 1933), 170-191; XLIV (September, 1933),
    238-261.

"Selections from the Correspondence of the Deceased Mathew
    Carey, Writer, Printer, Publisher." Records of the
    American Catholic Historical Society of Philadelphia
    IX (September, 1898), 352-384; XI (September, 1900),
    338-350.

Seton, Mother Elizabeth Bayley. Memoir, Letters, and
    Journal of Elizabeth Seton. Compiled and edited by
    Robert Seton. 2 vols. New York: P. O'Shea, 1869.

Shearer, Father Donald C., ed. Pontificia Americana: A
    Documentary History of the Catholic Church in the
    United States, 1784-1884. Washington: Catholic
    University of America Press, 1933.

A Short Abridgement of Christian Doctrine, Newly Revised
    for the Use of the Catholic Church in the United
    States of America. Georgetown: James Doyle, 1793.

A Short Account of the Establishment of the New See of
Baltimore, in Maryland, and of Consecrating the
Right Reverend Dr. John Carroll, First Bishop
thereof, on the Feast of the Assumption, 1790.
Philadelphia: Carey, Stewart & Company, 1791.

Spalding, Bishop Martin John. Sketches of the Life, Times
and Character of the Right Rev. Benedict Joseph
Flaget. Louisville: Webb & Levering, 1852.

_____. Sketches of the Early Catholic Missions of
Kentucky from their Commencement in 1787 to the
Jubilee in 1826-1827. Baltimore: John Murphy
Company, 1844.

Sundry Documents, submitted to the consideration of the
Pewholders of St. Mary's Church, by the trustees
of that Church. Philadelphia: Lydia R. Bailey,
1812.

Thayer, Father John. Controversy Between the Rev. John
Thayer, Catholic Missionary of Boston, and the
Rev. George Lesslie, Pastor of a Church in
Washington, New Hampshire. Newburyport: John
Mycall, 1793.

_____. An Account of the Conversion of the Reverend
John Thayer, lately a Protestant Minister, at Boston
in North America, who embraced the Roman Catholic
Religion at Rome, on the 25th of May, 1783.
Baltimore: William Goddard, 1788.

D. PRINTED WORKS: NON-CATHOLICS

Bentley, Reverend William. The Diary of William Bentley.
4 vols. Salem, Massachusetts: Essex Institute,
1905-1914.

Coke, Bishop Thomas, and Asbury, Bishop Francis. The
     Doctrines and Discipline of the Methodist Church in
     America. 10th ed. Philadelphia: Henry Tuckniss,
     1798.

The Constitution of the Presbyterian Church in America.
     Philadelphia: Robert Aitken, 1797.

Endfield, Reverend William. An Essay on Marriage. Phila-
     delphia: Zachariah Poulson, 1788.

Franklin, Benjamin. The Writings of Benjamin Franklin.
     Edited by Albert Henry Smyth. 10 vols. New York:
     Macmillan Company, 1905-1907.

Jefferson, Thomas. The Papers of Thomas Jefferson. Edited
     by Julian P. Boyd. Princeton: Princeton
     University Press, 1950-

Madison, James. The Writings of James Madison. Edited by
     Gaillard Hunt. 9 vols. New York: G.P. Putnam's
     Sons, 1900-1910.

_____. The Papers of James Madison. Edited by
     William T. Hutchinson and William M.E. Rachal.
     Chicago: University of Chicago Press, 1962-

Strictures on the Establishment of Colleges, particular
     that of St. Mary's. Baltimore: N.P., 1806.

West, Reverend Stephen. The Duty and Obligation of Christia
     to Marry Only in the Lord. Hartford: Watson and
     Goodwin, 1778.

Wharton, Reverend Charles Henry. A Letter to the Roman
     Catholics of the City of Worcester, from the Late
     Chaplain of that Society, Stating the Motives which
     induced him to relinquish their communion and become
     a member of the Protestant Church. Philadelphia:
     Robert Aitken, 1784.

_____. A Reply to an Address to the Roman Catholics of
the United States of America. Philadelphia:
Charles Cist, 1785.

SECONDARY SOURCES

A. BOOKS

Altfeld, E. Milton. The Jew's Struggle for Religious and
Civil Liberty in Maryland. Baltimore: M. Curlander,
1924.

Baisnée, Father Jules A. France and the Establishment of
the American Catholic Hierarchy: The Myth of
French Interference 1783-1784. Baltimore: John
Hopkins Press, 1934.

Bartlett, Father Chester Joseph. The Tenure of Parochial
Property in the United States of America.
Washington: Catholic University of America Press,
1926.

Baudier, Roger. The Catholic Church in Louisiana.
New Orleans, 1939.

Baumgartner, Apollinaris William. Catholic Journalism: A
Study of Its Development in the United States
1789-1930. New York: Columbia University Press,
1931.

Beitzell, Father Edwin Warfield. The Jesuit Missions of
St. Mary's County, Maryland. Abell, Maryland, 1960.

Billington, Ray Allen. The Protestant Crusade 1800-1860:
A Study of the Origins of American Nativism.
Quandrangle Paperbacks. Chicago: Quandrangle
Books, 1964.

Blied, Father Benjamin Joseph. Catholic Aspects of the
War for Independence, the War of 1812, the War
with Mexico, the War with Spain. Milwaukee, 1949.

Brant, Irving. James Madison: The Virginia Revolutionist.
New York: Bobbs-Merrill Company, 1941.

_____. James Madison: The Nationalist 1780-1787.
New York: Bobbs-Merrill Company, 1948.

Brent, Daniel. Biographical Sketch of the Most Rev. John
Carroll. Baltimore: John Murphy, 1843.

Brilioth, Yngve. A Brief History of Preaching. Preachers'
Paperback Library. Philadelphia: Fortress Press,
1965.

Brown, Stuart Gerry. The First Republicans: Political
Philosophy and Public Policy in the Party of
Jefferson and Madison. Syracuse: Syracuse
University Press, 1954.

Callahan, Daniel. The Mind of the Catholic Layman. The
Scribner Library. New York: Charles Scribner's
Sons, 1963.

Carthy, Mother Mary Peter. Old St. Patrick's: New York's
First Cathedral. New York: The United States
Catholic Historical Society, 1947.

Cassidy, Father Francis Patrick. Catholic College
Foundations and Development in the United States,
1677-1850. Washington: Catholic University of
America Press, 1924.

Cobb, Sanford Hoadley. The Rise of Religious Liberty in
America: A History. New York: Macmillan Company,
1902.

Daly, Father John M. Georgetown University: Origin and
    Early Years. Washington: Georgetown University
    Press, 1957.

Dehey, Elinor Tong. Religious Orders of Women in the
    United States. Revised edition. Hammond, Indiana:
    W.B. Conkey Company, 1930.

DeMarco, Father Angelus A. Rome and the Vernacular.
    Westminister, Maryland: Newman Press, 1961.

Dignan, Father Patrick J. A History of the Legal
    Incorporation of Catholic Church Property in the
    United States 1784-1932. Washington: Catholic
    University of America Press, 1933.

Dohen, Dorothy. Nationalism and American Catholicism.
    New York: Sheed and Ward, 1967.

Ellis, Monsignor John Tracy. Catholics in Colonial America.
    Baltimore: Helicon Press, 1963.

_____. Perspectives in American Catholicism.
    Baltimore: Helicon Press, 1963.

_____. American Catholicism. Chicago: University of
    Chicago Press, 1956.

Fecher, Father Vincent J. A Study of the Movement for
    German National Parishes in Philadelphia and
    Baltimore 1787-1802. Rome: Apud Aedes
    Universitatis Gregorianae, 1955.

Fell, Sister Marie Leonore. The Foundations of Nativism
    in American Textbooks 1783-1860. Washington:
    Catholic University of America Press, 1941.

Foik, Father Paul Joseph. Pioneer Catholic Journalism.
New York: United States Catholic Historical
Society, 1930.

Fox, Sister M. Columba. The Life of the Right Reverend
John Baptist Mary David 1761-1841. New York:
United States Catholic Historical Society, 1925.

Geiger, Sister Mary Virginia. Daniel Carroll: A Framer of
the Constitution. Washington: Catholic University
of America Press, 1943.

Godecker, Sister Mary Salesia. Simon Bruté de Rémur: First
Bishop of Vincennes. St. Meinrad, Indiana: St.
Meinrad Abbey Press, 1931.

Gorman, Father Robert. Catholic Apologetical Literature in
the United States 1784-1858. Washington: Catholic
University of America Press, 1939.

Greeley, Andrew M. The Catholic Experience: An Interpreta-
tion of the History of American Catholicism.
Doubleday Image. Garden City, New York: Doubleday
& Company, 1967.

Greene, Evarts Boutell. Religion and the State: The Making
and Testing of an American Tradition. Ithaca:
Cornell University Press, 1959.

_____. The Revolutionary Generation 1763-1790. New York:
Macmillan Company, 1946.

Griffin, Martin I.J. History of the Right Reverend Michael
Egan, D.D., First Bishop of Philadelphia.
Philadelphia: By the Author, 1893.

Guilday, Father Peter. The Life and Times of John Carroll,
Archbishop of Baltimore 1735-1815. 2 vols. in one.
New York: Encyclopedia Press, 1922.

_____. The Life and Times of John England: First
    Bishop of Charleston 1786-1842. 2 vols. New York:
    America Press, 1927.

_____. A History of the Councils of Baltimore 1791-1884.
    New York: Macmillan Company, 1932.

Herberg, Will. Protestant, Catholic, Jew: An Essay in
    American Religious Sociology. Anchor Books.
    Garden City, New York: Doubleday & Company, 1960.

Herbermann, Father Charles George. The Sulpicians in the
    United States. New York: Encyclopedia Press, 1916.

Hertkorn, Francis. A Retrospect of Holy Trinity Parish
    1789-1914. Philadelphia: F. McManus, Jr. &
    Company, 1914.

Hopkins, Father Thomas F. "St. Mary's Church, Charleston,
    S.C." Yearbook, 1897, City of Charleston, S.C.:
    Walker, Evans & Cogswell, 1897.

Howard, George Elliott. A History of Matrimonial
    Institutions. 3 vols. Chicago: University of
    Chicago Press, 1904.

Howlett, Father William J. Life of Rev. Charles Nerinckx.
    Techny, Illinois: Mission Press, 1915.

Humphrey, Edward Frank. Nationalism and Religion in America
    1774-1789. New York: Russell & Russell, 1965.

Kelly, Father Laurence J. History of Holy Trinity Parish,
    Washington, D.C. 1795-1945. Washington: Holy
    Trinity Parish, 1946.

Kirlin, Joseph L.J. Catholicity in Philadelphia.
    Philadelphia: John Jos. McVey, 1909.

Kremer, Father Michael N. Church Support in the United
    States. Washington: Catholic University of
    America Press, 1930.

Krout, John Allen, and Fox, Dixon Ryan. The Completion of
    Independence 1790-1830. New York: Macmillan
    Company, 1944.

Lemcke, Father Peter Henry. Life and Work of Prince
    Demetrius Augustine Gallitzin. New York:
    Longman's, Green & Company, 1940.

Lochemes, Sister Mary Frederick. Robert Walsh: His Story.
    Washington: Catholic University of America Press,
    1941.

Lord, Robert H.; Sexton, John E.; and Harrington, Edward T.
    History of the Archdiocese of Boston: In the
    Various Stages of Its Development 1604 to 1943.   3
    vols. New York: Sheed & Ward, 1944.

Lucey, Father William Leo. Edward Kavanagh: Catholic,
    Statesman, Diplomat from Maine 1795-1844.
    Francestown, New Hampshire: Marshall Jones
    Company, 1946.

Lynskey, Elizabeth M. The Government of the Catholic
    Church. New York: P.J. Kenedy & Sons, 1952.

McAvoy, Father Thomas Timothy. The Catholic Church in
    Indiana 1789-1834. New York: Columbia University
    Press, 1940.

McDonald, Father Lloyd Paul. The Seminary Movement in the
    United States: Projects, Foundations, and Early
    Developments 1784-1833. Washington: Catholic
    University of America Press, 1927.

Malone, Dumas. Jefferson and His Time. Vol. I: Jefferson the Virginian. Boston: Little, Brown and Company, 1948.

Mast, Sister M. Dolorita. Always the Priest: The Life of Gabriel Richard. Baltimore: Helicon Press, 1965.

Mattingly, Sister Mary Ramona. The Catholic Church on the Kentucky Frontier 1785-1812. Washington: Catholic University of America Press, 1936.

Maynard, Theodore. The Story of American Catholicism. Image Books. 2 vols. New York: Doubleday & Company, 1960.

Mead, Sidney E. The Lively Experiment: The Shaping of Christianity in America. New York: Harper & Row, 1963.

Melville, Annabelle M. Jean Lefebvre de Cheverus 1768-1836. Milwaukee: Bruce Publishing Company, 1958.

_____. Elizabeth Bayley Seton 1774-1821. New York: Charles Scribner's Sons, 1951.

_____. John Carroll of Baltimore: Founder of the American Catholic Hierarchy. New York: Charles Scribner's Sons, 1955.

Meyer, Jacob Conrad. Church and State in Massachusetts: From 1740 to 1833. New York: Russell & Russell, 1968.

Mol, J.J. The Breaking of Traditions: Theological Convictions in Colonial America. Berkeley: Glendessary Press, 1968.

Nemmers, Erwin Esser. Twenty Centuries of Catholic Church Music. Milwaukee: Bruce Publishing Company, 1948.

Nuesse, Celestine Joseph. The Social Thought of American Catholics 1634-1829. Westminster, Maryland: Newman Book Shop, 1945.

Nye, Russell Blaine. The Cultural Life of the New Nation 1776-1830. Harper Torchbooks. New York: Harper & Row, 1960.

O'Daniel, Father Victor F. The Right Reverend Edward Dominic Fenwick. Washington: The Dominicana, 1920.

_____. A Light of the Church in Kentucky or the Life, Labors, and Character of the Very Rev. Samuel Thomas Wilson. Washington: The Dominicana, 1932.

Paré, George. The Catholic Church in Detroit 1701-1888. Detroit: Gabriel Richard Press, 1951.

Ray, Sister Mary Augustina. American Opinion of Roman Catholicism in the Eighteenth Century. New York: Columbia University Press, 1936.

Riordan, Father Michael J. Cathedral Records From the Beginning of Catholicity in Baltimore to the Present Time. Baltimore: Catholic Mirrow Publishing Company, 1906.

Rowland, Kate Mason. The Life of Charles Carroll of Carrollton, 1737-1832. 2 vols. New York: G.P. Putnam's Sons, 1898.

Ruane, Joseph William. The Beginnings of the Society of St. Sulpice in the United States 1791-1829. Washington: Catholic University of America Press, 1935.

Ruskowski, Father Leo F. French Émigré Priests in the United States 1791-1815. Washington: Catholic University of America Press, 1940.

Ryan, Leo Raymond. _Old St. Peter's: The Mother Church of Catholic New York 1785-1935._ New York: United States Catholic Historical Society, 1935.

Sargent, Daniel. _Mitri or the Story of Prince Demetrius Augustine Gallitzin, 1770-1840._ New York: Longman's, Green & Company, 1945.

Scharp, Heinrich. _How the Catholic Church is Governed._ New York: Herder and Herder, 1960.

Schauinger, Joseph Herman. _Stephen T. Badin, Priest in the Wilderness._ Milwaukee: Bruce Publishing Company, 1956.

_____. _William Gaston: Carolinian._ Milwaukee: Bruce Publishing Company, 1949.

_____. _Cathedrals in the Wilderness._ Milwaukee: Bruce Publishing Company, 1952.

Shaughnessy, Father Gerald. _Has the Immigrant Kept the Faith? A Study of Immigration and Catholic Church Growth in the United States 1790-1920._ New York: Macmillan Company, 1925.

Shea, John Gilmary. _History of the Catholic Church in the United States._ Vol. II: _The Life and Times of the Most Reverend John Carroll._ New York: By the Author, 1888.

Smith, Ellen Hart. _Charles Carroll of Carrollton._ Cambridge: Harvard University Press, 1942.

Smith, Father John Talbot. _The Catholic Church in New York: A History of the New York Diocese from Its Establishment in 1808 to the Present Time._ 2 vols. New York: Hall & Locke Company, 1905.

Sparrow-Simpson, W.J. Roman Catholic Opposition to Papal
        Infallibility. Milwaukee: Young Churchman Company,
        1910.

Stokes, Anson Phelps. Church and State in the United
        States. 3 vols. New York: Harper & Row, 1950.

Walker, Father Fintan Glenn. The Catholic Church in the
        Meeting of Two Frontiers: The Southern Illinois
        Country 1763-1793. Washington: Catholic
        University of America Press, 1935.

Webb, Benedict J. The Centenary of Catholicity in Kentucky.
        Louisville: Charles A. Rogers, 1884.

Webber, Frederick R. A History of Preaching in Britain
        and America. 3 vols. Milwaukee: Northwestern
        Publishing House, 1952-1957.

Whitehall, Walter Muir. A Memorial to Bishop Cheverus with
        a Catalogue of the Books given by him to the Boston
        Athenaeum. Boston: Boston Athenaeum, 1951.

Williams, Robin M., Jr. American Society: A Sociological
        Interpretation. Second edition, revised. New York:
        Alfred A. Knopf, 1963.

Winslow, Father Francis Joseph. Vicars and Prefects
        Apostolic. Maryknoll, New York: Catholic Foreign
        Mission Society of America, 1924.

Zollmann, Carl Frederick Gustav. American Church Law.
        St. Paul, Minnesota: West Publishing Company, 1933.

B. ARTICLES

Bennett, William H. "Francis Cooper: New York's First
    Catholic Legislator." Historical Records and
    Studies, XII (1918), 29-38.

Brislen, Sister M. Bernetta. "The Episcopacy of Leonard
    Neale, Second Archbishop of Baltimore." Historical
    Records and Studies, XXXIV (1945), 20-111.

Browne, Father Henry J. "A New Historical Project:
    Editing the Papers of Archbishop Carroll."
    American Ecclesiastical Review, CXXVII (October,
    1952), 341-350.

Campbell, Bernard U. "Memoirs of the Life and Times of the
    Most Rev. John Carroll." United States Catholic
    Magazine, III (1844), 32-41, 98-101, 169-176,
    244-248, 363-379, 662-669, 718-724, 793-802; IV
    (1845), 249-260, 782-791; V (1846), 595-599,
    676-682; VI (1847), 31-38, 100-104, 144-148,
    183-186, 434-439, 482-486, 592-606.

Campbell, Jane. "Notes on a Few Old Catholic Hymnbooks."
    Records of the American Catholic Historical Society
    of Philadelphia, XXXI (June, 1920), 129-143.

Carthy, Mother Mary Peter. "English Influences on Early
    American Catholicism." Historical Record and
    Studies, XLVI (1958), 12-149.

Chaput, R. "Patronage, Canon Law of." New Catholic
    Encyclopedia, 1967, Vol. X.

Connolly, Arthur J. "Rev. Francis A. Matignon, D.D. First
    Pastor of the Church of the Holy Cross, Boston,
    Mass." United States Catholic Historical Magazine,
    III (1890), 129-150.

Connors, Father Daniel Joseph. "Archbishop Troy and the American Church, 1800-1823." Historical Records and Studies, XXII (1932), 168-183.

Curran, Father Francis X. "The Jesuit Colony in New York 1808-1817." Historical Records and Studies, XLII (1954), 51-97.

D'Arcy, Eric. "Freedom of Religion." New Catholic Encyclopedia, 1967, Vol. VI.

Dignan, Father Patrick J. "Peter Anthony Malou, Patriot and Priest 1753-1827." Records of the American Catholic Historical Society of Philadelphia, XLII (December, 1931), 305-344; XLIII (March, 1932), 62-96.

Ellis, Monsignor John Tracy. "Archbishop Carroll and the Liturgy in the Vernacular." Worship, XXVI (November, 1952), 545-552.

_____. "A Guide to the Baltimore Cathedral Archives." Catholic Historical Review, XXXII (October, 1946), 341-360.

Eminyan, Father Maurice. "Extra Ecclesiam Nulla Salus." New Catholic Encyclopedia, 1967, Vol. V.

_____. "Salvation, Necessity of the Church For." New Catholic Encyclopedia, 1967, Vol. XII.

Faulkner, Thomas A. "Bishop, Canon Law." New Catholic Encyclopedia, 1967, Vol. II.

Fellner, Father Felix. "Trials and Triumphs of Catholic Pioneers in Western Pennsylvania." Records of the American Catholic Historical Society of Philadelphia, XXXIV (September, 1923), 195-261; XXXIV (December, 1923), 287-343.

Fennell, Desmond. "Continental and Oceanic Catholicism." *America*, March 26, 1955, pp. 669-671.

Flick, Lawrence. "The French Refugee Trappists in the United States." *Records of the American Catholic Historical Society of Philadelphia*, I (1884-1886), 86-116.

Flynn, Daniel Vincent. "Vicar-General." *New Catholic Encyclopedia*, 1967, Vol. XIV.

Garraghan, Father Gilbert J. "John Anthony Grassi, S.J., 1775-1849." *Catholic Historical Review*, XXIII (October, 1937), 273-292.

Griffin, Martin I.J. "The Rev. Peter Helbron, Second Pastor of Holy Trinity Church, Philadelphia." *Records of the American Catholic Historical Society of Philadelphia*, XXIII (March, 1912), 1-21.

_____. "The Reverend John Nepomucene Goetz, Third Pastor and William Elling, Assistant, of Holy Trinity Church, Philadelphia." *Records of the American Catholic Historical Society of Philadelphia*, XXIII (June, 1912), 94-124.

Hamilton, Raphael N. "The Significance of the Frontier to the Historian of the Catholic Church in the United States." *Catholic Historical Review*, XXV (July, 1939), 160-178.

Hanley, Father Thomas O'Brien. "The Emergence of Pluralism in the United States." *Theological Studies*, XXIII (June, 1962), 207-232.

_____. "The Catholic Tradition of Freedom in America." *American Ecclesiastical Review*, CXLV (November, 1961), 307-318.

Hennesey, Father James J. "The American Experience of the
     Roman Catholic Church." Catholic Mind, November,
     1965, pp. 29-36.

_____. "Papacy and Episcopacy in Eighteenth and
     Nineteenth Century American Catholic Thought."
     Records of the American Catholic Historical
     Society of Philadelphia, LXXVII (September,
     1966), 175-189.

Henry, Monsignor H.T. "A Philadelphia Choir Book of 1787."
     Records of the American Catholic Historical Society
     of Philadelphia, XXVI (September, 1915), 208-223.

Herbermann, Father Charles George. "The Right Rev. John
     Dubois." Historical Records and Studies, I
     (January, 1900), 278-355.

Herbermann, Henry F. "The Reverend Lawrence Graessel."
     Historical Records and Studies, VIII (June, 1915),
     209-222.

Hurley, Father Philip S. "Father Robert Molyneux
     1738-1808." Woodstock Letters, LXVII (October,
     1938), 271-292.

Kenny, Father Lawrence. "The Mullanphys of St. Louis."
     Historical Records and Studies, XIV (May, 1920),
     70-111.

Kines, Father Louis B. "Lincoln in a Cassock: Life of
     Father John McElroy, S.J., 1782 to 1847." Woodstock
     Letters, LXXXVII (November, 1958), 335-398.

Lucey, Father William Leo. "Two Irish Merchants of New
     England." New England Quarterly Review, XIV
     (December, 1941), 633-644.

McAvoy, Father Thomas T. "Americanism and Frontier Catholicism." Review of Politics, V (July, 1943), 275-301.

_____. "The Catholic Minority in the United States 1789-1821." Historical Records and Studies, XXXIX (1952), 33-50.

_____. "The Formation of the Catholic Minority in the United States 1820-1860." Review of Politics, X (January, 1948), 13-34.

McCarthy, Father Charles F. "The Historical Development of Episcopal Nominations in the Catholic Church of the United States 1784-1884." Records of the American Catholic Historical Society of Philadelphia, XXXVIII (December, 1927), 297-355.

McGarity, Father John Edward. "Samuel Sutherland Cooper 1769-1843." Records of the American Catholic Historical Society of Philadelphia, XXXVII (December, 1926), 305-340.

MacMaster, Father Richard K. "Benedict Fenwick, Bishop of Boston: American Apprenticeship 1782-1817." Historical Records and Studies, XLVII (1959), 78-139.

McNamara, Father Robert F. "Trusteeism in the Atlantic States 1785-1863." Catholic Historical Review, XXX (July, 1944), 135-154.

_____. "Trusteeism." New Catholic Encyclopedia, 1967, Vol. XIV.

Maes, Father Camillus P. "John Francis Rivet." American Ecclesiastical Review, XXXV (July, 1906), 33-51; XXXV (August, 1906), 113-123.

Maier, Father Eugene F.J. "Mathew Carey, Publicist and Politician, 1760-1839." Records of the American Catholic Historical Society of Philadelphia, XXXIX (June, 1928), 71-154.

Meehan, Thomas F. "A Self-Effaced Philanthropist: Cornelius Heeney 1754-1848." Catholic Historical Review, IV (April, 1918), 4-17.

_____. "Some Pioneer Catholic Laymen in New York-- Dominic Lynch and Cornelius Heeney." Historical Records and Studies, IV (October, 1906), 285-301.

Merritt, Reverend Percival. "Sketches of the Three Earliest Roman Catholic Priests in Boston." Publications of the Colonial Society of Massachusetts, XXV (1923), 173-229.

Miller, Father N.H. "Pioneer Capuchin Missionaries in the United States 1784-1816." Historical Records and Studies, XXI (1932), 170-234.

Montani, Nicola A. "Early Church Music in America: An Example of the Style in Vogue in the Year 1814-- with Reflections on the Sacred Music of Today." Catholic Choirmaster, XIV (Winter, 1928), 7-11.

Nemmers, Erwin Esser, "Early American Catholic Church Music." Catholic Choirmaster, XL (Winter, 1954), 158-159, 190.

O'Connor, Thomas F. "Catholic Archives of the United States." Catholic Historical Review, XXXI (January, 1946), 414-430.

O'Daniel, Father Victor F. "Concanen's Election to the See of New York 1808-1810." Catholic Historical Review, II (April, 1916), 19-46.

Ong, Father Walter J. "American Catholicism and America." Thought, XXVII (Winter, 1952-1953), 521-541.

Parsons, Father Wilfred. "Early Catholic Publishers of Philadelphia." Catholic Historical Review, XXIV (July, 1938), 141-152.

_____. "Father Anthony Kohlmann, S.J., 1771-1824." Catholic Historical Review, IV (April, 1918), 38-52.

Purcell, Richard J. "Thomas Fitzsimons: Framer of the American Constitution." Studies, XXVII (June, 1938), 273-290.

Quirk, Father John F. "Father Ferdinand Farmer, S.J." Historical Records and Studies, VI (December, 1912), 235-248.

Ruggiero, Guido de. "Religious Freedom." Encyclopedia of the Social Sciences, 1934, Vol. XIII.

Ryan, Father Joseph Paul. "Travel Literature as Source Material for American Catholic History." Illinois Catholic Historical Review, X (January, 1928), 179-238; X (April, 1928), 301-363.

Siegman, E.F. "Women Clothed with the Sun." New Catholic Encyclopedia, 1967, Vol. XIV.

Smith, Elwyn A. "The Fundamental Church-State Tradition of the Catholic Church in the United States." Church History, XXXVIII (December, 1969), 486-505.

Smith, Sara Trainer. "Philadelphia's First Nun." Records of the American Catholic Historical Society of Philadelphia, V (December, 1894), 417-523.

Sturges, Walter K. "A Bishop and His Architect." Liturgical Arts, XVII (February, 1949), 53-64.

Tiffany, Father George E. "The Church and the Frontier in the Old Northwest 1699 to 1812." Historical Records and Studies, XXV (1946), 73-144.

Treacy, Father Gerald C. "Evils of Trusteeism." Historical Records and Studies, VIII (June, 1915), 136-156.

Weber, Father Francis J. "Episcopal Appointments in the U.S.A." American Ecclesiastical Review, CLV (September, 1966), 178-191.

Weller, Philip T. "Early Church Music in the United States." Caecilia, LXVI (September, 1939), 297-304.

Willcox, Joseph. "Biography of Rev. Patrick Kenny." Records of the American Catholic Historical Society of Philadelphia, VII (March, 1896), 27-79.

Winslow, Father Francis Joseph. "Prefect-Apostolic." New Catholic Encyclopedia, 1967, Vol. XI.

_____. "Vicar-Apostolic." New Catholic Encyclopedia, 1967, Vol. XIV.

C. UNPUBLISHED SOURCES

Barton, Fred Jackson. "Modes of Delivery in American Homiletic Theory in the Eighteenth and Nineteenth Century." 2 vols. Unpublished Ph.D. dissertation, State University of Iowa, 1949.

Hanley, Father Thomas O'Brien. "The Impact of the American
        Revolution on Religion in Maryland 1776-1800."
        Unpublished Ph.D. dissertation, Georgetown
        University, 1961.

Lambertson, Floyd Wesley. "A Survey and Analysis of
        American Homiletics Prior to 1860." 2 vols.
        Unpublished Ph.D. dissertation, State University
        of Iowa, 1930.

Madden, Richard Cain. "Joseph Pierre Picot de Clorivière
        1768-1826." Unpublished M.A. thesis, Catholic
        University of America, 1938.

The Heritage of
American Catholicisim